The Architectural Logic of Database Systems

E. J. Yannakoudakis

The Architectural Logic of Database Systems

With 69 Figures

Springer-Verlag
London Berlin Heidelberg New York
Paris Tokyo

E. J. Yannakoudakis, BSc, PhD, CEng, FBCS
Postgraduate School of Computer Sciences, University of Bradford,
Bradford, West Yorkshire BD7 1DP, UK

ISBN 3-540-19513-0 Springer-Verlag Berlin Heidelberg New York
ISBN 0-387-19513-0 Springer-Verlag New York Berlin Heidelberg

British Library Cataloguing in Publication Data
Yannakoudakis, E.J., 1950-
Architectural logic of database systems
1. Machine - readable files. Design
I. Title
005.74
ISBN 3-540-19513-0

Library of Congress Cataloging-in-Publication Data
Yannakoudakis, E. J., 1950-
The architectural logic of database systems.
Includes bibliographies and index.
1. Data base management.   2. Computer architecture.
I. title.
QA76.9.D3Y36 1988 005.74   88-3248
ISBN 0-387-19513-0 (U.S.)

©Springer-Verlag Berlin Heidelberg 1988
Printed in Great Britain

Filmset by Saxon Printing Limited, Saxon House, Derby
Printed by Page Bros (Norwich) Limited, Mile Cross Lane, Norwich.

2128/3916–543210

To Eve, John, Irene and Helen
who involuntarily allowed me to finish this book.

Preface

If we look back to pre-database systems and the data units which were in use, we will establish a hierarchy starting with the concept of 'field' used to build 'records' which were in turn used to build higher data units such as 'files'. The file was considered to be the ultimate data unit of information processing and data binding 'monolith'. Moreover, pre-database systems were designed with one or more programming languages in mind and this in effect restricted independent development and modelling of the applications and associated storage structures.

Database systems came along not to turn the above three units into outmoded concepts, but rather to extend them further by establishing a higher logical unit for data description and thereby offer high level data manipulation functions. It also becomes possible for computer professionals and other users to view all information processing needs of an organisation through an integrated, disciplined and methodical approach.

So, database systems employ the concepts field, record and file without necessarily making them transparent to the user who is in effect offered a high level language to define data units and relationships, and another language to manipulate these. A major objective of database systems is to allow logical manipulations to be carried out independent of storage manipulations and vice versa.

A rather accurate parallel between database systems and high level languages such as FORTRAN, COBOL and Pascal can be drawn here by stating that database systems form a natural progressive step from file systems in the way that high level languages form a natural progressive step from assembly or low level languages. The Data Base Management System (DBMS) is the software necessary to set up, manipulate and maintain the object database, that is, the data of the organisation including appropriate control information.

Since the establishment of this higher concept and its acceptance by the computer community as the next step towards an even more advanced information processing environment, the market has been stocked with a plethora of books on the subject, its implications and application environments. However, few books are available for the person who has elementary knowledge of programming and who wishes to have a general introduction to database principles and at the same time acquire knowledge of current database management system software and the various levels at which it is utilised, independent of any vendor-related software. The present book tackles this and also discusses the database environment under the following major areas:

(a) The logic behind database systems
(b) The architecture of database systems and related software
(c) How an entire organisation can be viewed with the aid of appropriate database software
(d) How data can be defined and manipulated using database languages as well as natural language
(e) Models which can describe an organisation accurately
(f) Database design methodologies and techniques to bind record types together
(g) Potential administrative and technical tasks to be performed.

A recent development has been the automation of database design following analyses of the different 'views' (applications) users may have of the same centralised data. The technique used is termed 'canonical database synthesis', where all user views are merged into a single unit which reflects the inherent structure of organisational data. The ultimate objective is to aid the design of the 'logical database structure' which:

(a) Is free from duplication
(b) Is optimised to reflect the organisation accurately
(c) Does not depend on specific vendor-software
(d) Can satisfy new applications without major restructuring

Canonical synthesis is presented here in a step-wise fashion with examples that illustrate the merging, analysis and grouping of user views to form closely related clusters of data elements. An algorithm for canonical sythesis has been implemented in Pascal and this is used to analyse a complete hospital database environment for a Regional Health Authority. Although the software we developed is not included in the book, the Appendix contains example reports it produces for the hospital database, starting with the input of user views followed by their processing and finally the design of the complete logical schema.

The American National Standards Institute (ANSI) and the International Standards Organisation (ISO) have adopted a new standard Relational Database Language (RDL) and a Network Database Language (NDL). Both RDL and NDL are presented here in their current form of development with our own extensions where appropriate, particularly for the definition of the storage structures. The book contains the syntax of the most important RDL and NDL commands for data definition and data manipulation functions. They are illustrated with simple examples that show the input, the statements the user actually types, and the end result.

The ultimate objective of this book is to demystify database concepts and methodologies and at the same time explain in as simple a manner as possible, three important approaches to defining relationships among attributes: the 'hierarchical', 'network' and 'relational'.

The emphasis is on the relational and network approaches to database management because they appear to be suitable for most data processing applications. Besides, we have not seen nor are we likely to see an international standard for the hierarchical approach to database design.

The material includes ample examples and realistic attributes and relationships among these. It is presented in a rather laconic and synoptic fashion by avoiding unnecessary long introductions to the various concepts and by making direct, factual and precise statements on 'what it is', 'how it works' and 'how it can be applied'. The material can in fact be split into four parts:

Part I   : The database environment and underlying data models (Chapters 1, 2 and 3).

Part II   : The architecture of database software and man-machine communication (Chapters 4 and 5).

Part III : Database design methodology (Chapters 6 and 7).

Part IV   : The relational and network database architectures (Chapters 8 and 9).

The concepts and method of presentation are completely independent of hardware and commercial software packages. The person who masters the material presented here will be in a strong position to judge and evaluate any type of database software, regardless of whether this is offered on a micro, mini or large mainframe. Moreover, the ISO database language discussed here will provide a yardstick for comparative assessment for some years to come.

The book will be useful to all people who wish to acquire a working, sound and up to date knowledge on the subject, its terminology and method of application. Since it does not require any a priori knowledge of database systems but only simple programming principles, it is recommended to students taking A-level courses in computer studies, University undergraduates, postgraduates who may wish to use the DBMS as a tool for data manipulation, computer programmers who are about to commence programming under a DBMS, systems analysts who may wish to assess the feasability of introducing a DBMS into their organisation, and database administrators who wish to acquire sufficient and integrated knowledge on logical database architecture, associated structures and software modules, and technical tasks behind setting up and maintaining a database. Finally, data processing managers will find the material useful, particularly the terminological dictionary; most importantly, though, they will be able, identify and establish appropriate administrative posts for the effective maintenance of a database.

Acknowledgements

I would like to thank Chris Stoker (University of Bradford) for the assistance he has given me in the production of the canonical synthesis reports for the hospital database presented in the Appendix. I would like particularly to thank Chi Pui Cheng (Hong Kong Polytechnic) for his invaluable comments in shaping up the chapter on RDL and NDL.

January 1988   E.J.Y.

Contents

1 FOUNDATIONS OF DATABASES

1.1 DATA AND INFORMATION

The principles of database systems are very simple and yet they have been, somehow, mystified by various implementations but particularly by the terminology which has been adopted. Study the following definition in order to appreciate the simple logic behind a database system and its associated environment:

> A database is a collection of well organised records within a commonly available mass storage medium. It serves one or more applications in an optimal fashion by allowing a common and controlled approach to adding, modifying and retrieving sets of data. The Database Management System (DBMS) is a suit of computer programs which perform these operations in a standardised and fully controllable manner.

We can therefore say that a DBMS forms the interface between a programmer or user and the computer hardware or devices upon which the data is stored. Standards can thus be introduced quite easily because of the need to go through a DBMS rather than directly to individual files on the devices [Yannakoudakis, 1984].

Evidently, an enterprise utilises computers to satisfy its own subjective requirements, in an efficient manner, through what we call 'decomposition': the breaking down of organisational requirements into autonomous but communicating environments. We call these 'applications', each carrying out well defined tasks pertinent to specific realms of thought.

To illustrate the appplications of an organisation we will take a look at a library. Here, details of each book, reader, supplier, staff etc, are held on computer files which are shared. For example, application CATALOGUING may use the files 'Book-details', 'Publisher-details' and 'Subject-details' in order to maintain the catalogue. Application RECALLS may use the files 'Name-address' and 'Book-details' to send recall notices to borrowers. The user of an application can be a member of the library staff, or a reader/borrower of books. Consider the following distinct applications:

(a) Maintain the catalogue holding all books in the library. Tasks: insert, delete, alter, classify, reorganise, etc.
(b) Retrieve details from catalogue to satisfy user-requests. Tasks: search, display, cluster records, interrelate records, etc.

(c)   Maintain the reader/borrower list. Tasks: insert, delete, alter, reorganise, renew, inform, etc.
(d)   Acquisitions and communication with other organisations. Tasks: issue order, receive order, control inter-library loans, etc.

The wide variety of requirements and operations within the library premises are now decomposed into distinct functional areas which can be managed effectively and efficiently. Order is imposed and each member of staff can be assigned tasks as and where necessary. The librarian is thus in a position to co-ordinate all the activities and communicate information within and between applications.

It is very important at this stage to make clear the distinction between 'data' and 'information'. An organisation may have complete and adequate data stored on a computer-readable medium but may not be capable of satisfying all user functional requirements. Computer files may for example contain all relevant data about each employee of a division but it may be difficult to extract the information necessary to answer a simple query such as 'which employees live in a specific geographic area ?'.

Thus, in order to provide information for management and users alike and thereby aid the decision-makers generally, it becomes necessary to perform a number of distinct but interrelated tasks upon the actual data. The tasks can be grouped under a number of headings as follows:

(a)   Identify; distinguish between alternative data
(b)   Locate; find the position of relevant data
(c)   Retrieve; transfer data into user-working areas
(d)   Associate; link all relevant data together
(e)   Correlate; determine levels of associations
(f)   Quantify; calculate and measure the connections
(g)   Control; control and supervise mechanisms or tasks
(h)   Present; present results for user-interpretation.

Following the completion of each of the above tasks, as and where appropriate, and after the presentation of results, we can say that 'information' is provided for further interpretation and use by the recipient. More specifically, data is manipulated by application-dependent programs and re-presented in different forms and shapes according to the logic built into the software used.

The generality of the above tasks, coupled with the fact that any kind or type of data can be manipulated by the DBMS, including numeric, text, voice, graphic or image, enables us to present an outline scenario of current modes of man-machine communication.

Figure 1.1 presents a general environment for man-machine communication containing current devices and tools. The disk represents the physical database which can be stored on ordinary hard disks (usually formatted according to the traditional three-dimensional architecture of cylinder, track and sector), or a laser-based device, or any other type of storage including the well known floppy disk. The Visual Display Unit (VDU) represents the user view of the database as well as a form of presenting numeric/textual or image information. The microphone represents the input of phonetic information. The image sensor represents the input of photographic information. The loudspeaker represents the output of acoustic information. The robot represents the control of a real time

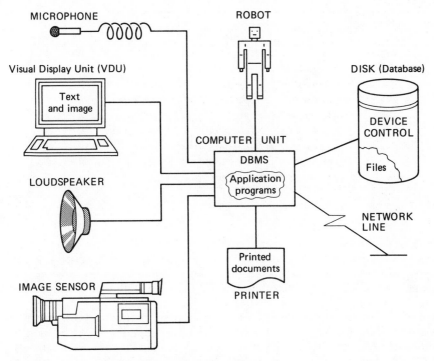

Figure 1.1   An environment for man-machine communication.

application. And finally, the printer represents printed information and generally the printed word, graph or image.

Figure 1.1 implies that the mappings between data and information, and between man and machine, are under the direct control of the DBMS. Besides, the user has a choice of media for communicating with the database or indeed other remote users and databases through a network line. A multiplicity of devices can of course be connected to the database enabling communication at both intra (within) and inter (between) organisation levels.

Our main objective here is to demystify the DBMS by revealing its logical architecture and software necessary to implement and drive surrounding applications in an orderly manner. We discuss the logic behind the DBMS itself and the way an enterprise can be 'translated' into appropriate computer structures which can then materialise through DBMS-dependent software modules (i.e very high level languages).

1.2 PROGRAM AND FILE COMMUNICATION

A DBMS can perform a number of functions by manipulating ordinary files which are defined and maintained with the aid of the DBMS itself. The records of the

File: PERSONNEL

Key	Name	Address		Sex	Job-title	Dept-code	Pay-code
		Street	Area				
1	N. Afghan	1 Pemberton Rd	Bingley	M	Clerk	B	6
2	J. Albanian	6 Keighley Rd	Keighley	M	Clerk	B	6
3	G. English	5 Oxford Str	Leeds	F	Lecturer	A	1
4	E. French	66 Bronte Rd	Howarth	F	Supervisor	B	4
5	J. Greek	23 Richmond Str	Bradford	M	Lecturer	A	1
6	F. Italian	12 Queen's Rd	Wakefield	F	Demonstrator	A	5
7	B. Mexican	13 Laisteridge La	Bradford	M	Clerk	B	6
8	V. Russian	31 Marx Str	Bradford	M	Assistant	A	2
9	C. Welsh	19 Newlands Rd	Bingley	F	Clerk	B	6

Figure 1.2 A simple personnel file.

files may be accessed directly, sequentially or on the basis of certain criteria which are application-dependent. In this section we will consider an example of a simple personnel file in order to discuss the interface between computer programs and data files.

Figure 1.2 shows nine records each containing pertinent fields for the employees of an organisation. These are the record number which is used to identify each of the employees, the name, address, sex (M for male, F for female), job title, department code and pay code. The address field in this case comprises two subfields, the street number and name, and area.

For any computer program written in any language to read this file it is necessary to define a number of variables which will hold control information. This may be the fact that there are seven fields per record and that there is a total of nine records. It may also be necessary to define the number of characters occupied by each field, as well as its type, such as string, integer, or real.

Regarding the file structure itself, it may be necessary to know whether it is held on disk, magnetic tape or any other device and whether it is a sequential or a direct access file. That is, whether each record is accessed one after the other starting with the first, or whether a record can be accessed directly by knowing only its relative position within the file (the number 1 to 9 in this example).

The system designer or programmer has therefore two choices regarding the provision of control data for the program manipulating the file:

(a) To include control data within the program in the form of constants or
(b) To request the user to provide control data during the execution of the program.

We must not confuse 'control data' which is necessary to interface programs to files, with 'session-dependent data'. In the latter case for example the user may request the program to display all records of department 'computer' in one session, and department 'finance' in another session.

Take approach (a) above where, for example, a program can only read a specific file because its name is held as a constant. Also, the number of records can be held as a constant and therefore the program will only be able to read as many records - the rest will be ignored. One can say that the program may have the ability to detect the end of file marker automatically, but what about the length of each field which can vary from file to file, or indeed the type of each field which can also vary from file to file ? We can carry on with numerous peculiarities under this case.

A fundamental assumption here is that it is desirable to develop programs which can read many different files, and similarly, it is desirable to design files which can be read by different programs.

Therefore, if we adopt approach (a) above but subsequently wish to read another file with different basic definitions, then the program will have to be edited and recompiled. It is the latter operations (editing and recompilation) which must be avoided wherever possible, unless of course the logic of the program itself has to change to accommodate changes in the application.

The programmer has to compromise and to determine what control information can be constant and what can be supplied during program execution. On the other hand, a session can become very tedious when the user is forced to supply numerous data (control or otherwise) before the program can actually commence or continue with the processing of the file.

Unfortunately, most high level programming languages impose restrictions on the definition of variables and the use of constants becomes a necessity rather than a choice. For example, if variable 'pay-code' is defined as integer within a Pascal program, then this definition is permanent and cannot vary from one program execution to the next, or from one file to another. Thus, a combination of the above approaches (a) and (b) involving both constant and variable data appears to be the only solution.

The DBMS approach to the design of files and programs aims to eliminate a number of the above peculiarities, or rather undesirable features of an information processing system in general.

Figure 1.3 shows an example of a program written in a FORTRAN-like language. It processes the file of Figure 1.2 by reading one record after the other, and identifies and displays all people who live in the area of Bradford. Capital letters indicate a program statement or keyword and small letters indicate user-defined variables or constants. A comma at the end of a line indicates that the statement continues to the next line. Constant control information is held on 'filename', 'totalrecords' and within the definition of each field.

The characteristics of the file as a whole are defined within the OPEN command. We can of course use the constants 'personnel' and '9' directly without having to assign these to the variables 'filename' and 'totalrecords' respectively. The choice is left to the programmer/designer of the application.

Our primary objective here is to demonstrate the current state of affairs regarding programming in an ordinary high level language, and the complexity of the approach, no matter how simple the task is. Study the following analytical description of each program statement (as shown in Figure 1.3) and its relationship to others:

1. Define the beginning of the program called 'readfile'.
2. Define all integer fields, namely, key, paycode, totalrecords, and var1, and allocate a maximum field-width of one digit.
3. Define all string fields, and allocate 11 characters for name, 12 characters for street, 8 characters for area.

4. Continue the definition of the remaining string fields.
5. Transfer the value 'personnel' upon variable filename.
6. Transfer the value 9 upon variable totalrecords.
7. Open the corresponding file held on disk and prepare for reading sequentially. The channel establishes a logical line for transferring data from the file.
8. Continue with the definition of the open command.
9. Start a loop using variable var1 which is to receive values from one to totalrecords in increments of 1.
10. Read the value of each field in turn, assuming a maximum field-width for each as defined under steps 2, 3 and 4 above.
11. Continue reading the rest of the values.
12. Test to see whether the current value of field area is equal to 'Bradford'. If the test establishes that the current value of area is 'Bradford', then the current value of variable name and variable street will be displayed.
13. Terminate the IF test.
14. Test the current value of var1 and, provided it is less than or equal to the value of variable totalrecords, then return to the statement following the starting of the loop (i.e statement 10) after incrementing variable var1 by one as specified within statement 9 which defines the loop. If the value of variable var1 is greater than the value of variable totalrecords (in this case 9), then continue with the next statement, that is, number 15.
15. Close logical channel 1 and its associated file.
16. Stop the execution of the program.
17. End the session and delete the program from the memory.

The above steps are of course very elaborate and tedious to put together even though the task carried out by the program is very simple indeed. It becomes, therefore, necessary to design an even higher level programming language in order to define and manipulate data independently and by means of very high level statements.

```
1    PROGRAM readfile
2    INTEGER key*1, paycode*1, totalrecords*1, var1*1
3    CHARACTER name*11, street*12, area*8,
4                      sex*1, job*18, dept*1, filename*9
5    filename='personnel'
6    totalrecords=9
7    OPEN(CHANNEL=1,FILE=filename,ACCESS='sequential',
8          DEVICE='disk')
9    FOR var1=1 TO totalrecords STEP 1
10       READ(CHANNEL=1)key,name,street,area,sex,job,
11                          dept,paycode
12       IF(area = 'Bradford')THEN DISPLAY name, street
13       ENDIF
14   NEXT var1
15   CLOSE(CHANNEL=1)
16   STOP
17   END.
```

Figure 1.3   A program with fixed control data.

1.3 PROGRAM AND META-FILE COMMUNICATION

Clearly, each program performs a specific task by following an algorithm of some fixed logic. In our example of Figure 1.3 the program displays the names and addresses of all personnel who live in Bradford. The simplicity of the logic does not necessarily imply simplicity in implementation.

Techniques and application-dependent software have been developed so that programs can create other programs (or rather tailor existing software to a user-defined specification) but this topic is beyond the scope of the present book.

Let us return to the pre-database environment and discuss the current approach to providing control data. If this is supplied during execution time, then the program can prompt the user to simply type in the value of each variable in turn. Alternatively, the program can read all control information from another file before the file-proper is processed. In either case we cannot avoid the need to supply at least the file name during the activation of the program if we wish to have a general purpose facility.

One method of naming the control file is to postfix the name of the data file with a standard code and thus create a new identifier automatically. Figure 1.4 shows a program which performs this task by prompting the user to type in the name of the file to be processed. This is then postfixed with the string '.meta' and a new file name is established. The corresponding control file is read first, the variables are defined and the file-proper is then processed in exactly the same way.

Note that control information about the auxiliary file is now constant as for example the number of digits or characters allocated for each field. We also have the constant 'Bradford' but this can be transferred to a variable, say, currentarea, through an assignment statement or it can be supplied by the user during execution time as is the case with the variable filename.

Each variable used in the program of Figure 1.4 corresponds to a real-world object regarding the file of Figure 1.2 as follows:

n1 : Field-width for object key
n2 : Field-width for object name
n3 : Field-width for object street
n4 : Field-width for object area
n5 : Field-width for object sex
n6 : Field-width for object job title
n7 : Field-width for object dept. code
n8 : Field-width for object pay code
n9 : Total records in main data file
n10 : Method of access of main data file records
n11 : Name of device where main data file is stored
var1: A variable holding current record number read

The rest of the variables used bear the names of the actual real-world objects, such as, name, street and area.

An example control file referring to Figure 1.2 is presented in Figure 1.5 with the following assumptions:

(a)   The maximum number of records which can be read is 999,999 by definition of variable n9.

(b) The maximum number of characters in the filename itself is 13 by definition of variable filename.
(c) The type of each field is fixed.
(d) The maximum number of characters per field is 999 by definition of variables n1 to n8.

In conclusion, we shall give the following definition:

> Files which hold control or descriptive data regarding the structure and format of other files are called 'meta-files'.

Meta-files can be used in conjunction with main data files so that a certain degree of independence is established between data files and programs.

Any changes or insertions which occur in the data file must also be communicated to the meta-file so that it is kept updated at all times.

The concept of meta-file forms a fundamental principle in the design of file structures for databases. This simple but powerful technique, in effect, forces the designer to distinguish between data and meta-data and to treat each in a different manner.

The DBMS offers the designer a set of very high level language statements which can: define meta-data and therefore data proper, suppress meta-data at the user interface and finally, manipulate meta-data and data proper independent of each other. So, the designer can concentrate on the logic and application environment in general.

```
 1   PROGRAM readfile
 2   {The following define and read control data}
 3   INTEGER n1*3,n2*3,n3*3,n4*3,n5*3,n6*3,n7*3,n8*3,
 4             n9*6,var1*6
 5   CHARACTER filename*13,filename2*13,n10*12,n11*12
 6   DISPLAY'type in file name';
 7   READ filename
 8   filename2=filename+'.meta'
 9   OPEN(CHANNEL=1,FILE=filename2,ACCESS='sequential',
10        DEVICE='disk')
11   READ(CHANNEL=1)n1,n2,n3,n4,n5,n6,n7,n8,n9,n10,n11
12   CLOSE(CHANNEL=1)
13   {The following define and read main data file}
14   INTEGER key*n1, paycode*n8
15   CHARACTER name*n2, street*n3, area*n4,
16             sex*n5, job*n6, dept*n7
17   OPEN(CHANNEL=1,FILE=filename,ACCESS=n10,DEVICE=n11)
18   FOR var1=1 TO n9 STEP 1
19       READ(CHANNEL=1)key,name,street,area,sex,
20                         job,dept,paycode
21       IF(area = 'Bradford')THEN DISPLAY name, street
22       ENDIF
23   NEXT var1
24   CLOSE(CHANNEL=1)
25   STOP
26   END.
```

Figure 1.4 A program with variable control data.

File: PERSONNEL.META

			Length of each field					Total records	Access mode	Device name
n1	n2	n3	n4	n5	n6	n7	8n	n9	n10	n11

| | 1 | 1,1 | 1,2 | 8 | 1 | 1,8 | 1 | 1 | 9 | S,E,Q,U,E,N,T,I,A,L | D,I,S,K |

Figure 1.5   An example of meta-file of file 'personnel' in Figure 1.2.

Now, let us assume that file 'personnel' exists on disk and that a very high level language is available for general file interrogation. Consider the following statements written in the language SQL (Structured Query Language) which is part of a DBMS and allows such tasks to be carried out very effectively:

SELECT name, street
   FROM personnel
   WHERE area = 'Bradford'

The above statements, by default, read the associated meta-file, scan the file proper and display the name and street of each record containing the value 'Bradford' under the field area. They are simple, easy to remember and take overall control of the opening, manipulation and closing of file 'personnel'.

It may be that these three statements are in effect translated (expanded) into a set of Pascal, FORTRAN or COBOL instructions before they are executed, or that they are part of an independent language. Either way, this technical detail is of no concern to the user of the database. In other words, the statements can be part of an application program or they can be issued from an on-line environment.

1.4 TOWARDS A DATABASE SYSTEM

If we look back to the first data processing systems and the way files were set up and processed, we will see that it was the lack of flexible programming languages which restricted the standardisation of the program-data interface. Perhaps the idea of a database system would have crystallised earlier if it hadn't been for the fact that most systems were developed and implemented with a specific language in mind. In retrospect, the weaknesses are obvious from the following [Date, 1986]:

(a)   There was lack of coordination among files. They were set up individually without any common standards or compatibility among themselves let alone with files in other sites.

(b)   Files were both program and language dependent. For example, information regarding the number of fields and the number of bytes allocated to each in a specific file was held within the data division of a COBOL program as constants rather than as variables which received values from a meta-file.

(c)   There was lack of multiple access paths. This meant that each record could
       only be accessed through pre-defined strict processes or single identifiers
       (i.e keys).
(d)   There was data redundancy. For example, if two different applications
       such as 'production control' and 'payroll' required the same information
       on individual employees, then this was frequently duplicated because files
       could not be shared. Updating, thus, became a problem by having to
       access the same fields/values twice or more and to repeat the process.
(e)   Existing data could not be shared or accessed concurrently and this in turn
       created a queuing problem.

In order to illustrate a pre-database environment we will use an example with
three applications, say, APL1, APL2, APL3, and three files, say, FIL1, FIL2 and
FIL3. Figure 1.6 shows three separate programs (PRO1, PRO2, PRO3) each
accessing a file independently of the others and through independent channels.
Figure 1.7 shows the same environment under the control of a DBMS; we still
have separate programs communicating with the files but through a Database
Control System (DBCS). The files however are integrated and the applications
remain autonomous.

By autonomous we imply that applications are independent of each other but
able to communicate among themselves when necessary. An example of
independence may be that the user of application, say, APL1 is not aware of the
functions of APL2 and vice versa.

By file integration we mean that unique record types need only be defined once
and simply invoked during subsequent executions of the application program. An
example record type is that of Figure 1.2 where the rows of the file are the actual
record occurrences. File integration, generally, helps to eliminate duplicate or
redundant data.

Moreover, within a database, files are not isolated as simple information unit
carriers, but component parts of a conceptual framework offering a total

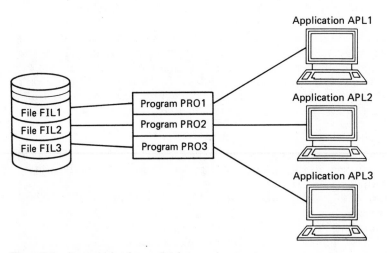

Figure 1.6   An example of a pre-database environment.

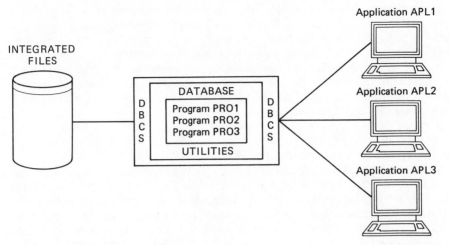

Figure 1.7   An example of a database environment.

solution to all informational needs of each and every application realm in an organisation [Everest, 1986]. Here, unique and desirable features are: propagation of information, accessibility at both intra- and inter-file levels, and accessibility by content (e.g 'Bradford') as well as by storage address (e.g record numbers 5, 7 and 8 of Figure 1.2).

Standards are imposed by virtue of the fact that all applications are implemented and operationalised through a DBMS. Because the built-in DBMS software is at a very high level, well above ordinary utilities, programmer productivity also increases substantially.

The first steps towards standardisation were made by a group of users and manufacturers who met in 1967 and formed the Database Task Group (DBTG). It was not until April 1971 that a draft proposal for a DBMS was published [CODASYL, 1971]. The group soon acquired an international reputation and the CODASYL (Conference On DAta SYstems Languages) committee was established. Its task was to specify a common computer language for the design and processing of database systems.

Present efforts to design a new database system [ANSI, 1986] are primarily efforts to establish a common standard or a language for defining the various record types (a Data Description Language (DDL)), and a language for manipulating these (a Data Manipulation Language (DML)) [Yannakoudakis, 1984].

The problem however is that most DBMS languages are designed for the specialist without any consideration for the ordinary user, the person who is not even familiar with a programming language such as COBOL, FORTRAN or Pascal.

A recent development has been the design of friendly interactive 'query languages' for the casual user who wishes to interrogate the database and to store or retrieve small sets of data. Current efforts are also directed to the specification of a common syntax for a universal language to define as well as manipulate database structures.

The concept 'database structure' implies a system of inter-related information organised in such a way as to reflect human levels of connectivity or associations between individual facts, figures or knowledge in general [McFadden & Hoffer, 1985]. The task of identifying inherent structures of human knowledge is not trivial. In many situations we are forced to superimpose the structure we are familiar with on knowledge we intend to classify, cluster and mechanise. Classification and clustering of knowledge, in turn, necessitate 'relationships' between elements of knowledge.

Because the concepts 'structure' and 'relationship' are frequently used with database management systems, we will present a simple example here to illustrate their relevance to our subject matter.

Consider factual knowledge about a University in terms of subject details and student details. Let this knowledge be structured under two record types: (a) SUBJECT containing title, lecturer, prerequisites and assessment details; (b) STUDENT containing name, address, course, department, supervisor and year. Now, a student may attend a number of subjects and a subject may be studied by many students. We say that types SUBJECT and STUDENT are related and can denote this as follows:

The double arrows indicate this situation which is an example of what is called a many-to-many (M:M) relationship. The other categories of relationships are: one-to-many (1:M), many-to-one (M:1) and one-to-one (1:1). The overall and complete definition of SUBJECT, STUDENT and relationship forms a structure. Whether SUBJECT and STUDENT become distinct record types has to be clarified by the analyst of the enterprise and before he attempts to implement the structure with the aid of a DBMS.

The detailed study of the 'real world', in our stated example the University environment, staff, students, etc., is otherwise referred to as 'conceptual database analysis' and enables the creation of the 'conceptual schema' of the database [ANSI, 1985]. The conceptual schema is then studied further and the 'logical schema' is derived incorporating the definitions of all record types and relationships.

Whereas the conceptual analysis and resultant conceptual model are completely independent of existing software (e.g operating system, DBMS), the logical schema is designed with a specific DBMS in mind and should thus be capable of satisfying the requirements of all applications within the enterprise. Evidently, each application utilises only those sections of the logical schema which are relevant to its functional requirements. Therefore, it makes sense to define these as a virtual unit, otherwise referred to as 'subschema'.

The logical schema incorporates multiple record types interrelated in many different ways so that the overall structure reflects the enterprise itself accurately. Such a structure is otherwise referred to as 'data model' of which there are a number of different categories, depending on the level and degree of abstraction. However, the models often discussed by database designers are the 'conceptual', 'logical' and 'storage'.

In conclusion, there are two essential guiding rules for the analysis of an enterprise, the establishment of an appropriate model and its subsequent implementation. The rules form in effect two principles [ANSI, 1985]:

The conceptualisation principle

The conceptual analysis stage and the resultant conceptual schema must include relevant information (static and dynamic) which describes and defines the universe of discourse including staff, procedures, rules and inherent data relationships, but not instances of information types. Moreover, conceptual information must not refer to storage, physical, hardware or a specific DBMS implementation.

The self-sufficiency principle

The conceptual schema contains the total, relevant and complete information about the enterprise and is therefore used as the basis for deriving the logical schema. In other words, it is self-sufficient and so information which is not part of the conceptual schema cannot be considered during the design of the logical schema. Moreover, the logical schema must enable the evolution of the universe of discourse in order to meet all dynamic aspects of the enterprise.

1.5 HIGH LEVEL DATABASE SOFTWARE

As explained in the previous sections, database systems offer a high level approach to storing and retrieving data effectively. In order to appreciate this, we will introduce a complete set of high level commands (part of the DBMS software) which enable the user to:

(a)   Create files
(b)   Insert records on files
(c)   Update individual fields of records
(d)   Interrogate the contents of files

Let us examine a high level database language, part of the DBMS software [Date, 1983; ANSI, 1986], which offers appropriate commands where the concept of 'table' becomes synonymous to the concept of 'file' for our purposes here. We will use the example file of Figure 1.2 as the basis to illustrate some of the facilities available.

All commands and keywords are presented in upper case letters and all parameters are presented in lower case letters. Square brackets ([ ]) are used to denote optional keywords, qualifiers or entries. Also, character or string values are presented in single quotes (e.g '1 Richmond Rd') whereas numerical values are presented without quotes.

Create

This command enables the creation of files/tables and has the following format:

CREATE TABLE table-name
  (field-name1 data-type [NOT NULL]
  [,field-name2 data-type [NOT NULL]]...)

where data-type may be INTEGER, CHAR(n) n being the maximum number of characters for the field, FLOAT to indicate a floating point number, etc. [Yannakoudakis & Cheng, 1987]. The keyword NOT NULL forces the user of the table to supply a value under a field when a record is inserted, rather than leave it empty. This is particularly important with the primary key (e.g key/code of Figure 1.2) which identifies each record uniquely. The following command will actually create the file of Figure 1.2 and its associated meta-file in Figure 1.5:

CREATE TABLE personnel
  (key INTEGER NOT NULL,
   name CHAR(11),
   street CHAR(12),
   area CHAR(8),
   sex CHAR(1),
   job-title CHAR(18),
   dept-code CHAR(1),
   pay-code INTEGER)

At this stage, the file will not contain any record occurrences as such. Note that the command does not expect the user to specify the type of file (e.g SEQUENTIAL or DIRECT) nor the type of device upon which it will be stored (e.g DISK or TAPE).

Insert

This command enables the user to transfer values upon the file, one record at a time. Its general format is as follows:

INSERT
  INTO table-name [(field-name1 [,field-name2]...)]
  VALUES (value-for-field1 [,value-for-field2]...)

The following statements will transfer a complete record on file 'personnel' where the primary key is 1:

INSERT
  INTO personnel (key, name, street, area, sex,
                   job-title, dept-code, pay-code)
  VALUES(1, 'N. Afghan', '1 Pemberton Rd.', 'Bingley',
         'M', 'Clerk', 'B', 6)

Update

This command enables the user to change the contents of any field in a file. Its general format is as follows:

UPDATE table-name
    SET field-name1 = expression
      [,field-name2 = expression]...
    [WHERE logical test]

where expression is more or less the same as the right-hand side of an assignment statement in another high level language, such as FORTRAN. The logical test defines the criteria for selecting pertinent record occurrences which are to be updated. The following statements will update the record with key equal 1 by changing the contents of the street field:

UPDATE personnel
    SET street = '8 Hope View'
    WHERE key = 1

Select

This command allows the interrogation of files and the retrieval of record occurrences or subsets of each satisfying user-supplied requirements. Its general format is as follows:

SELECT [DISTINCT] field-name1 [,field-name2]...
    FROM table-name1 [,table-name2]...
    WHERE logical test

This command can include other keywords (e.g GROUP BY, ORDER BY) which are discussed in Chapter 4. The keyword DISTINCT asks the system to display only distinct values (not duplicate) from records which satisfy the logical test supplied with the keyword WHERE. Only the corresponding values of the fields defined at the SELECT level will actually be offered to the user. For example, the following statements find and display the name and job-title of all employees in department 'A':

SELECT name, job-title
    FROM personnel
    WHERE dept-code = 'A'

The result from the execution of the above statements is in fact another table (file) which contains the following records (extracted from the file presented in Figure 1.2):

name	job-title
G. English	Lecturer
J. Greek	Lecturer
F. Italian	Demonstrator
V. Russian	Assistant Lecturer

1.6 SUMMARY

In this chapter, we introduced the concept of database (i.e a highly organised and commonly available collection of data/records), and the Database Management System (DBMS) which is a software package that enables the user to create appropriate data structures and to perform various operations on the database, such as locate, retrieve, update records, etc.

The basic principle behind the organisation, structure and usage of the database is the *meta-file*, that is, a special control file which describes another file. It is through the adoption of appropriate meta-files that the DBMS provides and maintains a standardised, fully controllable, and shared pool of data.

The DBMS offers a high level approach to storing and retrieving data effectively. In this chapter, we presented four examples of high level commands for (a) creating files, (b) inserting records on files, (c) updating individual fields of records, and (d) interrogating the contents of files.

1.7 REFERENCES

ANSI, X3H2, 'Concepts and Terminology for the Conceptual Schema and the Information Base', (ISO TC97/SC5/WG3), 1985.

ANSI, X3H2 Technical Committee on Databases, 'Relational Database Language', 1986.

CODASYL, Database Task Group Report, April 1971.

Date, C. J., 'An Introduction to Database Systems', Vol. I, 4th Edition, Addison-Wesley, 1986.

Date, C. J., 'Database: A Primer', Addison-Wesley, 1983.

Everest, G., 'Database Management: Objectives, System Functions, & Administration', McGraw-Hill, 1986.

McFadden, F. R. & Hoffer, J. A., 'Database Management', Benjamin/Cummings, 1985.

Yannakoudakis, E. J.,'The Logic of Database Systems', D.P. International, Institute of Data Processing Management, London, pp. 169-174, March 1984.

Yannakoudakis, E. J. & Cheng, C. P., 'A Rigorous Approach to Data Type Specification', Computer Bulletin, Vol 3, Part 4, pp. 31-36, 1987.

2 THE LOGIC OF THE DATABASE ENVIRONMENT

2.1 THE PRINCIPLE OF DATA INDEPENDENCE

Before a database can be designed and implemented for general purposes, it becomes necessary to consider the different levels of data analysis which must be carried out. In order to appreciate the relationships between these, we will introduce and subsequently adopt a terminology pertinent to each level.

At the conceptual level, the data analyst will investigate the so called 'entities' (e.g PERSON, BOOK, SUBJECT) and appropriate 'attributes' under each (e.g Name, Address, Subject code). Also, the relationships among entities must be identified and described accordingly.

At the logical level, the analyst will investigate the relationships (logical connections) among possible 'logical record types' which are defined so as to reflect conceptual entities. Logical record types are designed with a specific DBMS in mind, each containing one or more 'data items' (e.g Name CHARAC-TER(5) defining Name as type character with a maximum length of 5 bytes). A conceptual entity may be translated to one or more logical record types, and similarly, an attribute may give rise to one or more data items. For our purposes here and depending on context, when we talk of entities or attributes at the logical level we will imply that a one-to-one correspondence exists between the conceptual and logical definitions.

At the storage level, the analyst will investigate the translation of logical record types to 'storage record types' or simply 'record types', and the translation of data items to 'fields'. Also, the physical connections (e.g pointers, chains, storage indexes) reflecting the logical equivalent must be implemented accordingly.

The above terms are necessary, not only for communication purposes, but also because of the distortive mappings which take place between storage and presentation of values/information to the user. For example, what is known to the user of a database as a single record occurrence containing the values 'E J Yannakoudakis, The Architectural Logic of Database Systems, Springer, 1988' can in fact be stored on two, physically separate, storage record types. Also, the value '1988' may be stored under a field defined as 11 bits rather than 4 bytes long.

So, database systems allow data to be structured and stored on physical devices independent of the applications accessing it. Similarly, informational changes or variations in the processing logic of applications do not affect data at the storage level.

Data independence [Stonebraker, 1974; Fry & Kahn, 1976; Fry & Sibley, 1976] forms part of the immunisation of information and data against side-effects from organisational growth, and changes in structures, requirements, procedures, computer hardware and system software. Data independence is one of the most important principles in database design.

In this section we will discuss the operations that can take place at both application level and storage level, without any reference to marketed DBMS software, although most of the functions presented are possible in one form or another.

The degree of data independence can be judged under a series of well defined criteria which can be grouped broadly under two major areas: physical (storage) and logical.

2.1.1 Physical Independence

Data and associated structures can be manipulated on the devices without disturbing existing views at the logical or user levels. For example, when one or more record types or indeed clusters of record occurrences are accessed more frequently than others, then their access paths can be altered to improve the response time. This can take place without affecting the processing logic of existing programs or any views that users may have of the database.

We must point out here that a number of manipulative operations at the physical level can be performed by the operating system in use, although we envisage a DBMS which simply issues calls to operating system functions and utilities. If this is possible, then there will be no need for the designers of the DBMS to re-invent the wheel and to by-pass the operating system. However, the utilisation of the operating system need not be transparent to the database user or programmer.

So, the operating system and the DBMS should be considered as two interacting components of the overall information system and not as a DBMS under the control of the operating system. One can go as far as to say that DBMS functions and operating system functions should not be distinguishable.

Storage manipulations can be understood in the following terms:

(a) Change the general structure of records, that is, the way they are connected together so that a record type becomes accessible from another. Create new connections so that records can be linked uni-directionally, bi-directionally, hierarchically, or in a general manner resulting in a network.

For example, if an employee has a number of history records (one for each job carried out in the past), then these can be linked bi-directionally so that we can instruct the system to fetch the next or prior occurrence in an efficient manner.

The actual linking mechanisms can be implicit and hidden from the user/programmer, or explicit through fields that are common to two or more record types.

(b) Change the order of a series of record occurrences so that they are stored numerically or lexicographically according to the values under one or more fields.

(c) Split the records in a file into two or more subfiles in a horizontal or vertical manner. This may in fact be necessary when the file is either too large to be stored within a single device or limited physical slot, or when the operating system in use imposes restrictions on the size of files. Alternatively, we may wish to split files into subfiles in order to optimise their accessibility.

(d) Compress the stored values of records in order to save storage space.
(e) Code the stored values cryptographically for reasons of security.
(f) Analyse the stored values and merge where necessary, without affecting logical occurrences, in order to eliminate redundancy or overlap between different files.

For example, if 'employee-address' is common to two or more record types, then its values can be stored separately in a single file with appropriate links from the original record types.

(g) Split or combine physical records in order to conform with physical device features or restrictions.

For example, if the capacity of a block or sector on disk is 512 bytes and if each physical record is 600 bytes long, then it will have to be split between two blocks. Alternatively, the DBMS may offer the facility to create a virtual block (otherwise known as a 'page') which is 600 bytes long.

(h) Transfer the stored records to new devices with new features, capacities or capabilities. We are all well aware of the ever-changing market and the technological advances in computer hardware. The survival of an organisation may depend on its ability to adapt to new technologies.

(i) Reorganise overflow or other expansion areas as and where necessary in order to optimise the accessing of records.

2.1.2 Logical Independence

Logical records and structures, as viewed by the user, can be manipulated or redefined without disturbing existing storage structures or physical characteristics in general. Logical manipulations are of course application-dependent and change with time. Here, we will discuss manipulative operations from the functional point of view applicable to all user-defined (local) environments.

It is important to emphasise here that the DBMS approach allows each application to be as independent (functionally) of others as is the case with clerical or general information processing environments. For example, while a user in the advertising department is printing address labels by accessing pertinent values from a file, another user in the finance department can be accessing the same file in order to produce the weekly payroll.

Another important feature of DBMSs is that application-dependent functions or redefinitions do not affect other users or applications. For example, while a user manipulates data item 'Salary' as a real number, another may be manipulating the same data item as an integer number. Moreover, because all applications are implemented through the DBMS, it is possible to receive global information on what is happening around you if and when necessary.

Logical independence and corresponding manipulative operations can be understood in the following terms:

(a) Define and proceed to utilise only those entities and attributes which are relevant to the processing needs of an application environment. In other words, instruct the DBMS to suppress information that is not relevant to an application.

(b) Define a new application-dependent structure with its own subjective and local information in terms of relationships (connections) between entities.

Alternatively, alter an existing structure to cater for changes in the application environment.

(c)   Derive a new entity from existing ones. The result can be a subset of a single entity or a combination of two or more entities.

(d)   Redefine an existing attribute by associating it with a new data type. For example, if an existing attribute is of type 'decimal', then redefine it as type 'integer' and use it as such throughout an application.

(e)   Rename an entity or attribute to suit the needs of application users.

(f)   Change the order of values presented to the user from application to application or even from session to session. The new order can of course be a 'logical order' without necessarily affecting the way data is actually stored on the devices.

(g)   Apply different record selection criteria as and when required. These can vary from application to application or from session to session.

All the above logical functions can be carried out on request by the DBMS which will utilise specific field values during the execution of the application program. Moreover, the application programmer or database administrator has the option to make the changes on the database permanent, or to allow the DBMS to create the necessary conversions/transformations upon activation of an application.

2.2 STANDARD SOFTWARE AND THE DATABASE

Evidently, the majority of people today become familiar with a 'computer system' by using the software interface offered for man-machine communication. This can take the form of a special package (e.g wordstar, visicalc, paymaster), a programming language environment (e.g BASIC, Pascal, FORTRAN), an integrated and total program development environment (e.g Integrated Programming Support Environment (IPSE) using the language Ada), or an operating system (e.g UNIX, MS-DOS) offering a combination of all these. It is the latter category of interface that this section analyses in order to study its relationship to the DBMS.

As part of the standard computer software, we envisage a number of 'service functions' which can be called in a 'stand-alone' mode, or be offered as part of the operating system itself. Usually, it is a mixture of both resulting in a 'hotch-potch' of software. An attempt is thus made here to look at these service functions from the DBMS point of view, that is, database-related activities.

Service functions must be studied very closely and very carefully before any type of software is built around or in conjunction with the operating system. Possible design combinations from the set-theoretic point of view are as follows:

(a)   Custom-built software is totally independent of the operating system

(b)   Custom-built software is a subset of the operating system

(c)   Custom-built software is equivalent to the operating system

(d)   The operating system is a subset of custom-built software

Our approach to defining the co-existence of the DBMS and the operating system results in a strong interaction between the two [ANSI, 1984] and it is because of this property that we identify and present a list of fundamental functions as prerequisites to any potential co-existence. We identify the following operating system functions:

(a) Dynamic memory allocation and management
(b) Security services for unauthorised access
(c) Concurrency and parallel processing control
(d) Scheduling of resources or services
(e) Control of input, output, disk and file buffers
(f) Error detection/correction and communications

At a very much lower level (i.e close to the machine) we can consider what is called a 'layer', that is, a group of services, functions and communication protocols (i.e standards for the transfer of data) which is complete from the conceptual point of view.

Seven communication protocol layers, all very close to the computer hardware necessary for Open Systems Interconnections (OSI) [BSI, 1984], have been agreed upon by computer manufacturers and users and are presented below

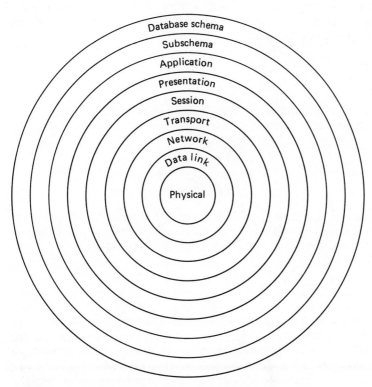

Figure 2.1   Architectural layers for data communication.

(layers 1 to 7) with examples of tasks performed. Layer numbers 8 and 9 are introduced here in order to place the DBMS in the right context and to denote the hierarchical structure implied by these layers. Each layer is enclosed within another (see Figure 2.1), starting with layer number 1 (the inner layer) so that each takes over 'control' from the immediately preceeding (i.e inner) layer. In other words, each layer prepares the ground for its successor.

1.   Physical; establish external, device-dependent features.
2.   Data link; notify local errors, link to physical device.
3.   Network; identify route, establish route, switch data.
4.   Transport; carry data through channel, check for errors.
5.   Session; set work area, connect, disconnect, maintain.
6.   Presentation; code, decode, display, transform data.
7.   Application; access remote files, secure files, records.
8.   Subschema; record types and relationships pertinent to one or more applications.
9.   Database schema; record types and relationships for the organisation as a whole.

Physical

The physical layer is concerned with the electronic and mechanical aspects of the devices and their effective inter-communication so that bits can be transmitted and received in a standardised manner.

Link

The aim here is to set up and maintain appropriate data links among a network of nodes (i.e transmitters and receivers). The link layer also aims to detect and possibly correct errors produced at the physical layer.

Network

The network layer is concerned with the activation and de-activation of connections between systems which communicate application-dependent data. It also offers the procedural means to exchange data between systems.

Transport

This layer offers the means to transport data across channels in a transparent manner and thereby enable the transport of data between session-dependent nodes. Transport of data is optimised in order to provide the performance required by each node and at the minimum possible cost. Optimisation factors are of course dependent on the complexity and size of concurrent demands upon the transport layer, as well as upon the quality of the network service itself.

Session

The session layer is concerned with the cooperation and orderly synchronisation of nodes so that their data exchange and general 'dialogue' is carried out effectively. It offers the necessary services for the above tasks to be implemented accordingly.

Presentation

This layer is concerned with the presentation of data to the user and therefore syntax and meaning of data are of primary importance.

Application

The purpose of this layer is to provide the necessary services to the users by acting as a 'window' whereby meaningful data is communicated to the application environment.

These layers can provide a framework for distributed database management and the DBMS need only concentrate on levels 7, 8 and 9 (layers 8 and 9 are discussed in more detail later). After that it can utilise existing software modules (usually part of the operating system itself) in order to carry out high level operations effectively.

Finally, where existing DBMS software is not sufficient or able to map peculiar or exceptional application requirements, it becomes necessary to use the facilities of other high level languages such as Pascal and FORTRAN or even low level languages (e.g assembly). These languages are otherwise known as 'host languages'. Problems may arise here due to the mixed programming mode and its inherent data communication difficulties (see Section 1.3) and so the database administrator must take care to reduce inter-dependence to the minimum.

2.3 THREE ARCHITECTURAL LEVELS

A high level architectural approach to analyse the complexity of the DBMS and to master its design as well as its usage, is to break the software down into three major components or levels on the basis of entities, relationships, users, applications and computer storage devices.

The levels here are, the logical, external and internal [Tsichritzis & Klug, 1978; ANSI, 1985], each resulting in what is generally referred to as a 'schema' (or 'schemata' in the plural form). So, we talk of the logical schema, the internal schema, and the external schema (otherwise referred to as 'subschema'). Each of these can, in fact, be supplied by different vendors, provided consistency is ensured through plug compatible software.

In order to appreciate the connection between the nine layers of software presented under Section 2.2 and the above three organisational levels, we present the following groupings:

Logical : Application layer, Schema
External: Subschema, Presentation layer
Internal: Layers 1 to 5, namely, Physical, Data link,
        Network, Transport and Session.

Figure 2.2 presents an overview of the three levels (to be studied in connection with the immediately following sections) using an example with three applications, namely, APL1, APL2, APL3 and therefore three subschemata, namely, SUB1, SUB2 and SUB3, and finally, three application programs, namely, PRO1, PRO2 and PRO3 [Yannakoudakis, 1984]. These mnemonic names (APL1, SUB1, PRO1, etc) can in fact be the keywords whereby the corresponding database levels are invoked, but they can become more meaningful, such as, PAYROLL, LABELS, PRODUCTION-CONTROL, etc.

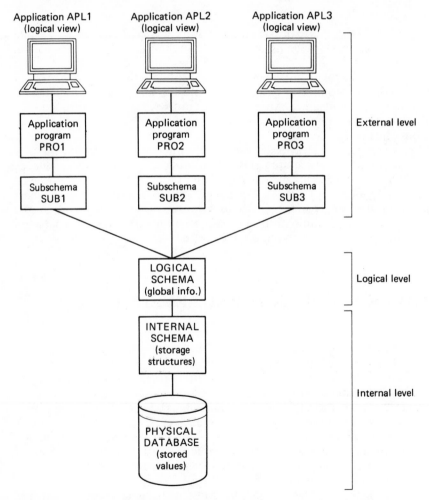

Figure 2.2   An example database architecture.

Ideally, an appropriate DBMS procedure will identify the type of user (see under Section 2.4) automatically and will proceed to establish the necessary connection. In turn, appropriate commands will be offered for further clarification of user requirements. The simple use of a password system can for example achieve this quite satisfactorily.

2.3.1 Logical Schema

This incorporates appropriate definitions for each of the various types of logical records, relationships, security and integrity checks. Generally speaking, the logical schema forms the collective view of all different types of records, relationships, and all applications, reflecting the global model of an enterprise. Throughout the book, and unless otherwise stated, when we refer to schema we will imply the logical schema.

If data independence is to be maintained, then the definitions at the schema must exclude any references to physical data organisation, that is, the way fields or records are accessed or structured on the actual physical devices such as magnetic disks.

The use of a suitable DBMS sublanguage, the Data Description Language (DDL), enables the creation of the schema including logical records, data items, relationships, etc. An appropriate DBMS utility then compiles the schema and creates the 'object schema' of the organisation.

A logical record can be considered equivalent to record type and a data item can be considered equivalent to a field type. We must however point out that the terms 'logical record' and 'data item' are closer to the concepts of the user whereas the terms 'record' and 'field' are closer to the format of data at the physical level.

2.3.2 Logical Subschema

This is a subset of the database schema and corresponds to the view of the user or individual application. It is often referred to as a 'view'. A suitable DBMS sublanguage, along the lines of a schema DDL, can be used to compose and compile the subschema.

The subschema incorporates the definitions of only those logical records and data items relevant to an application. Obviously, we have as many subschemata as there are distinct applications (see Figure 2.2) but it also makes sense for a subschema to be shared by different applications.

A subschema then comes closer to the users than its parent schema since it represents a collective view regarding an application. For example, the external view of users concerned with payroll may be 'a set of employee records each containing the name, department, pay code, bank account, National Insurance number, tax details'.

To a certain extent, the subschema is a convenient way to protect the database and to prevent users from accessing data which is of no concern to them or indeed irrelevant to their subject.

We must stress that the definition of a subschema should not introduce any new information whatsoever and all its needs should be directly mapped from the logical schema. If however, the subschema cannot be derived fully from the schema, then the database administrator has to change the schema itself to accommodate this rather than to expand the subschema locally and independently. A decent DBMS should not, in any case, allow the latter to take place.

2.3.3 Internal Schema

This level is concerned with the way data is actually structured and stored on the physical devices (see Figure 2.2). An appropriate sublanguage, the Data Storage Description Language (DSDL), enables definitions of all types of internal records, structures and storage slots and attempts to accommodate the requirements of the complete logical schema.

However, the DSDL handling the physical component should allow the development of the internal schema to proceed in a step-wise fashion. This may in fact be necessary where the logical schema itself is developed in a similar manner.

So, the implementation of the database can take place incrementally, application by application, from one human process to the next, or from one software module to the next. The choice here is debatable and heavily dependent on the type of enterprise using the database and of course the facilities offered by the DBMS.

The internal schema, otherwise referred to as 'storage schema', concentrates on alternative forms for efficient access with respect to storage devices, concurrent database access, file and record clustering, paging, coding of values, stored order, etc.

For an internal schema to be tailored to the hardware in order to map the logical schema effectively, the database administrator or software engineer must have information regarding access frequency, access type (e.g direct or sequential), clusters required, and general storage features.

The only problem here is that when the database is first set up usage frequency statistics may not always be available - unless the enterprise is converting from a file-based system to a DBMS and past statistical data is available. With all due respect for file-based systems, their statistical data may not always be accurate and in any case, it may not be consistent with the adopted database structure or record types defined in the logical schema.

Thus, the only sure way to proceed is to allow the DBMS itself to collect usage statistics from the point 'go' and subsequently to utilise these in order to tune the database. Physical performance modelling can play an important role here provided it is carried out objectively and with database-related internal records and values.

Several database researchers and authors make use of the terms 'internal record' or 'device record'. However, the main point is how far down the storage level the internal schema can afford to go. Let us discuss this further by analysing the subject matter in an objective way and by considering the various layers or shells within the internal schema.

Before we look at the database records, we will attempt to make a parallelism with computer software records. Let the assembly instruction LDX 1 NUM load accumulator 1 with the contents of variable NUM. This low level instruction can be called the internal software record. Now, consider a string of bits 01000010001011010100011011001 to be the translation of the low level instruction to an equivalent word in a 32-bit word computer. The bits refer to an operator, operand and accumulator as held on the operation decoder. This string of bits can be referred to as the device software record.

Returning to the database records: If we start in a 'bottom up' manner from the innermost record to the outermost record, then we end up with a series of shells where 'Device record' becomes the innermost layer of data and 'Conceptual record' becomes the outermost layer of data:

1.   Device record; one or more internal computer words.
2.   Physical record; one or more storage slots (e.g sectors).
3.   Storage record; as may be defined by an internal schema DSDL.
4.   Logical record; as defined by a schema or subschema DDL.
5.   Conceptual record; a conceptual entity of the real world.

In our opinion, a DSDL cannot afford to go below layer number 3 as it will be re-inventing the wheel. Appropriate functions and software tools operating below this layer will already exist as part of the operating system and in the form of standard services. However, we must point out here that the inadequacy and innefficiency of many operating systems force DBMS designers to re-write standard software.

Research in database management systems can lose sight of its main objectives and therefore attempt to establish as many internal schemata as there are layers of internal data, that is, storage, physical and device schemata. This is in fact what is being attempted by many database gurus today: the design of a Device Media Control Language (DMCL) offering yet another software layer between hardware and storage schema. However, for our purposes here, when we refer to an internal schema we will consider it synonymous or rather tautologous to storage, physical and device schema.

2.4 TYPES OF USERS

For an organisation to be managed effectively it becomes necessary to identify specific tasks and to define these accurately for the benefit of all. Of course the organisation ticks in a dynamic and ever evolving fashion, but so should tasks and people evolve and adapt to the current trends. Change and dynamicism then become the keywords.

Dynamicism is particularly important for an information system and demands a methodological approach to the design, set up, maintenance, tuning and tailoring of the database as well as surrounding software. In this section we identify and outline the role of each key database-related post relevant to all enterprises regardless of size or complexity.

Figure 2.3 presents the operational levels of the database environment according to the three-level architecture (logical, internal, subschema). It also shows the depth and level of responsibility for each of the major database posts to be studied in connection with the following sections.

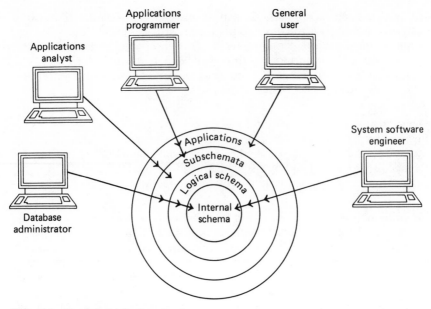

Figure 2.3   Operational database levels.

2.4.1 Database Administrator (DBA)

This person has overall responsibility for all operational data within the database. He must have a high degree of technical expertise in order to control the structure of data, relationships among entities, relationships among application environments and users.

In most cases, it will be the DBA who creates, compiles and maintains all schemata and surrounding subschemata. Besides, any changes in the characteristics of data (e.g size and length of a data item) are authorised by the DBA.

Another important function of the DBA is to report to top management and to communicate information extracted from the database for decision-support activities, as well as information regarding database growth, usage, priorities, hardware upgrades and budgetary requirements. State of the art reports to management and users alike also become an essential part of the DBA's responsibilities.

Finally, the DBA ensures that standards are adopted and maintained at all software levels of schema, subschema, application programs and internal schema.

2.4.2 System Software Engineer (SSE)

The complexity of database software requires a highly trained person to ensure that it is used effectively and efficiently. It becomes the responsibility of the SSE to see that database software (including the operating system and other attached modules and packages) is introduced and maintained properly and that it is not interfered with by unauthorised database users.

A trendy proverb states that 'the best way to debug software is to release it for general use'. We are all aware of this unacceptable malpractice by designers and implementors of software and must therefore be prepared to accept the so called 'new version' or rather 'fewer bugs' syndrome. The SSE ensures that software updates are carried out effectively and also co-ordinates all reported bugs and other unexpected responses from the system and attempts to resolve these appropriately.

2.4.3 Applications Analyst

This person is responsible for communicating with and establishing the needs of both management and application users. He forms a link between the applications programmer, the application user, the DBA and management. An important task involves the specification of all application procedures and layouts including input and output formats.

A parallel can be drawn here between traditional systems analysts and applications analysts although the applications analysts are more specialised in terms of familiarity with specific environments, such as, medical, engineering, financial, library, etc.

2.4.4 Applications Programmer

This person utilises subschemata and develops the necessary software for applications. Obviously, he collaborates closely with the applications analyst and observes the standards laid down by the DBA.

His tasks are similar to those of other high level programmers although familiarity with database principles and database software becomes an essential prerequisite.

2.4.5 General User

This is the person using the DBMS and who can of course be the DBA, the analyst, the programmer or general user of an application.

It is clear that the DBMS must be able to differentiate between categories of users and to enable appropriate levels of connection with the database as well as database software. Appropriate passwords or login procedures can be employed to identify and establish the desired and legitimate mode of connection between a user and the database.

2.5 SUMMARY

There are two important principles behind the operation of any DBMS:

(a) Physical independence implying that data and associated structures are manipulated on the devices without disturbing existing views at the logical level.

(b)   Logical independence implying that logical records and structures, as
       viewed by the users, are manipulated without disturbing existing storage
       structures or physical characteristics in general.

For the DBMS to perform effectively it is important to consider other standard
software (e.g the operating system of the computer in use, communication
software) and their integration. In this chapter, we presented an overview of the
possible *coexistence* of these, paying particular attention to the seven architectural
layers for Open Systems Interconnection (OSI), that is, physical, link network,
transport, session, presentation and application, and the levels at which the
functions of the DBMS converge with those of standard computer software.

The logical architecture of the database environment can be studied under
three major levels:

(a)   The logical schema which incorporates the definition of each of the various
       types of logical records, relationships, security and integrity checks.
(b)   The logical subschema which is a subset of the logical schema and
       corresponds to the view of a user or an individual application.
(c)   The internal schema which is concerned with the way data is actually
       structured and stored on the physical devices.

In accordance with this three-level architecture which we adopted, we
proceeded to describe the major classes of users (i.e database administrator,
system software engineer, applications analyst, applications programmer, and
general user) and their responsibilities.

2.6 REFERENCES

ANSI, X3/SPARC Database System Study Group, 'Reference Model for DBMS Standardisation',
    1984.
ANSI, X3H2, 'Concepts and Terminology for the Conceptual Schema and the Information Base',
    (ISO TC97/SC5/WG3), 1985.
BSI, 'Basic Reference Model for Open Systems Interconnection', BS 6568, 1984.
Fry, J. P. & Kahn, B. K., 'A Stepwise Approach to Database Design', Proc. ACM Southeast Reg.
    Conf., pp. 34-43, 1976.
Fry, J. P. & Sibley, E. H., 'Evolution of Database Management Systems', Computing Surveys, Vol. 8,
    No. 1, pp. 7-42, March 1976.
Stonebraker, M. R., 'A Functional View of Data Independence', Proc. ACM SIGMOD Workshop
    on Data Description, Access and Control, May 1974.
Tsichritzis, D. C. & Klug, A. (editors), 'The ANSI/X3/SPARC DBMS Framework: Report of the
    Study Group on Database Management systems', Information Systems, Vol. 3, 1978.
Yannakoudakis, E. J.,'The Logic of Database Systems', D.P. International, Institute of Data
    Processing Management, London, pp. 169-174, March 1984.

3 DATA STRUCTURES AND DATA MODELS

3.1 INTRODUCTION

A data item, in the present context, is the most elementary building block of records and therefore a database. It can represent a *conceptual object* (e.g the edition number of a book) or a *structural object* (e.g an internal value, pointing to a book held by a reader and therefore linking entities READER and BOOK together). A data structure is an organised system of relationships among data items, structural objects and record types, the totality of which provides the means of mapping the logical schema onto an internal equivalent.

It is the type of data structures which are supported by a DBMS, that will determine the viability and flexibility of accessing the various data items of a given organisation. The types of data structures supported, will also dictate the features of the data storage description language itself. Our aim here is to outline the criteria whereby data items can be analysed, in order to bind together logical record types capable of supporting the needs of an organisation. To this end, it becomes necessary to adopt an appropriate conceptual data model which is independent of logical or internal models.

The conceptual model is established following a detailed data analysis and functional analysis of the enterprise, application by application. After the conceptual model has been established, the logical model can be designed by utilising only the information contained within the conceptual model and an appropriate Data Definition Language (DDL) of the DBMS.

In the present context, a 'data model' represents and reflects accurately the relationships that exist among a set of record types, data items or fields; we often discuss these with the generic term 'node' or 'element'. The relationships, in effect, exemplify a bondage of elements, the totality of which defines a comprehensive structure that is capable of embodying the information flow between and within different applications in an enterprise.

In further analysis of the relationships among a set of data items, it becomes clear that they can be exemplified through two different types of structures:

(a) Intra-record structures, that is, the way data items are placed in each record [Olle, 1969]
(b) Inter-record structures, that is, the way records are placed in files [Navathe & Fry, 1976]. In other words, relationships among record types

Let us investigate possible intra-record structures. A data item can be defined as

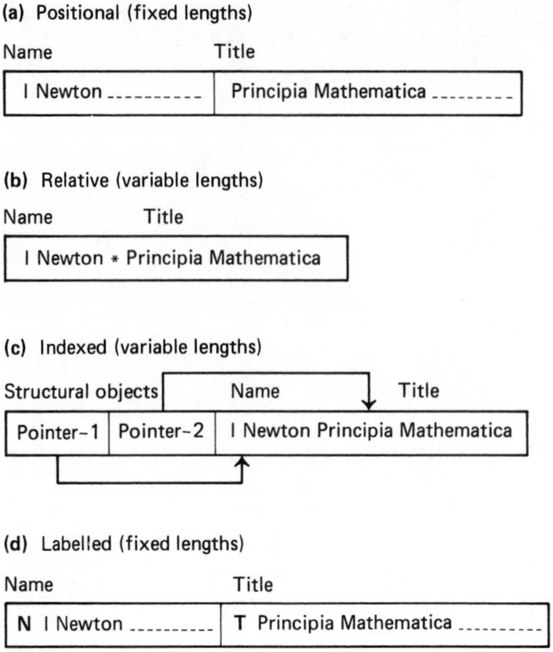

(a) Positional (fixed lengths)

Name   Title

| I Newton _____ | Principia Mathematica _____ |

(b) Relative (variable lengths)

Name   Title

| I Newton * Principia Mathematica |

(c) Indexed (variable lengths)

Structural objects | Name ↓ Title

| Pointer-1 | Pointer-2 | I Newton Principia Mathematica |

(d) Labelled (fixed lengths)

Name   Title

| **N** I Newton _____ | **T** Principia Mathematica _____ |

Figure 3.1   Intra-record structures.

a pair <data-item-name, value> where 'data-item-name' identifies an object and 'value' conveys the value associated with it. Examples are: <name, Clark B E>, <name, Smith J>, <reader-identifier, R101>. There are basically four different ways of storing data items within records. These are termed: (a) Positional, (b) Relative, (c) Indexed and (d) Labelled. Figure 3.1 presents examples of each using two different data items, namely, 'Author' of book and 'Title' of work.

Under positional, relative and indexed, data items are assumed to be stored in the correct sequence and, therefore, it is not necessary to store the names of the objects which are, in effect, implicit from the ordering of values. The positional technique (Figure 3.1 (a)) allocates fixed length storage, at a fixed displacement from the beginning of a record, for every data item. If the value to be stored is shorter than the allocated space, then the value may be left- or right-justified.

The relative and indexed techniques can be used when there is a storage problem and, therefore, a need to store only the actual values of data items. Under the relative technique (Figure 3.1 (b)), successive storage locations are used to store values, each separated by a predefined delimiter (e.g a '*'). Where a value is missing or is not relevant to a specific record occurrence, the delimiter will still be present to indicate the order of the data items. Under the indexed technique (Figure 3.1 (c)), the record is augmented with a set of pointers or indices (the structural objects), which indicate the first and/or last locations of successive data items. The values of the pointers can be actual addresses or relative displacements of values within records.

Under the labelled technique (Figure 3.1 (d)), data items are assigned unique identifiers or codes (e.g. 'N' for name, 'T' for title) thereby eliminating the need to store missing or unwanted values. Moreover, the presence of codes, waives the need to have a predefined order of data items in each record type. Labelled storage can of course be used in conjunction with a positional technique, as is the case with the example of Figure 3.1 (d).

Clearly, the design of appropriate files (e.g. sequential, direct, indexed), incorporating the above techniques, and the ordering of values under data items (in a 'vertical' manner), is enterprise-dependent and is determined by the operations that are to be performed upon the values themselves. A combination of the above techniques may by implented within a single record type. Also, where overflow occurs (i.e. where a value requires more storage than has been catered for), then other structural data items can signify the continuation of a value.

While the choice of data items and associated operations depends on the requirements of each application, the design of storage structures (including inter- and intra-record relationships), to a certain extent, allows for independent development and innovation [Kouvatsos & Yannakoudakis, 1982]. After the components of logical records have been analysed, the design of storage records can take place and storage structures can be determined accordingly. It is important, at that stage, to distinguish between computer-dependent storage slots (e.g. blocks, pages) and computer-independent data elements and relationships of accessibility or ordering among these.

Following detailed analyses of conceptual entities [Chen, 1976], we will be in a position to create stable groups of attributes which can then be turned into appropriate logical record types [Senko, 1975]. This is no trivial task and the designer must adopt objective criteria [Kouvatsos & Yannakoudakis, 1982] whereby these units can be established. To this end, a number of fundamental questions must be answered during the analysis of data items. These include:

(1)   To what extent the presence of a data item contributes towards the description of a record type.
(2)   To what extent a data item is compatible with others in the same record type.
(3)   Whether the presence of a data item necessitates the presence of others.
(4)   To what extent a data item contributes towards non-unique identification of record occurrences.
(5)   To what extent a data item contributes towards unique identification of record occurrences
(6)   How can we determine the interaction, if any, between two or more data items.

Other more immediate considerations are: The type of each data item (e.g. string, numeric), the length of each data item, how frequently a data item appears within different applications

Record structures are designed so that the data items themselves can be processed in an optimal way. This may mean ease of access of a data item (i.e. its value(s)), in the minimum possible time [Teory & Fry, 1982]. To this end, data items must be placed within record types in such a way that they conform with the access requests which are likely to occur. When access requirements change frequently, the database structure should be able to accommodate the changes, without major restructuring or inconvenience to the user community.

Following detailed analyses of different applications and corresponding logical record types, we will be in a position to model a structure and to assess its effectiveness, by studying: (a) distinct and well defined record types, (b) relationships between record types, and (c) operations performed upon record types. Because a 'record' is considered to be the basic logical unit of input and output (as far as the user and applications programmer are concerned), it becomes necessary to investigate a number of fundamental points, such as:

(1)   Number of record occurrences under each record type
(2)   Access and coaccess of records within an application
(3)   Access and coaccess of records between applications
(4)   Direct and indirect relationships among records
(5)   Frequency of access of records
(6)   Frequency and type of operations performed upon records

Inter-record structures can be investigated from the global point of view (i.e as applied to the totality of the logical schema), by considering the different ways two or more record types can be bound together. Current state of the art in database design, recognises three different types of logical structures and therefore models [Date, 1986]. These are, the *tree* (or hierarchic) where each record occurrence does not have more than one 'parent' record occurrence, the *network* where a record occurrence may have more than one 'parent' record occurrence associated with it, and finally, the *relational* where the presence of common data items (otherwise known as keys) among record types forms the basis of binding record types together. (Other data models proposed include the 'Entity-Relationship' [Chen, 1976], 'Binary', 'Semantic Network', and 'Infological' [Tsichritzis & Lochovsky, 1982].)

Under the tree and network models the binding of record types has to be stated explicitly, whereas under the relational model, the relationships are implicit. In other words, under the relational model, certain data items may also be considered as structural objects (e.g pointers and indicators). Each of these models is discussed in some detail later.

It is clear from the preceding discussion that the design of stable and structured records should achieve a union, resulting in a harmony between two realms:

(a)   The definition of the problem in terms of a set of elements imposing demands on the structure/model itself, and
(b)   The final structure/model (the solution) which should also be under the direct and independent control of the DBA or system software engineer.

3.2 DATA STRUCTURES AND RELATIONSHIPS

At the conceptual level of database design, the relationships among attributes are formed without regard to their implementation at the storage level or efficiency in

(a) Repeating attribute 'Book' viewed as a linear structure

BOOKS-BORROWED

Reader– no	Book			
R101	B100	B110	B901	B909

(b) Repeating attribute 'Book' viewed as a tree

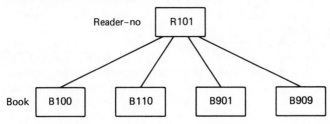

Figure 3.2 Two different views of a repeating attribute.

access. The logical level aims to analyse conceptual entities so that they can be mapped onto appropriate logical and subsequently storage structures. Our aim here, is to investigate, in an integrated manner, the underlying storage structures upon which the logical schema is based, independent of programming language or database utility. We also look at the use of primary and secondary keys and how they influence the structuring of data.

3.2.1 Data Structures on Keys

Generally speaking, keys are important because they establish 'natural' relationships among elements and therefore clusters of related values, without having to state relationships explicitly. The clusters are formed as a result of multiple record occurrences that can be analysed 'vertically' (i.e one or more columns at a time) [Yannakoudakis, 1979].

In simple terms, a *primary* key is unique to a given record, whereas a *secondary* key may be common to two or more records. It is essential that all unique records within a database be allocated unique keys in order to enable their isolation and extraction from the database. On the basis of these considerations, it becomes clear that it is possible to establish and represent any type of linkage between elements [Bachman, 1969], by choosing appropriate keys as *binding* data items.

The concept of secondary keys enables us to include a data item, which may be the primary key of a record type, within another record type. We can, for example, include the data item 'Book' (repeating this as many times as we wish) within record type BOOKS-BORROWED, in order to establish the linear structure shown in Figure 3.2 (a). An alternative way to denote this, is a tree structure such as the one presented in Figure 3.2 (b) where reader number R101 becomes the *owner* of occurrences B100, B110, B901 and B909.

The allocation of fixed length storage (e.g a maximum of four entries for data item 'Book', as shown in Figure 3.2 (a)), may not reflect conceptual requirements accurately. Besides, with fixed length records there is bound to be some wastage of storage since not all of the reserved locations will be taken up (e.g not all library users will hold the maximum number of books allowed at any point of time); naturally occurring information values are in most cases variable in length.

The conceptual requirements implied by the example of Figure 3.2 aim to create a bond between entities READER and BOOK, so that, given a reader number, we can trace all the books he is currently holding; but it is also desirable to be able to trace the reader of a given book. What we are highlighting is a two-way communication structure where values under one entity can be used to retrieve values under another.

The primary key is otherwise known as the 'identifier of a record', whereas the secondary key is known as the 'identifier of a set of records' [Yannakoudakis, 1979], that is, a set of records which have a common secondary key, enabling requests involving boolean algebra to be performed upon the files. For example, 'find all books-borrowed where reader-no='R101' AND subject-code='computing'. Here, the key value 'R101' will be used to trace all the book numbers associated with it, then each of these will be used to retrieve the corresponding book details in order to determine whether the key value 'computing' exists under an appropriate data item or not.

Although advances in database systems enable users and programmers alike to utilise any data item as a key, it is important for us to clarify the techniques employed to trace record occurrences. There are basically two different classes of keys: the *physical* and the *symbolic*. A physical key points to the physical address of a record on a storage medium, such as a disk, whereas a symbolic key carries an ordinary value (e.g string, number) under a data item.

A symbolic key must be either hashed (i.e manipulated before an address can be derived), or be traced in an index which will contain its corresponding physical address. It should therefore be clear that when a database is reorganised and records are moved around or sorted for reasons of efficiency, a physical key may not point to the same record as before the reorganisation took place. This of course is not the case with symbolic keys because they are unaffected by physical database reorganisation, that is, their contents do not change, but only the parameters of the manipulative operations which derive the physical address. Obviously, symbolic keys are not as efficient as physical keys because of the extra time required to calculate the physical address.

The example we presented earlier involved a single type of secondary key (i.e 'Book'). There are also cases where multiple data items become secondary keys in order to satisfy more complex requests. The ability of database management systems to handle multiple secondary keys does, in fact, form one of the strongest arguments for their adoption. In what follows, we discuss this aspect by considering the terms 'data item' and 'key' to be synonymous.

When multiple secondary keys become necessary, then it may be possible to separate the records in one file and the keys in another. The keys can then be manipulated independent of the actual data, that is, without reading the source records themselves. This approach, in effect, provides a front-end to the actual retrieval of source records and may become necessary, especially where the records are large.

(a) One-way list (one pointer per element)

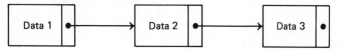

(b) Two-way list (two pointers per element)

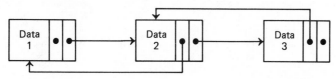

(c) Circular list (one pointer per element)

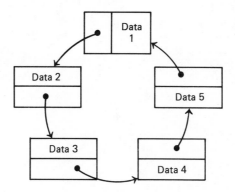

(d) Multiple list (three pointers per element)

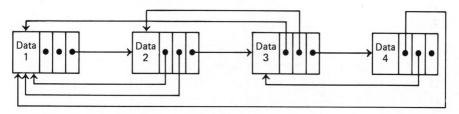

Figure 3.3 Example types of lists.

The file containing the keys can be represented by linked lists, such as, one-way, two-way, circular or multiple, as presented in Figure 3.3 [Knuth, 1973]. Multiple lists allow two or more pointers to be created for each element, and so two or more alternative paths can be offered when the list is traversed. In other words, while we traverse a multiple list, we have a choice to change direction when necessary.

Each path links elements [Bachman, 1969] with common characteristics or on the basis of some prespecified order (e.g numeric, lexicographic).

Figure 3.3 (a) shows a one-way list where each element is connected to the *next* by a single pointer. Figure 3.3 (b) shows the same data elements (i.e Data 1, Data 2 and Data 3) connected in the form of a two-way list (i.e two pointers per element, next and *prior*). Figure 3.3 (d) presents a multiple list structure where each of the three data elements also contains three pointers, the *next*, *prior* and

(a) File on 'Subject' (unique 'Location')

Subject	Location
Algebra	681.1
Botany	582.2
Computing	682.2
Philosophy	400.1
Physics	403.6

(b) File on 'Location' (unique 'Subject')

Location	Subject
400.1	Philosophy
403.6	Physics
582.2	Botany
681.1	Algebra
682.2	Computing

(c) File on 'Subject' (overlapping 'Location')

Subject	Location
Algebra	681.1
Arts	700.2
Botany	582.2
Computing	682.2
Electronics	682.2
Philately	700.2
Philosophy	400.1
Photography	700.2
Physics	403.6

Figure 3.4 Inverted files for secondary key processing.

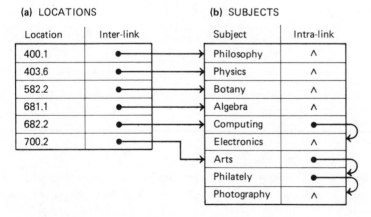

(a) LOCATIONS   **(b)** SUBJECTS

Figure 3.5 Inter- and intra-links with fixed length records
(∧ = last entry).

first. The 'first' pointer is used to connect each element to the first element in the list. Note that, both the 'first' and 'prior' pointers of the first element are empty. Also, the 'next' pointer of the last element in the list is empty.

With lists, the 'connections' among elements can be made through common keys or 'invisible' internal pointers. However, in the general case, linked lists are not efficient when they are used to process secondary keys. This is particularly evident when existing keys are deleted or new ones are inserted regularly (e.g where readers borrow and return books daily). In many cases, large sets of records have to be altered to accommodate an update, or even expanded to incorporate incoming keys. The latter case implies that extra storage space has to be allocated to all affected elements. When a multiple list is expanded, usually all elements have to be updated to incorporate the extra pointer field(s).

An alternative method of storing keys is by means of *inverted* files. Here, each type of secondary key is stored in a separate file which is usually ordered numerically or lexicographically and enables fast access by traversing efficient structures, such as trees (these are discussed later).

Consider the example presented in Figure 3.4 where the keys are: 'Subject' (Figure 3.4 (a)) and 'Location' (Figure 3.4 (b)). Record occurrences are sorted by primary key 'Subject' in Figure 3.4 (a) and by 'Location' in Figure 3.4 (b). This arrangement is acceptable provided secondary keys are unique and we do not, for example, have a situation where the same 'Location' is shared by more than one 'Subject', as is the case with the file in Figure 3.4 (c); the value 700.2 has been triplicated and the value 682.2 has been duplicated. The problem here is that the structure will give rise to unacceptable levels of duplicate values.

In order to understand the handling of non-unique secondary keys, we will use the example of Figure 3.4 (c) which points to two alternatives for overcoming the problem of redundancy or overlap.

The first alternative considers the key 'Location' as a repeating group, and proceeds by splitting the file into two: (a) LOCATIONS and (b) SUBJECTS as shown in Figure 3.5. The new structure enables direct access of records through primary key 'Location', or sequential access through the secondary key 'Subject'. Besides, intra-links can be used to connect all related subjects, as is the case with the entries 'COMPUTING', 'ELECTRONICS', 'ARTS', 'PHILATELY' and 'PHOTOGRAPHY'. Note that all entries within the file SUBJECTS are fixed in length.

The second alternative adopts variable length records within file SUBJECTS, as shown in Figure 3.6. This structure is obviously more complex to program and

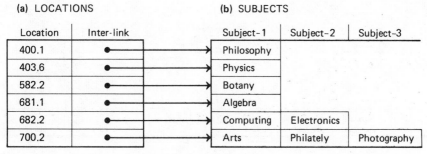

(a) LOCATIONS

Location	Inter-link
400.1	●
403.6	●
582.2	●
681.1	●
682.2	●
700.2	●

(b) SUBJECTS

Subject-1	Subject-2	Subject-3
Philosophy		
Physics		
Botany		
Algebra		
Computing	Electronics	
Arts	Philately	Photography

Figure 3.6 Inter-links and variable length records.

to maintain because storage devices usually offer fixed length slots (e.g sectors, blocks). So, for reasons of efficiency, we are forced to transform entities into record types which are fixed in length.

In summary, a combination of both linked lists and inverted files offers an efficient environment for the processing of database records with multiple secondary keys. In order to demonstrate the logic of utilising inter- and intra-record structures, in a co-ordinated manner, we present the following procedure which manipulates the files LOCATIONS and SUBJECTS (see Figure 3.5) and traces and displays all related (linked) record occurrences, from any given record occurrence identified by a key (K) in LOCATIONS:

(1)   Accept a key K holding a value under 'Location' in file LOCATIONS
(2)   Find the position of a record in file LOCATIONS using K
(3)   Read the record with key K and associated link L from file LOCATIONS
(4)   Repeat
(5)   Find the position of the corresponding record in file SUBJECTS using L
(6)   Read the record and its associated link M from file SUBJECTS
(7)   Display the record read from file SUBJECTS
(8)   Set L = M
(9)   Until L = 'NULL' (i.e until link L is empty)
(10) End

3.2.2 Tree Structures

A special class of a linked system of elements, forming a discrete structure, is the 'tree' or hierarchy [Knuth, 1973] as is better understood in business. Trees impose a discipline on data structures by not allowing 'cycles' (i.e elements which refer to themselves). Each value of an element in a tree has a single 'parent', for example, a book which may be held by a single reader at any point of time. In other words, each element has a single pointer coming in, except the top element which can have many pointers to it. Moreover, the elements in a tree are ordered.

The top element in a tree is called the *root* and the bottom elements are referred to as the *leaves*. The maximum number of *children* (i.e non-leaf elements) per

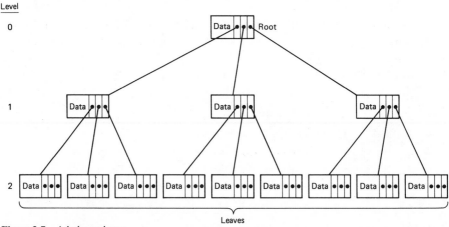

Figure 3.7   A balanced tree.

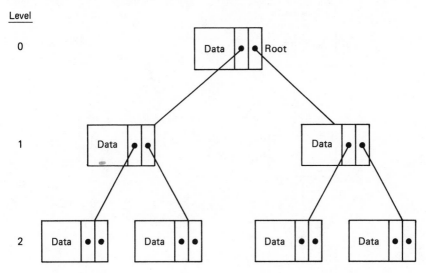

Figure 3.8   A binary tree.

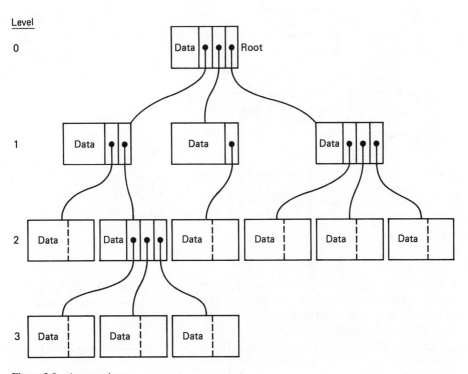

Figure 3.9   A general tree.

(a) The model

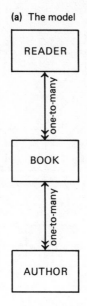

(b) An occurrence of the model

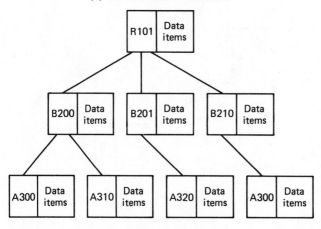

Figure 3.10   An example hierarchic model - Case A.

parent is otherwise referred to as the *degree* of the tree. Also, the *level* of a tree element signifies the number of branches required to reach the root, and the *depth* of a tree signifies the maximum number of levels available. Figure 3.7 presents an example tree of depth 2 and degree 3.

Basically, there are three different types of trees: the balanced, binary and general. A *balanced tree* requires that each element has associated with it the same number of elements. An example of this is presented in Figure 3.7. A *binary tree* requires that each element has associated with it exactly two elements, as is the case with Figure 3.8.

A *general tree* does not impose any restrictions on the number of children per element and although this may appear to be the best solution, the structure will generally be very inefficient because each element has a variable number of storage slots allocated to it. This imposes extra overheads in terms of control information necesary to maintain the structure. An example of a general tree is presented in Figure 3.9.

A special class of balanced tree, with a degree greater than or equal to 3, is the B-tree [Bayer & McCreight, 1972; Comer, 1979] where each leaf has exactly the same path length from the root (i.e all leaves have the same level). For practical reasons, the degree of a B-tree should be an odd number. It has been established that B-trees are very efficient for database design.

The elements of a tree can be keys (primary or secondary) which can be manipulated independent of the source records. The well known binary search technique utilises a binary tree, where only one of the two branches is chosen for further comparisons; the elements here are sorted in ascending or descending order. B-trees are also popular for secondary key processing, as well as in cases where large indexes are required [Held & Stonebraker, 1978]. Finally, we must point out that trees can be represented by linked lists.

3.3 HIERARCHIC DATA MODELS

Because a hierachic model is very similar to a tree, the same terminology applies. What we must stress here is that a hierarchic model can only handle one-to-one and one-to-many relationships among elements. The relationship many-to-one is not allowed in a hierarchy. So, an occurrence under an element, say, book number B100, can have a single parent, say, reader number R101. Generally speaking, an element in a hierarchy can be thought of as a distinct record type which may own one or more other distinct record types.

In all types of hierarchies (binary, balanced and general) the root corresponds to the most binding record type which establishes a pre-defined order among all elements. Nested hierarchies are possible where a child is also a parent. We could, for example, consider READER as the most binding record type, in order to establish the hierarchy shown in Figure 3.10 (a) where READER owns BOOK and BOOK owns AUTHOR. Figure 3.10 (b) shows an actual occurrence with this hierarchy.

The hierachic model binds record types together so that occurrences under a given level can be used to retrieve others directly below it. Now, if a record occurrence is not directly below another, then it cannot be accessed directly. For example, if an author has published two or more books, as is the case with the occurrence shown in Figure 3.10 (b), then we will not be able to cluster the books B200 and B210 which have been written by author A300. Clearly, a certain amount of redundancy is introduced because a record occurrence (e.g A300) is actually repeated under two different sub-trees (e.g B200 and B210). So, the designer must estimate the degree of redundancy, before a specific binding order is utilised. But above all, he must ensure that any changes/updates to the values of elements, are propagated consistently and throughout the overlapping elements.

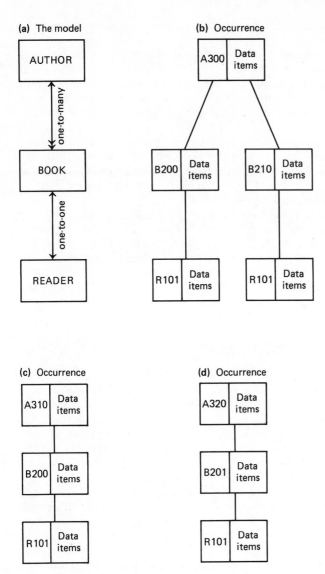

Figure 3.11   An example hierarchic model - Case B.

An alternative binding order for the record types of Figure 3.10 is presented in Figure 3.11. Here, AUTHOR owns BOOK and BOOK owns READER. The corresponding occurrence hierarchies are presented in Figure 3.11 (b), (c) and (d), showing clearly an even greater amount of redundancy than has been the case with the example of Figure 3.10. However, with one-to-one relationships (see Figure 3.11 (a) where BOOK owns READER), we can combine the child with the owner and therefore reduce the level by one, as is the case with the model of Figure 3.12. This will ultimately reduce the access path of a leaf from the root and therefore optimise its access time.

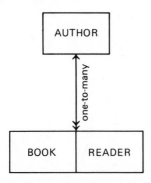

Figure 3.12   An example hierarchic model - Case C.

In conclusion, the hierarchic model offers a simple and natural way to represent database models, and although a certain amount of data redundancy will always be present, related data can be retrieved efficiently by traversing pointers (usually starting with the root element). However, inverted files can also be employed to represent hierarchies. In many practical situations, it is difficult (if not impossible) to model data using hierarchies. It is not therefore advisable to impose a hierarchic model upon the enterprise, if the data itself does not direct the designer to such a course of action. Evidently, it is easy to form unbalanced trees and thereby increase the complexity in database design and programming.

3.4 NETWORK DATA MODELS

A network differs from a hierarchy in that its elements can have more than one owner each, and all relationships are stated explicitly between two or more record types. In other words, a record occurrence can be owned by two or more other record occurrences. This helps reduce the redundancy introduced in the hierarchic model, by defining appropriate multiple incoming pointers to each record occurrence.

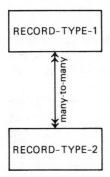

Figure 3.13   General representation of a network model.

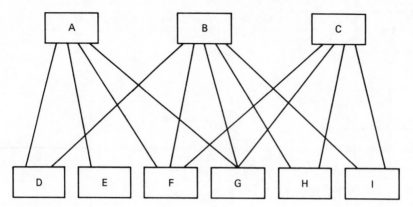

Figure 3.14   An example of a network model.

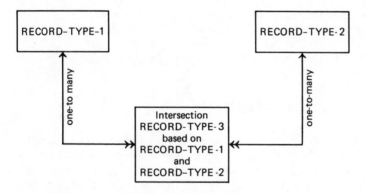

Figure 3.15   Decomposition of the network in Figure 3.13 into two one-to-many relationships.

The general representation of a network model is shown in Figure 3.13; note the many-to-many relationship between record types '1' and '2'. An example occurrence of a network model is presented in Figure 3.14 where the elements A, B and C can be considered as the 'owners' of D, E, F, G, H and I.

A network of record occurrences can materialise under the following different clusters:

(a)   A single record occurrence with a single owner. For example, a department with a single manager.

(b)   A single record occurrence with multiple owners. For example, a book written by two or more authors.

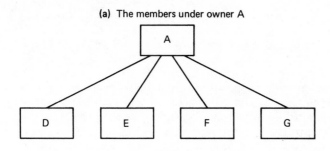

(a) The members under owner A

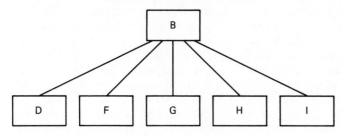

(b) The members under owner B

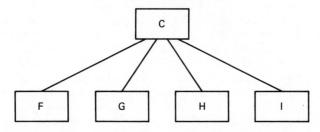

(c) The members under owner C

Figure 3.16   Three trees derived from the network of Figure 3.14.

(c)   Multiple record occurrences with a single owner. For example, many
       history records for an employee.
(d)   Multiple record occurrences with multiple owners. For example, many
       library locations with many books and common (identical) books in
       different locations.

Moreover, the above clusters can materialise under different classes of
relationships among distinct record types. The classes (arrangements) here can be
discussed as follows:

(a)   A single record type owner of a single record type member.
(b)   A single record type owner of multiple record type members.

(c)   Multiple record types assumed to form an owner of a single record type member.
(d)   Multiple record types assumed to form an owner of multiple record type members.

The complexity of implementing appropriate database software to handle the above, particularly the classes (c) and (d), makes it necessary for vendors to restrict the class of relationships which can be supported by the DBMS. For example, the CODASYL proposal we discuss in Chapter 9 states that: within a set of related record types, only one can be defined as the 'owner' and all the rest as its 'member' record types; multiple relationships can be defined under multiple set types, with common (overlapping) record types [CODASYL, 1978].

In many cases, it becomes necessary to create an *intersection* record type which aims to link other record types, and therefore bind these together in order to resolve logical requirements which cannot be implemented directly with a DBMS. One way to create an intersection record type is to use, as its components, the primary keys of the corresponding record types (note that it is also possible to include other data items within an intersection record type). So, the general network model corresponding to a many-to-many relationship, as shown in Figure 3.13, can be transformed into the model presented in Figure 3.15, where the many-to-many relationship is represented by two one-to-many relationships.

Networks can also be decomposed into a number of hierarchies, as is the case with Figure 3.16 which shows three trees derived from the network of Figure 3.14. Decomposition, however, can cause duplication of elements, as is the case in Figure 3.16 where elements D, F, G, H and I are repeated (duplicated) under different trees. So, the problems of the hierarchic model are also present here.

In some cases duplication is acceptable but in some others it is not. If duplication is bound to occur as a result of network decomposition, then the designer must carry out a thorough study of the degree of duplication, so that alternative structures which aim to reduce this can be considered. If the record occurrence being duplicated involves lengthy data items, such as textual strings, then it will be worthwhile to carry out a thorough data analysis exercise and to consider, for example, the use of pointers to access each occurrence from an independent file, rather than to incorporate the information within each element of the hierarchy.

The most common method of processing networks is to establish multiple links or pointers at each element, on the basis of which the structure itself can be traversed to retrieve the corresponding data. It is also customary to use the same number of links per element, since variable length records are difficult to represent physically. While the structure is being utilised and where extra links are required, then a tag within each element may indicate the presence of an overflow area which contains the rest of the links. The overflow area itself can have a fixed number of links per element.

It is not the number of record types which determines the degree of complexity of a network model, but rather the links it contains. Consider, for example, the model of Figure 3.17 where a BOOK is common to two or more subjects, and where a SUBJECT has more than one book. Besides, a SUBJECT can be found at specific locations in the library and a LOCATION may be shared by two or more subjects. Now, the example in Figure 3.17 implies that, the location of a book can be retrieved directly as well as through SUBJECT which is also related to

LOCATION. The major task facing the designer here, is the identification and elimination of redundant links.

Networks sometimes result in cycles or loops where an element appears to be linked to itself. Take the case of a BOOK type linked to itself when multiple element values refer to its constituent parts; for example, repeated record occurrences, referring to each and every joint author of a given book. This category of cycle occurs when a record type is defined as member and owner of the same single record type set. Let us discuss another example. Suppose record type EMPLOYEES holds the details of all the employees of an organisation, where some of the employees are classed as 'managers' and the rest as 'employees under named managers'. The definition of a set, say, MANAGES (see Figure 3.18) where record type EMPLOYEES is the owner and only member of the set, enables the logical 'partitioning' of all employees by manager.

There is another category of cycle that incorporates two or more record types. Consider an example of a manufacturer producing different guns. Some of the guns may be sub-contracted out to other manufacturers, and a contract may refer to several guns. The loop in this example incorporates the record types

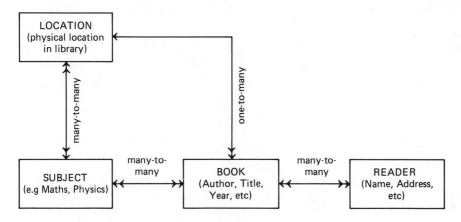

Figure 3.17   A network model of a library system.

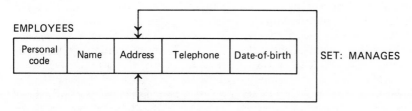

Figure 3.18   A single-type cycle.

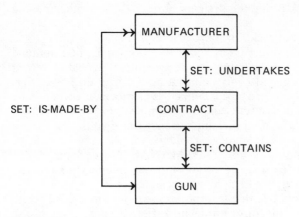

Figure 3.19   A three-type cycle.

MANUFACTURER, CONTRACT and GUN, as presented in Figure 3.19 which shows three different sets as follows:

SET: UNDERTAKES
Owner : MANUFACTURER
Member: CONTRACT

SET: CONTAINS
Owner : CONTRACT
Member: GUN

SET: IS-MADE-BY
Owner : GUN
Member: MANUFACTURER

Although a logical schema can be designed so that unnecessary cycles/loops and redundant links are excluded, subsequently, it may be altered to accommodate new requirements. If the designer or DBA is not careful, alterations and amendments can introduce redundancy which, in many cases, is very difficult to detect without exhaustive analysis of existing relationships.

In order to demonstrate the way logical requirements are mapped onto network models, and how these are affected following changes in the requirements, we consider a University environment, as depicted in Figure 3.20, showing one-to-many relationships. Each department is responsible for running a number of courses, with its own academic and technical staff. The model contains four record types, namely, DEPARTMENT, TECHNICAL, COURSE and ACADEMIC, and three sets (i.e direct relationships), namely, DEPARTMENT-TECHNICAL in set-1, DEPARTMENT-COURSE in set-2 and DEPARTMENT-ACA-DEMIC in set-3. Clearly, record type DEPARTMENT is related to three different sets.

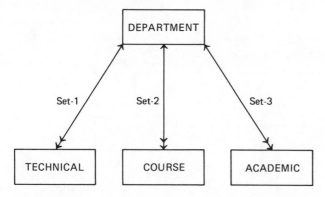

Figure 3.20 A University environment (one-to-many relationships).

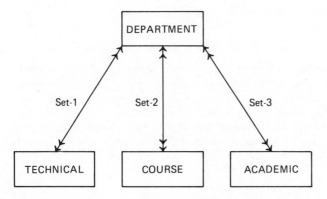

Figure 3.21 A University environment (many-to-many relationships).

The model of Figure 3.20 implies that each department is independent of others, that is, its resources are not shared. Suppose, however, that a reorganisation is envisaged where academic and technical staff are shared by different departments. Also, depending on our definition of a 'course', this may also be shared by different departments where, for example, a course refers to a single subject, such as programming in FORTRAN, rather than to a degree course. Thus, the new model introduces many-to-many relationships, as shown in Figure 3.21.

If the DBMS cannot support many-to-many relationships directly, then decomposing the network into one-to-many relationships, by employing intersection record types, produces the model presented in Figure 3.22. Each intersecting record type, therefore, becomes the 'medium' of communication between the two original types and must be used as the basis for traversing the structure itself.

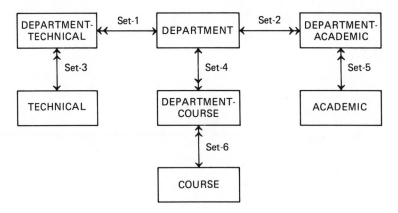

Figure 3.22   A University environment (final structure).

In conclusion, the network model appears to offer a very powerful approach to modelling our logical requirements, but it can also give rise to duplication of elements and data redundancy, as is the case with the hierarchic model. The multiplicity of links (paths) makes it rather difficult to keep track of where we are, while traversing the network. Maintenance of the database is complicated and error prone, especially as we try to trace and isolate the required 'owner' records from multiple owner occurrences.

3.5 RELATIONAL DATA MODELS

The relational model can be characterised as the simplest way to represent data relationships, since it conforms with the external database level which, in most cases, exemplifies a tabular form [Codd, 1970]. Here, the columns refer to the attributes (i.e data items) and the rows to the entries of the table (i.e record occurrences). An example table called READER (i.e library user) with six columns, each corresponding to an attribute, is presented in Figure 3.23. The attributes are 'Reader-code', 'Reader-name', 'Address', 'Sex', 'Status', and 'Department'.

READER

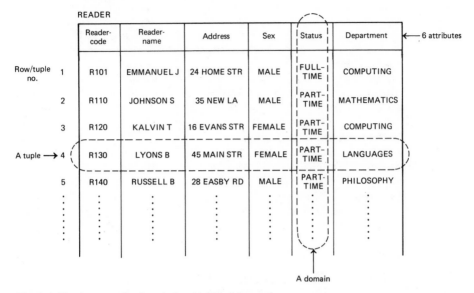

Figure 3.23   An example of a relational table of degree 6.

The relational model has adopted its own terminology and although this may appear confusing to the student, we must point out that its underlying principles are based on matrix theory, relational algebra and relational calculus. Its main aim is to use primary and secondary keys as the basis to form the relationships among record types. In other words, the relationships are established through keys which are common between record types; the relationships are implicit and independent of physical implementations.

3.5.1 Relational Terminology

A set of attributes which form a viable combination, representing a valid logical entity or sub-entity, is called a *relation* and is assigned a unique name; for example, READER in Figure 3.23. As we shall see in Chapter 6, the process of creating viable relations (otherwise known as *normalisation*) follows strict rules and regulations [Codd, 1970].

Each relation has associated with it a table which can be permanent and is otherwise referred to as a *base table* (i.e a table which exists in the database exactly as viewed by the user). A *virtual* table on the other hand, is derived upon invocation of the corresponding virtual relation.

The *degree* of a table or relation signifies the number of atrributes it incorporates. For example, the table of Figure 3.23 is of the 6th degree.

A *tuple* can be considered as a row of values, forming a complete record occurrence the attributes of which receive values from prespecified lists. For example, Figure 3.23 highlights the 4th tuple containing the values: R130, LYONS B, 45 MAIN STR, FEMALE, PART-TIME, LANGUAGES

A *domain* is the complete and prespecified list of values an attribute can receive during its usage. Clearly, there are as many domains as there are degrees in a table or relation, although a domain can be shared by two or more attributes. For example, the domain of attribute 'Status' (see Figure 3.23) is the values: FULL-TIME and PART-TIME.

The *cardinality* of a table is the number of tuples it contains at any point of time. Obviously, this is bound to change dynamically, from run to run, or it can even become zero when all tuples are deleted. In the latter case, it may still be desirable to maintain the relation within the database for possible use in the future. The cardinality of the table in Figure 3.23 is 5.

The *primary key* of a relation is one or more attributes which can be thought of as a single attribute, capable of identifying each tuple uniquely. For example, the primary key of the table in Figure 3.23 is 'Reader-code'. A primary key containing two or more attributes is also known as a *composite key*. Although a relation may have more than one combination of attributes which can identify tuples uniquely, only one combination is designated as the primary key; the rest remain as *candidate keys*.

3.5.2 Basic Characteristics of Relational Models

The relational model excludes repeating groups from relations, as it considers these to be peculiar cases introducing redundancy which must therefore be dealt with separately. In further understanding of a repeating group, we will take the case where an order is raised with a supplier for a number of books. Each order raised will obviously have a variable number of items (i.e books) and

BOOKS-ORDERED

Order-no	Description	Supplier	Date	Book-no	Price	Quantity
OR114	Biology books	Dillons	13-3-88	B501	£10.50	1
				B510	£11.95	2
				B520	£8.50	3
				B530	£15.95	1

Figure 3.24   An example of a repeating group.

BOOKS-ORDERED

Order-no	Description	Supplier	Date
OR114	Biology books	Dillons	13-3-88

ORDER-ITEMS

Order-no	Book-no	Price	Quantity
OR114	B501	£10.50	1
OR114	B510	£11.95	2
OR114	B520	£8.50	3
OR114	B530	£15.95	1

Figure 3.25   Result of removal of the repeating group in Figure 3.24.

therefore, a repeating group can be thought of as a special class of a variable length record.

Consider the table of Figure 3.24 where attributes 'Book-no', 'Price' and 'Quantity' are repeated four times under order OR114. The primary key of the table is composite and comprises the attributes 'Order-no' and 'Book-no'. In order to convert this table into a relational equivalent, we can break it into two, namely, BOOKS-ORDERED with primary key 'Order-no' and ORDER-ITEMS with a composite primary key 'Order-no, Book-no', as shown in Figure 3.25. Note that table BOOKS-ORDERED has a single tuple, whereas table ORDER-ITEMS has as many tuples as there were items repeated in the original table. It is clear that, attribute 'Order-no' is common to both tables BOOKS-ORDERED and ORDER-ITEMS. Although this will appear as another form of duplication, it may not give rise to redundancy, at the physical level, because duplication can be avoided through efficient data storage structures which can of course be implemented through linked lists, as discussed earlier.

Repeating groups must be identified well before the physical structures are designed, otherwise it may be necessary to reorganise the complete database at a later stage; reorganisation can prove rather inconvenient after the database has been used for a while.

Once the relations of an organisation have been identified and normalised accordingly (note that elimination of repeating groups is only one aspect of the normalisation process), the logical model can be designed and the corresponding tables can then be populated.

The matrix-like structure of tables enables the adoption of relational algebra and predicate calculus concepts to manipulate their contents effectively. To this end, it becomes necessary to define relations and associated tables precisely, by means of axioms or rules which must be obeyed during the design of the relational model. In what follows, we present the major rules in terms of properties which must characterise the elements of the relational model.

(1)   Each relation has a distinct name and comprises of one or more attributes.
(2)   Each column of a table refers to an attribute with a name.
(3)   Within a given column all entries are homogeneous. In other words, they are derived from a single domain.
(4)   Each base table has a prespecified primary key which is capable of identifying tuples uniquely.
(5)   Each row in a table represents a unique tuple, that is, a record occurrence. Duplicate tuples are not allowed.
(6)   Each addressable cell in a table contains the value of a single conceptual object. Its logical address forms the intersection of a given column with a given tuple number.
(7)   Repeating groups are not allowed. These are removed into a separate table or flat file.
(8)   No one column has more significance than another, and the order of values under a column can be specified dynamically.
(9)   No one row has more significance than another, and the order of columns in a table can be specified dynamically.

3.6 AN EXAMPLE SCHEMA MODEL

In order to appreciate the complexity in the design of database models as well as their functioning, we will present a realistic logical model for a library information system, by adopting the relational approach.

Assume that the conceptual analysis stage has established the following entities, each with a specific set of attributes which are presented in brackets:

BOOK   (Book-no, Author, Title, Publisher-details, Year,
                      Volume, Edition)
SUBJECT   (Subject-code, Description & Keywords, Location)
READER   (Reader-no, Name, Address, Telephone, Sex, Status,
                      Books-held)
ORDER   (Order-no, Instructions, Date, Supplier, Books-ordered,
                      Price-of-each)

Following a detailed functional analysis of the library, we decide that, where multiple copies of a book exist, then each copy will be allocated a unique identification number. Besides, each book may refer to more than one subject, such as the 'psychology of computer programming' where the subjects are 'psychology' and 'programming'. Also, each order will be issued with a single supplier but may incorporate a number of books. Clearly, each reader may borrow a number of books, but a given book is issued only to a single reader at a time. Figure 3.26 presents a data model diagram which reflects these considerations accurately. The actual relationships among the four entities are presented below:

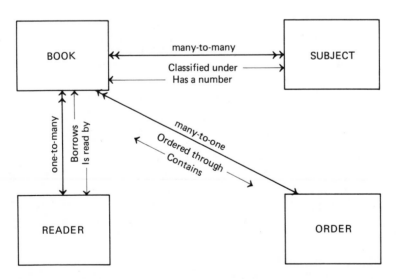

Figure 3.26   An example library data model.

Entity		Entity
BOOK	many-to-many	SUBJECT
READER	one-to-many	BOOK
ORDER	one-to-many	BOOK

Now, entity BOOK contains the attribute 'Publisher-details' which will of course be repeated (duplicated, triplicated, etc) under as many record occurrences as there are books in the library that are published by the same publisher. It becomes therefore necessary to split this entity into two, by storing 'Publisher-details' under a separate entity, say, PUBLISHER, where each record occurrence is unique. Similarly, because different orders can be issued with the same supplier, the attribute 'Supplier' will be duplicated, triplicated, etc. The establishment of a new entity, say, SUPPLIER, resolves duplication here.

Generally, the exclusion of 'duplicating attributes' from entities, creates the need for some mechanism to get to the information they carry from the original entity. This is achieved by including the identification key (the primary key) of the duplicating attributes within the original entity.

Let us examine the relationship between BOOK and SUBJECT. Here, the entities do not appear to have any common attributes and unless they are linked together (logically and physically) it will not be possible to find, say, all books under 'psychology' by searching entity SUBJECT and displaying the title and author of each. A link between the two can be established by creating a new entity, say, BOOK-SUBJECT, which contains the primary keys of BOOK and SUBJECT. This is also a form of indexing which speeds up the location of relevant record occurrences and proceeds to retrieve the full records.

The above considerations, together with further detailed analysis of each attribute and its relationships to the rest, at both intra-entity and inter-entity levels, result in a refined model of relations, such as the one presented on Figure 3.27. This is by no means the best arrangement of attributes, but can form the basis for the design of the actual logical database schema with the aid of a DBMS.

Each relation in Figure 3.27 incorporates a set of attributes which belong to a predefined set of conceptually operational data for the library system. The interconnecting lines may be considered as links from one relation to another, implemented here through common keys. The schema incorporates definitions for each attribute, in terms of its type and length as follows:

X(n): Any character of n bytes long
A(n): An alphabetic string of n bytes long
I(n): An integer number of n decimal digits
R(n,m): A real number with n digits for the integer part and m digits for precision

We chose to create the links between the different relations by means of their primary keys, indicated by the symbol '#' at the bottom corner of appropriate attributes (see Figure 3.27). We must point out here that internal (invisible) pointers can equally be implemented in the design of the internal model, in order to link record occurrences together. The relational model of database design insists that all relationships be established through 'visible' keys which are under the direct control of the programmer or user of an application.

The relations BOOK-SUBJECT and ITEM, as presented in Figure 3.27, contain two attributes, each marked as a key. (A relation is allowed only a single

Logical record type

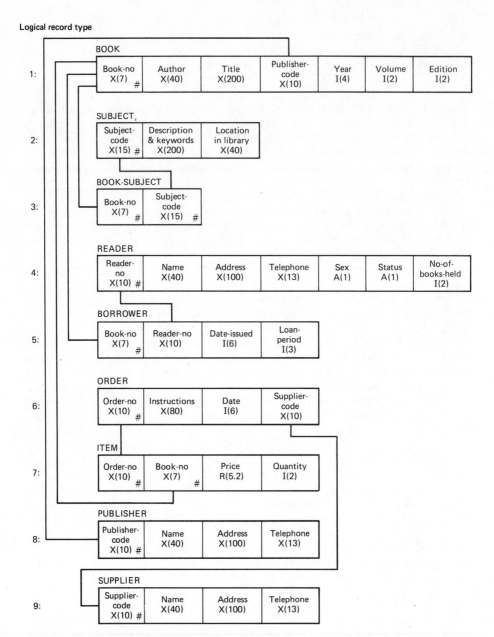

Figure 3.27   An example diagrammatic logical schema
(# = Primary attribute, A(n) = Alphabetic type,
X(n) = String type, I(n) = Integer type,
R(m,n) = Real type).

primary key which can be composite, that is, comprising two or more attributes.) Thus, the primary key of BOOK-SUBJECT is 'Book-no, Subject-no' and the primary key of ITEM is 'Order-no, Book-no'. Of course, a subset of a primary key can be the primary key of another relation, as is the case with the key 'Book-no' in relation ITEM.

In order to appreciate the need for a composite key in relation ITEM, we point out that, because within an ITEM table an order may contain two or more books, the attribute 'Order-no', on its own, is not sufficient to identify all order items uniquely. Therefore, a composite primary key is essential in this case.

3.7 AN EXAMPLE SUBSCHEMA MODEL

Before a subschema can be derived, it is necessary to analyse the requirements of the application in some detail (structurally and functionally), and to specify only the required sections and subsections (e.g sub-relations) of the logical schema. Moreover, within a subschema, it should be possible to specify only that portion of the attribute length necessary to satisfy the application. For example, if the logical schema defines a book title as a string of 200 bytes, but the application requires only the first 80 bytes, then the subschema must ensure that this truncation takes place effectively.

Let us consider the library schema of Figure 3.27 and an application which performs searches on BOOKS and BORROWERS, in order to satisfy queries, such as:

1. Find who is the current holder of a book
2. Display all the books held by a reader
3. Find whether a book is on loan or not
4. Print recall notices for selected readers
5. Display the author and the first line (80 bytes) of the title of a book

Clearly, information about orders, subjects, publishers and suppliers, is not required for this application and so, the relations needed are BOOK, BORROWER and READER. Moreover, under each of these relations only a subset is necessary to satisfy the above enquiries. Therefore, the subschema can incorporate the following relations and associated attributes (noting that attribute 'Sex' is needed only to determine the title Mr or Ms):

SS-BOOK (Book-no, Author, Title)
SS-BORROWER (Book-no, Reader-no, Date-issued, Loan-period)
SS-READER (Reader-no, Name, Address, Sex)

The corresponding diagrammatic model of the application is presented on Figure 3.28, where the primary keys of subschema relations form the necessary links between record occurrences. Where the length of an attribute is not specified, this is assumed to be the same as that defined within the logical schema (see Figure 3.27). The record types SS-BOOK and SS-READER are subsets of

Logical record type

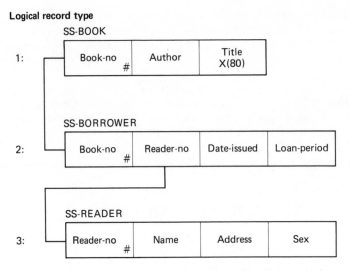

Figure 3.28   An example diagrammatic subschema (# = Primary key).

the corresponding schema record types, whereas SS-BORROWER remains the same.

After the subschema model has been derived, a Data Definition Language (DDL) can be employed to define and generate the object subschema. Moreover, an application program may invoke the subschema and proceed to utilise all the data items, as though they had already been defined under, say, the data division section of the program.

In conclusion, a subschema can be derived from the information contained only within a logical schema, although it can be argued that there will be cases where extra information becomes necessary. We also point out that, similar arguments may be put forward to support the derivation of a subschema from two or more logical schemata. At the relation level, one can also argue that the subschema must not 'expand' attributes (physically), but only 'contract' these where necessary. The availability and flexibility in implementing these transformations, and general mappings from schema to subschema, depend on particular DBMS models, but most importantly, on the internal structure of the database.

3.8 SUMMARY

A data structure is an organised system of relationships among data items (attributes) and record types, offering the means to define and map the logical schema onto an internal equivalent. To this end, it becomes necessary to study well established techniques of binding data to form stable and flexible structures.

In this chapter, we discussed traditional data structures and the criteria for their adoption and usage by a DBMS. The data structures we discussed are: lists (one-way, two-way, circular, and multiple), inverted files, trees (binary, balanced, and general), and networks.

The type of data structures which are supported by a DBMS, determine the viability and flexibility of accessing the various data items of a given organisation.

A data model represents real-world objects and their associations, or relationships within an organisation. Its main aim is to aid the analyst or user, in general, to understand the binding of entities, activities, events, associations, etc.

There are three basic data models whereby the relationships that exist among a set of records can be reflected accurately:

(a)   The hierarchic model, which binds record types together so that occurrences under a given level, can be used to retrieve others directly below it.

(b)   The network model, which differs from the hierarchic in that its elements (e.g record types) can have more than one owner each, and all relationships are stated explicitly between two or more elements.

(c)   The relational model, which uses simple tables to define clusters of attributes; attributes which are common between tables provide the means to bind the tables (record types) together. Within a relational table, each column corresponds to an attribute, and each row corresponds to a record occurrence, otherwise referred to as a 'tuple'.

To further understand the concepts *data model*, *logical schema* and *subschema*, we presented a realistic example of a library schema, incorporating nine record types, and proceeded to derive a subschema with three record types. The example we presented was based on the relational model which appears to be gaining favour within the academic, as well as the industrial community.

3.9 REFERENCES

Bachman, C. W., 'Data Structure Diagrams', Database, Vol. 1, No. 2, pp. 4-10, 1969.

Bayer, R. & McCreight, E. M., 'Organisation and Maintenance of Large Ordered Indices', Acta Informatica, Vol. 1, No. 3, pp. 173-189, 1972.

Chen, P. P., 'The Entity-Relationship Model: Toward a Unified View of Data', ACM TODS, Vol. 1, No. 1, pp. 9-36, 1976.

CODASYL, Report of the CODASYL Data Description Language Committee, Pergamon Press, 1978.

Codd, E. F., 'A Relational Model of Data for Large Shared Databases', CACM, Vol. 13, No. 6. pp. 377-387, 1970.

Codd, E. F. & Date, C. J., 'Interactive Support for Non-Programmers: The Relational and Network Approaches', In: Data Models: Structure Set vs. Relational', Randall & Rustin (editors), Proc. ACM SIGMOD Workshop on Data Description, Access and Control, Vol. II, May 1974.

Comer, D., 'The Ubiquitous B-tree', ACM Computer Surveys, Vol. 11, No. 2, June 1979.

Date, C. J., 'An Introduction to Database Systems', Vol. I, 4th Edition, Addison-Wesley, 1986.

Held, G. & Stonebraker, M., 'B-trees Reexamined', CACM, Vol. 21, No. 2, pp. 139-143, 1978.

Knuth, D., 'The Art of Computer Programming: Sorting and Searching', Vol. 3', Addison-Wesley, 1973.

Kouvatsos, D. D. & Yannakoudakis, E. J., 'A New Approach to the Design of Structured Bibliographic Records', Information Technology: Research and Development, Vol. 1, No. 4, pp. 285-300, 1982.

Navathe, S. B. & Fry, J. P., 'Restructuring for Large Databases: Three Levels of Abstraction', ACM TODS, Vol. 1, No. 2, pp. 138-158, 1976.

Olle, T. W., 'Data Structures and Storage Structures for Generalised File Processing', File Organisation Selected Papers from File-68 - An I.A.G. Conference, Swets & Zeitlinger N.V., pp. 310-315, 1969.

Senko, M. E., 'Information Systems: Records, Relations, Sets, Entities, and Things', Information Systems, Vol. 1, No. 1, pp. 1-13, 1975.

Sibley, E. H. (editor), 'Special Issue on Database Management Systems', ACM Computing Surveys, Vol. 8, No. 1, 1976.

Teorey, T. J. & Fry, J. P., 'Design of Database Structures', Prentice-Hall, 1982.

Tsichritzis, D. C. & Lochovsky, F. H., 'Data Models', Prentice-Hall, 1982.

Yannakoudakis, E. J., 'Towards a Universal Record Identification and Retrieval Scheme', J. of Informatics, Vol. 3, No. 1, pp. 7-11, 1979.

4 THE ARCHITECTURE OF DATABASE SOFTWARE

4.1 INTRODUCTION

In previous chapters we discussed the DBMS and database from a number of different angles as well as the types of users, architectural levels, structures and models necessary to describe the database. This chapter presents database software under well defined modules (languages or sublanguages - all part of the overall DBMS) and outlines the main objectives and tasks performed by each.

The primary aim here, is to highlight architectural aspects for the benefit of software engineers and users at large. We look at database software in an integrated manner and use appropriate commands to illustrate database operations. We assume the availability of a Relational Database Management System (RDBMS) and associated structured query language (SQL) with a common syntax for both data description and data manipulation statements. We then proceed to illustrate the overall structural components of the operations.

In order to create the three architectural modules of schema, subschema and internal schema and to maintain these effectively, the DBMS must provide certain commands which enable the following tasks to be performed satisfactorily:

(a) Define the logical schema of an organisation and derive all necessary subschemata.
(b) Define the internal (storage) schema of the database and initialise all storage structures.
(c) Manipulate the database indirectly, for example, by invoking DBMS commands from a high level language such as Pascal.
(d) Manipulate the database directly, for example, through commands which are typed from a terminal and are then interpreted and executed by the DBMS under an on-line mode.
(e) Document the database, associated software, users, applications, and organisation resources generally.

What we need therefore is a number of high level utilities or computer software either in the form of modules which are part of the DBMS, or independent high level languages. In either case the objectives and tasks each one performs can be defined quite clearly.

In the following sections we present a complete set of high level commands for schema, subschema (view), data manipulation and storage schema definition. The commands are very similar to the current proposal by the American National

Standards Institute (ANSI) for a Relational Database Language (RDL). The ANSI proposal [ANSI, 1986] does not include a Data Storage Description Language (DSDL) and for reasons of completeness we present a number of commands under DSDL in an attempt to illustrate the most important functions pertinent to a storage schema.

All commands and keywords are presented in upper case letters, and all parameters are presented in lower case letters. (The assumption we make here is that casing (i.e the use of upper and lower case letters) is insignificant when reference is made to attribute or relation names.) Square brackets ([]) are used to denote an optional keyword, qualifier, or entry. Also, character and string values generally, are presented in single quotes (e.g '25 Carnoustie Grove') whereas numerical values are presented without quotes. The symbol 'I' is used to separate alternatives from a multiple choice list of qualifiers, keywords or components of commands. Such a list is presented in braces ({}). Finally, three full stops (...) immediately after a statement or list indicate that this can be repeated a number of times. For example,

SELECT [DISTINCT] {* I column-name1 [, column-name2]... }

where the keyword (clause) DISTINCT is optional and from the rest the user may choose the '*' or one or more column names separated by commas.

4.1.1 Data Types and Qualifiers

The basic building block of a database is the attribute or column of a table. We shall use these terms interchangeably to refer to the same object. The definition of a column corresponds to the lowest level of data description and it becomes therefore necessary to study this in some detail and to consider appropriate data types and qualifiers.

With a Relational Database Language (RDL), the values of a column can take the form of a single data type which can also be qualified further regarding its range and usage. The actual specification of a column name can take the form: table-name.column-name. In this section we present the most important data types [Yannakoudakis & Cheng, 1987] (i.e INTEGER, SMALLINT, DECIMAL, REAL, DOUBLE PRECISION, FLOAT, and CHAR) and two qualifiers (i.e NOT NULL and UNIQUE) as used by RDL.

INTEGER

This is a signed binary integer number the length of which depends on the hardware used. For example, in a 32-bit computer, that is, a computer which offers 32 bits per complete computer word, this will be 31 bits because a single bit is used for the sign of the number (i.e plus or minus).

SMALLINT

This is a signed binary integer number which is half the length of a full integer. For example, in a 32-bit computer, this will be 15 bits. Again, a single bit is used to represent the sign of the number.

DECIMAL (m [,n])

This is a signed decimal number with a maximum of m digits before the decimal point, and n digits after the decimal point. The variables m and n must be included in round brackets - the square brackets indicate that n is optional.

REAL

This specifies a real number the length of which is implementor defined but based on the computer architecture in use, that is, the number of bits per computer word. Compare this with the equivalent in FORTRAN.

DOUBLE PRECISION

This allocates a storage space for a number which is twice that of a real number. Its length (in bits) is dependent on the computer architecture used. Compare this with the equivalent command in FORTRAN.

FLOAT ([n])

This specifies a floating point number with precision n. When n is omitted, then the number will have the default length defined by the implementor. This is dependent on the computer architecture.

CHAR (n)

This specifies a character string which may comprise alphanumeric or other symbols selected from the character set available on a computer. When n is ommitted, then 1 is assumed.

NOT NULL

This is an extra qualifier (not a data type as such) for a column of a table. When used, it specifies that an attribute must be given a value when a tuple is populated or updated. This is particularly useful when the primary key of each table is defined because we cannot afford to have tuples with null primary keys [Date, 1984]. Also, non-key attributes can be defined as NOT NULL when a value is necessary to describe a valid tuple. For example, attribute 'name' (i.e the name of an employee) must have a value before a salary slip can be produced. So, the designer must differentiate between attributes which can receive the values: zero, blank, or null. Each of these will signify a different attribute state.

UNIQUE

This is an extra qualifier (not a data type as such) for a given column of a table. It specifies that the values under a column must be unique, that is, no two or more tuples may contain the same value at any point of database usage. The 'unique' qualifier is particularly useful when primary key attributes are defined so that each tuple can be identified uniquely.

4.2 DATA DESCRIPTION LANGUAGE (DDL)

For a database to serve different applications it becomes necessary to describe and define a global schema which encapsulates the structural and functional requirements of each, in an optimal fashion and with minimum overlap. Understandably, different applications may have conflicting requirements and the DBA must ensure that these are resolved satisfactorily.

The adoption of certain common standards to define the logical schema and subschemata, namely, a common data description language (DDL), helps the DBA to identify intersecting or conflicting requirements. However, the main objective of a DDL is to define data at the logical level, independent of any programming languages (host or otherwise), excluding any references to physical data structures or hardware features [CODASYL, 1978].

We assume that a common DDL is used to define both logical schema and subschemata. The following tasks are equally applicable to both:

1. Define all record types and data items and associate these with their conceptual counterparts.
2. Specify the logical order of data items.
3. Define logical standard values, domains and ranges for all data items in the schema.
4. Define all data items to be used as search keys (i.e primary and secondary keys).
5. Define all 'links' among record types reflecting their logical relationships and levels of connectivity.
6. Define privacy locks and passwords in order to prevent unauthorised reading or modification of data items.

Because each subschema is derived from a logical schema, it becomes necessary for the DDL to offer certain subschema-dependent commands. Some of the tasks which are specific to a subschema DDL, and therefore application environment, are:

1. Exclude data items from record types.
2. Rename record types and data items.
3. Impose a new order on selected values under data items.
4. Redefine the data type of a data item (e.g from real to integer).
5. Define new (virtual) record types by selecting data items from one or more schema record types.

6.   Define 'virtual links' (relationships) between record types.
7.   Compress, decompress, concatenate or code data item values.

4.2.1 RDL Commands

In this section we discuss the most important RDL commands used to define or
alter the logical schema and existing subschemata otherwise referred to as views of
the database. We must point out that although RDL enables the definition of
views during the actual manipulation of the database tables, we consider these to
be user-derived views rather than essential application structures.

CREATE SCHEMA

CREATE SCHEMA AUTHORISATION schema-authorisation-identifier
    [CREATE TABLE table-name1 [CREATE TABLE table-name2]...]
    [CREATE VIEW view-name1   [CREATE VIEW view-name2]...]

The schema-authorisation-identifier is a name which identifies a schema
uniquely, assuming that the database may contain two or more schemata. The
statements CREATE TABLE and CREATE VIEW are amplified in the
following paragraphs. Because these are optional here, the DBMS must offer a
facility whereby all the tables and views pertinent to a schema can be specified
after each has been defined independently.

CREATE TABLE

CREATE TABLE table-name
    (column-name1 data-type [NOT NULL] [UNIQUE]
    [,column-name2 data-type [NOT NULL] [UNIQUE]]...)

This command creates a base table containing one or more columns each based
on a single data type which can be: INTEGER, SMALLINT, DECIMAL,
REAL, DOUBLE PRECISION, FLOAT or CHAR. The qualifiers NOT NULL
and UNIQUE may also be used with selected columns. The following statements
create a table called 'publisher' with primary key 'publisher-code' and three non-
prime keys, 'name', 'address', and 'telephone' all of type character.

CREATE TABLE publisher
    (publisher-code CHAR (10) NOT NULL UNIQUE
    name CHAR (40)
    address CHAR (100)
    telephone CHAR (13))

ALTER TABLE

ALTER TABLE table-name
  ADD column-name1 data-type [NOT NULL] [UNIQUE]
    [,column-name2 data-type [NOT NULL] [UNIQUE]]...

This command enables the addition of one or more columns to an existing table of the database. For example, the following statements add the columns 'status' and 'telephone' to table 'supplier':

ALTER TABLE supplier
  ADD status CHAR (2), telephone CHAR (13)

DELETE TABLE

DROP TABLE table-name

This command deletes (withdraws) a table from the database. For example,

DROP TABLE publisher

CREATE VIEW

CREATE VIEW view-name
  [(column-name1 [,column-name2]...)]
  AS
  SELECT [DISTINCT] { * | column-name1 [,column-name2]... }
    FROM table-name1 [,table-name2]...
    [WHERE select-condition]
    [GROUP BY column-name1 [,column-name2]...
        [HAVING select-condition]]
    [ENABLE UPDATES]

The ENABLE UPDATES specifies that the view can actually be used to insert/ update new tuples. The omission of this clause implies that the view cannot be updated.

Because a view can be based on one or more tables, there may be cases where an insert or update of view tuples gives rise to inconsistencies [Cosmadakis & Papadimitriou, 1983; Furtado & Casanova, 1986]. For example, if a view contains the attributes: 'reader-id' and 'reader-name' from table 'reader', and attributes: 'book-held' and 'return-date' from table 'holdings', then the insertion of a new reader will omit his/her address (assuming that attribute 'address' is included in the table 'reader').

The DISTINCT clause specifies that only distinct (non-duplicate) tuples will be used to create the table. If the DISTINCT clause is omitted, then duplicate tuple occurrences may be present.

The asterisk ('*') indicates that all the columns of the source table will be incorporated in the resultant (derived) table.

The select-condition specifies the logic to be applied while the table(s) is searched. The full version of the SELECT command is discussed later under Section 4.3.1 including the options WHERE and GROUP BY.

Let us see a view/subschema which enables the identification of all users who have not returned the books they have borrowed by a specified (advance) date. Assume that the following relations/tables exist:

reader (reader-no, name, address)
holdings (book-held, reader-no, return-date)

The following statements create an appropriate view to deal with books overdue:

```
CREATE VIEW books-not-returned
   (reader-id, reader-name, reader-address,
    book-held, return-date)
   AS
   SELECT reader.reader-no, reader.name, reader.address,
          holdings.book-held, holdings.return-date
     FROM reader, holdings
     WHERE reader.reader-no = holdings.reader-no AND
           holdings.return-date < CURRENT-DATE
```

The value of CURRENT-DATE can be established automatically by the DBMS following the invocation of the view and an appropriate system call. The join dependency between the tables 'reader' and 'holdings' is specified by the statement:

```
WHERE reader.reader-no = holdings.reader-no ...
```

DELETE VIEW

```
DROP VIEW view-name
```

This command deletes (cancels) an existing view from the database. For example,

```
DROP VIEW books-not-returned
```

SECURITY COMMANDS

The security aspects of databases are absolutely vital, particularly with the advent of multi-user, multi-processing, and concurrent environments. Usually, the person who creates a table is also its owner and no other persons can access its tuples. The owner (e.g the DBA) can however grant permission to individual persons and for specific operations upon tuples of the table.

In the following sections we present some of the most commonly used commands that enforce security on tables of relational database structures.

Grant permission

GRANT {ALL | {DELETE | INSERT | SELECT |
                    UPDATE [(column-name1 [,column-name2]...)] }... }
    ON table-name
    TO {PUBLIC | user-identifier1 [,user-identifier2]... }

The above command grants authorisation to a user or the public at large (i.e the database user community) so that they can carry out one or more specific operations upon a given table. The operations can involve the deletion, insertion, selection or update of values under specific columns.

This facility is particularly useful where different users access the same table but for different reasons. For example, in a financial division the chief accountant may have UPDATE privilege (in order to upgrade the salary column), but the payroll production clerk may have SELECT only privilege (in order to print the payroll slips). Assuming the presence of a table called 'employees' containing appropriate attributes one of which specifies the salary, the following commands will grant the privileges described above:

GRANT UPDATE (salary)
    ON employees
    TO Nick;
GRANT SELECT
    ON employees
    TO George

There are cases where the DBA wishes to grant authority to specific users and for specific tuples in database tables. Suppose for example the chief programmer is to be given authority to retrieve data from tuples which contain information about programmers; assume the presence of a table called 'jobs' containing appropriate attributes one of which specifies the job-title, and a chief programmer called 'Emmanuel'. The following statements implement this by, first of all, creating a view called 'programmers':

CREATE VIEW programmers
    AS
    SELECT *
        FROM jobs
        WHERE job-title = 'programmer'
GRANT SELECT
    ON programmers
    TO Emmanuel

Permit access

PERMIT {ALL I {DELETE I INSERT I SELECT I
                  UPDATE [(column-name1 [,column-name2]...)] }... }
  ON table-name
  TO {PUBLIC I user-identifier1 [,user-identifier2]...}
  AT terminal-identifier
  [FROM time1 TO time2]

This command is clearly an extension of the GRANT command and allows
users to access a database table at specific times of each day and from a specific
terminal. This facility is particularly useful under multi-processing environments
where the DBA wishes to restrict the use of the database to groups of people so
that the system does not become overloaded and as a result provide unacceptable
response times.
   The following command gives permission to Nick to update tuples on the table
employees between 1400 and 1500 hours each day using a terminal known to the
DBMS as VDU10:

PERMIT UPDATE
  ON employees
  TO Nick
  AT VDU10
  FROM 1400 TO 1500

Revoke permision

REVOKE {ALL I {DELETE I INSERT I SELECT I
                  UPDATE [(column-name1 [,column-name2]...)] }... }
  ON table-name
  FROM {PUBLIC I user-identifier1 [,user-identifier2]...}

The above command in effect cancels an authorisation (permission) previously
granted to database users. For example, prevent the user called 'George' from
displaying values under column 'salary' in table 'employees':

REVOKE SELECT (salary)
  ON employees
  FROM George

INTEGRITY COMMANDS

Integrity and consistency of databases can be ensured through appropriate
commands, although very few database management systems today actually
provide a comprehensive set of facilities or mechanisms for this. For the reader to
appreciate the importance of integrity, we present the following example. Let a
schema contain the tables:

book   (book-no, author, title, publisher-no, year, edition, price)
borrower (book-no, reader-no, return-date)

If column 'book-no' in 'borrower' contains a value which is not already included under column 'book-no' in 'book', then obviously the database has not been used consistently since it holds a borrower responsible for a book that does not exist in the database. In other words, the integrity of the database is in doubt. It becomes therefore necessary to impose integrity constraints regarding the usage of database tables and columns. For example, we must be able to instruct the DBMS not to include a book number in 'borrower' before this is checked against table 'book'.

Another type of constraint checks the values which may be processed under any given column. For example, it may be necessary to instruct the DBMS not to accept any values under column 'price' unless these are greater than zero.

In order to appreciate how a constraint might be set up and maintained we present the following component of an integrity command specifying that the values of column 'price' must be greater than zero:

... CHECK price > 0

Now, if the user issues a statement asking the DBMS to read (accept) a value from a terminal (e.g a VDU) with the following:

ACCEPT price

then the DBMS will automatically extend this command to include the predefined constraint as follows:

ACCEPT price WHERE price > 0

Create constraint

CREATE CONSTRAINT constraint-name
    ON table-name1 [,table-name2]...
    AS { column-name1 IN column-name2}
        [,column-name2 IN column-name3]...}
    [CHECK column-name1 operator expression
        [,column-name2 operator expression]...]

This command creates a constraint on one or more database tables each of which may have two or more constraints active at any point of time.

The IN clause checks for the presence of a column value under another column.

The CHECK clause checks the value of a column against an expression which can be considered equivalent to a valid expression (the right hand side) of an assignment statement in a high level programming language.

The CHECK clause must not be confused with the domain of a column which aims to specify its data type and general format. We must however point out that the range of values a column takes can be specified independent of any constraints which may also be imposed upon it.

The following combinations form valid operators which compare the value of a column with the value of an expression:

Operator	Meaning
>	Greater than
<	Less than
=	Equal to
>=	Greater than or equal to
<=	Less than or equal to
<>	Not equal to

Let us use an example to illustrate the definition of a constraint. Suppose the DBA wishes to check every incoming value under attribute 'borrower.book-no' to see whether or not this is already held in the catalogue, that is, whether or not a value under 'borrower.book-no' is equal to a value under another attribute, say, 'book.book-no'. This simple test implies that a borrower cannot be held responsible for a book that the library does not hold. Suppose also that the DBA wishes to ensure that every date recorded under each book borrowed is greater than or equal to the current date. Let the corresponding table be 'book' (holding the catalogue) and 'borrower' (holding details on each registered borrower). The following statements define these restrictions accurately:

```
CREATE CONSTRAINT check1
    ON book, borrower
    AS borrower.book-no IN book.book-no
        CHECK book.price > 0,
                borrower.return-date >= CURRENT-DATE
```

The value of CURRENT-DATE can be established automatically by the DBMS following an appropriate system call. In other words, assume that CURRENT-DATE is a DBMS key word that activates a function call.

Drop constraint

DROP CONSTRAINT constraint-name

This command cancels an existing constraint which may be operational (active) on one or more tables. Only the named constraint is cancelled. For example,

DROP CONSTRAINT check1

4.3 DATA MANIPULATION LANGUAGE (DML)

A DML is used to manipulate data in order to satisfy the requirements of each application. If the language allows simple record storage and retrieval, then it becomes necessary to interface the DML to an ordinary programming language such as FORTRAN or COBOL which will allow further analyses and processing of data items. The two languages can communicate through standard and common memory blocks or they can call the software modules of each other to perform a number of tasks.

Where a DML forms an extension of a high level programming language, then clearly it can be independent of the DBMS and available for use in conjunction with software from different vendors. Thus, a DML becomes a separate 'self-contained language'. Alternatively, where the DML forms part of the DBMS software, then it can be completely independent of any programming language.

Some of the major tasks carried out by a DML are presented below.

1. Traverse existing data structures (e.g trees, networks, relations) and links already established within the schema and subschema.
2. Access records by address.
3. Access records by contents.
4. Modify existing values of data items through the overlaying of values held within the application or session environment.
5. Insert, delete and reorganise records as required by each application.
6. Reorder data items to satisfy application requests.
7. Define transactions and error conditions.

4.3.1 RDL Commands

Here, we present the most important RDL commands which may be part of a data manipulation language, such as SQL. We refer to the table holdings with the attributes: book-held (the primary key), reader-no (secondary key indicating the user number holding a book), and return-date (indicating the return date):

HOLDINGS

book-held	reader-no	return-date
B200	R100	15–03–88
B300	R100	15–03–88
B400	R100	17–03–88
B410	R110	17–03–88
B210	R110	17–03–88
B220	R120	19–03–88

SELECT/SEARCH TUPLES IN TABLES

This facility forms the basis for data manipulation, including joining tables, imposing an order on the retrieved tuples, grouping tuples, and finally, transferring the result onto a separate table. The general format of the select statement is as follows:

```
SELECT [DISTINCT] {* I column-name1 [,column-name2]... }
    FROM table-name1 [,table-name2]...
    [WHERE select-condition]
    [GROUP BY column-name1 [,column-name2]...
            [HAVING select-condition]]
    [ORDER BY column-name1 [ASC I DESC]
            [,column-name2 [ASC I DESC]]...]
    [INTO table-name]
```

The specification of a column may take the form: table-name.column-name. The asterisk ('*') indicates the selection of the complete set of columns available under the table being searched.

The FROM clause specifies the table(s) to be used as the basis for data manipulation.

The WHERE clause specifies the logic to be followed while selecting pertinent tuples from the table(s). This clause can incorporate column names and expressions with operators as is the case with the CHECK clause of the 'create constraint' command.

The GROUP BY clause arranges the tuples retrieved into groups with common values so that each distinct set of values under the columns specified by the GROUP BY clause is presented only once. Subsequently, the HAVING select-condition is applied only to each distinct tuple retrieved by the GROUP BY clause. Therefore, the HAVING clause must only be used in conjunction with the GROUP BY clause. Thus, the WHERE clause applies the logic to tuples from the original table, whereas the HAVING clause applies the logic only to tuples produced by the GROUP BY clause.

The ORDER BY clause enables the presentation of the selected tuples (or sub-tuples for that matter) in ascending or descending order using the qualifiers ASC and DESC respectively.

The INTO clause specifies the table upon which the result is to be transferred. This will contain only those columns specified in the SELECT clause and associated values satisfying the logic of the WHERE/HAVING clause. So, the derived table - which must not already exist in the database - can be used subsequently for further processing.

Because the clauses WHERE, GROUP BY/HAVING, and ORDER are optional, when they are not specified, then the table columns specified will be extracted as they are from the source table(s). In other words, the SELECT statement can be used to derive projections from one or more tables.

Now, there are cases where users do not have complete knowledge of the contents of the tuples they wish to retrieve. For example, a user may know that the title of the book required contains the words 'nuclear physics' which can be thought of as a subset of the complete title. It becomes therefore necessary to provide a facility (part of the DML) which accepts incomplete input and proceeds to search the tables by means of string and substring matching of relevant values under specific columns. So, the select condition of both the WHERE and HAVING clauses can incorporate a column specification with the following form:

... table-name.column-name [NOT] LIKE pattern

where pattern encapsulates user input as well as wildcard delimiters. Two frequently used delimiters are '?' which matches any single character in the same position, and '*' which matches any characters preceding or following the string provided by the user. Consider the following examples which can be applied in the same way with the HAVING clause:

(a)   Trace the book(s) which contain the string 'nuclear physics':

    ... WHERE title LIKE '*nuclear physics*'

(b)   Trace all books which contain the string 'nuclear' in the leftmost position
       of the title:

       ... WHERE title LIKE 'nuclear*'

(c)   Trace all books with a title not more than 20 characters in length and
       where the substring 'nuclear' is in the leftmost position of the title:

       ... WHERE title LIKE 'nuclear?????????????'

Another important clause here allows the definition of the range of numerical
values that are to be manipulated at any point of time. The BETWEEN clause
enables the specification of a range comparison and can be used in conjunction
with the WHERE or the HAVING clauses; the limits specified are inclusive. This
clause takes the form:

... WHERE table-name.column-name
        [NOT] BETWEEN expression AND expression

The following example locates and displays all holdings where the book held is
in the range 'B200' and 'B210', inclusively:

SELECT *
    FROM holdings
    WHERE book-held BETWEEN 'B200' AND 'B210'

To further understand the SELECT operation, we present the following
example DML statements as applied to table holdings and the result they
produce:

Example 1

Find all books held by reader 'R100' and retrieve all columns of table holdings:

SELECT *
    FROM holdings
    WHERE reader-no = 'R100'

Result:

book-held	reader-no	return-date
B200	R100	15-03-88
B300	R100	15-03-88
B400	R100	17-03-88

Example 2

Find all readers who are expected to return the books they hold before the 18-03-88:

SELECT reader-no, return-date
  FROM holdings
  WHERE return-date < '18-03-88'

Result:

reader-no	return-date
R100	15–03–88
R100	15–03–88
R100	17–03–88
R110	17–03–88
R110	17–03–88

Example 3

Find all distinct and current readers of library books:

SELECT reader-no
  FROM holdings
  GROUP BY reader-no

Result:

reader-no
R100
R110
R120

Example 4

Find all distinct and current readers who are expected to return all the books they hold before the 18-03-88:

SELECT reader-no
  FROM holdings
  GROUP BY reader-no
  HAVING max(return-date) < '18-03-88'

(The function 'max' selects the maximum value under the column specified; the function is described later under the section 'Simple mathematical functions'.)

Result:

reader-no
R100
R110

Example 5

Find all books held by reader number 'R100' and where the return date is before the 19-03-88. At the same time, sort the output in descending order of return date:

SELECT return-date, book-held
   FROM holdings
   WHERE reader-no = 'R100' AND return-date < '19-03-88'
   ORDER BY return-date DESC

Result:

return-date	book-held
17–03–88	B400
15–03–88	B200
15–03–88	B300

JOIN/COMBINE TABLES

There are cases where the user wishes to retrieve information from two or more tables at the same time. Take for example a table, say, 'pay' containing the columns 'employee-code', 'employee-salary' and 'employee-tax-code', and another table, say, 'details' containing the columns 'employee-code', 'employee-address' and 'employee-department'. In order to produce the payroll (including the printing of address labels), we must retrieve a tuple at a time from table 'pay' and the corresponding tuple from table 'details'. So, tables 'pay' and 'details' must be joined (combined) through a common key, in this case, 'employee-code'.

In the following examples we adopt multiple tables per data manipulation statements in order to illustrate how tuples from different tables can be joined to answer complex queries. The following three tables are used:

book   (book-no, author, title, publisher-no, year, edition, price)
borrower   (book-no, reader-no, return-date)
reader   (reader-no, name, address)

Example 1

Find all book titles and book numbers held by reader R100:

```
SELECT book.title, book.book-no
   FROM book, borrower
   WHERE book.book-no = borrower.book-no
         AND borrower.reader-no = 'R100'
```

The join dependency between tables 'book' and 'borrower' is specified by the statement:

```
WHERE book.book-no = borrower.book-no ...
```

Example 2

An alternative approach to joining two or more tables can involve set operators which check for the presence of common values/tuples between tables. Consider the following statements which perform the same task as in Example 1 above using the 'IN' clause:

```
SELECT book.title, book.book-no
   FROM book
   WHERE book.book-no
        IN (SELECT book-no
               FROM borrower
               WHERE reader-no = 'R100')
```

Example 3

Find all the book numbers and book titles currently on loan:

```
SELECT borrower.book-no, book.title
   FROM book, borrower
   WHERE borrower.book-no = book.book-no
```

Example 4

Find all readers who have not returned the books they hold by a specified date and transfer the reader number and book title onto a separate table called 'reminder'. Subsequently, use table 'reminder' to retrieve the name and address of each reader in order to produce reminder slips (one for each book overdue):

```
SELECT borrower.reader-no, book.title
   FROM borrower, book
   WHERE book.book-no = borrower.book-no AND
           borrower.return-date < '19-03-88'
   ORDER BY borrower.reader-no
   INTO reminder;
SELECT reader.name, reader.address, reminder.title
   FROM reminder, reader
   WHERE reminder.reader-no = reader.reader-no
```

SIMPLE MATHEMATICAL FUNCTIONS

The tabular structure of relational tables make it easy to scan a column at a time and to perform simple mathematical tasks, such as summation, averaging, counting, etc. In simple terms, we can apply a select condition which retrieves relevant tuples and displays these so that we can count the occurrences. Ideally, what we need is a set of built-in functions which can be incorporated within the SELECT statement. The Relational Database Language (RDL) provides the following simple functions:

AVG   Average a numeric column
COUNT   Count the total occurrences
MAX   Find the largest value of a column
MIN   Find the smallest value of a column
SUM   Sum a numeric column

Each of the above functions takes the form:

function-name ([DISTINCT] column-name)

where the keyword DISTINCT is optional and specifies that only distinct (non-duplicate) values be considered during the evaluation of the corresponding function. The specification of a column-name can take the form:

table-name.column-name

Study the following examples which manipulate the table 'item' with attributes: order-no, book-no, price, quantity. The primary key is the composite attribute 'order-no, book-no' because there may be two or more different books specified under the same order number.

Example 1

Find the average price of a book on order:

SELECT AVG (price)
    FROM item

Example 2

Count the orders which have been raised:

SELECT COUNT (DISTINCT order-no)
    FROM item

Example 3

Find the most expensive book on order:

```
SELECT book-no, price
    FROM item
    WHERE price = (SELECT MAX (price)
                            FROM item)
```

Example 4

Find the cheapest book on order:

```
SELECT book-no, price
    FROM item
    WHERE price = (SELECT MIN (price)
                            FROM item)
```

Example 5

Calculate the total cost of all current orders:

```
SELECT SUM (price * quantity)
    FROM item
```

Example 6

Calculate the total cost of order number '01150':

```
SELECT SUM (price * quantity)
    FROM item
    WHERE order-no = 'O1150'
```

DELETE TUPLES

The following command enables the deletion of a tuple from a table:

```
DELETE
    FROM table-name
    [WHERE select-condition]
```

Because the WHERE clause is optional, when omitted all the tuples of the table will be deleted, but not necessarily the table definition itself. The latter can only be achieved with the command: DROP table-name. The following statements delete all tuples of order number 'O1150':

```
DELETE
    FROM item
    WHERE order-no = 'O1150'
```

INSERT TUPLES

The following syntax enables the insertion of new tuples in a table:

INSERT
    INTO table-name [(column-name1 [,column-name2]...)]
    { VALUES (value1 [,value2]...) |
      SELECT entry }

Obviously, for the creation of a complete tuple, we must supply as many values/
expressions as there are columns in a table. Because the column names are
optional, when omitted the values supplied will be assigned, one after the other,
starting with the leftmost column.

The user has a choice here to supply the values directly using the VALUES
clause, or to employ the SELECT command in order to retrieve tuples from other
tables and then transfer these to the table concerned. The latter case is equivalent
to a 'copy' operation where one or more tuples are copied from one table to
another. The specification of the SELECT entry here is the same as the one we
discussed earlier.

An important point to remember when the INSERT command is used, is that
each new tuple must have a primary key which can identify its occurrence
uniquely. Otherwise, the command gives rise to an error, in effect informing the
user that a tuple with the same primary key value already exists in the table. So,
the user must differentiate between the 'update' of an existing tuple and the
'insertion' of a completely new tuple. The following statements introduce a new
tuple in the table item:

INSERT
    INTO item
    VALUES ('O1165', 'B300', 15.95, 2)

UPDATE TUPLES

The following syntax enables the user to supply new values under specific columns
of a table:

UPDATE table-name
    SET column-name1 = expression1
      [,column-name2 = expression2]...
    [WHERE select-condition]

Because the WHERE clause is optional, when omitted all the values under the
specified column(s) will be updated accordingly.

A valid expression here can be considered equivalent to a valid component (the
right hand side) of an assignment statement in a high level programming language.
Examples of complete SET clauses are:

SET salary = salary + 10 * salary / 100
SET count = count + 1
SET address = '25 Carnoustie Grove, Cottingley, Bingley'
SET status = 'full-time'

Example 1

The following statements update the quantity column of an item under order number 'O1150' and book number 'B200' by ordering in effect an extra book:

UPDATE item
  SET quantity = quantity + 1
  WHERE order-no = 'O1150' AND book-no = 'B200'

Example 2

The following statements update the salary of all employees in department 'biology' by awarding a 7.5% increase:

UPDATE employees
  SET salary = salary + 7.5 * salary / 100
  WHERE department = 'biology'

DEFINE AND MANIPULATE CURSORS

Most high level programming languages available today operate on a single record at a time, that is, a single tuple in the case of the relational model. However, when a DML statement is issued it usually scans the complete relational table as is the case with the statements:

REPEAT

  . statements

UNTIL EOF {END OF FILE}

Therefore, it becomes necessary to define subsets of pertinent tables (rather than complete tables) upon which specific operations can then be carried out on a single tuple at a time and thereby offer a means of interfacing an RDL language with a high level language (the host language).

A cursor is a set of tuples which are extracted from one or more base or view tables and stored on a temporary table. The cursor table is created when the cursor is 'opened' and destroyed when the cursor is 'closed'. Another way to visualise a cursor is to assume that the tuples on the source tables (base or view) are 'marked' and declared as a named logical unit which can be processed further independent of any other tables in the database.

So, a cursor is declared, opened, manipulated and closed as required. While a cursor is open, an appropriate command (e.g FETCH) can be used to access a tuple at a time, starting from the beginning of the cursor table. Accessing of cursor tuples then takes place sequentially one after the other and at any point of time there will be a specific tuple which can be retrieved by the FETCH command (assume there is an 'invisible' current pointer to a tuple). When a tuple is deleted or inserted, it is reasonable to expect the pointer to point to the tuple after the one which has been deleted or inserted. We are now in a position to present the general format of statements which operate on cursors.

Create cursor

```
DECLARE cursor-name CURSOR
  FOR
  SELECT [DISTINCT] {* I cursor-column1 [,cursor-column2]... }
    FROM table-name1
    [WHERE select-condition]
    [GROUP BY column-name1 [,column-name2]...
        [HAVING select-condition]]
    [ORDER BY column-name1 [ASC I DESC]
        [,column-name2 [ASC I DESC]]...]
    [ENABLE UPDATES]
```

A cursor-column defines a column in the cursor table whereas a column-name defines a column in a database table (the source) from which cursor tuples are derived. The ENABLE UPDATES clause permits updates on cursor tuples and therefore source tables. The rest of the clauses are identical to those presented under the SELECT command.

The following example creates a cursor for all tuples in table 'borrower' where the return date is less than the current date:

```
DECLARE books-overdue CURSOR
  FOR
  SELECT book-no, reader-no, return-date
    FROM borrower
    WHERE return-date < CURRENT-DATE
    ORDER BY reader-no ASC
    ENABLE UPDATES
```

Open cursor

OPEN cursor-name

This command opens a cursor and positions the internal pointer to the first tuple in the cursor table. Obviously an error occurs when the user attempts to open a cursor which has not been defined. The following command opens an existing cursor called 'books-overdue':

OPEN books-overdue

Close cursor

CLOSE cursor-name

This command closes an open cursor and destroys the temporary cursor table from the database. An error occurs when the user attempts to close a non-existent cursor. The following command closes the cursor called 'books-overdue':

CLOSE books-overdue

Fetch a tuple from a cursor

FETCH cursor-name
    INTO variable1 [,variable2]...

This command advances the pointer to the next tuple in the cursor table and transfers its contents to the variables specified in the INTO clause. A single tuple is transferred in the User Work Area (UWA).

Obviously, the variables specified by the INTO clause must be compatible with the data types of the corresponding columns in the cursor, although most vendors allow for simple mappings (conversions). For example, if the length of a value in the source table is greater than the variable it is assigned to, then the leftmost bytes/bits are transferred. The following statements retrieve a tuple from cursor 'books-overdue' and store the values on the variables 'book-code', 'reader-number' and 'return-date':

FETCH books-overdue
    INTO book-code, reader-number, return-date

Delete a tuple from a cursor

DELETE
    FROM table-name
    WHERE CURRENT OF cursor-name

Here, the table name must be the same as the one specified within the FROM clause of the command DECLARE cursor. Only the current tuple (a single occurrence) pointed to by the invisible pointer is actually deleted with the above command. For example,

DELETE
    FROM borrower
    WHERE CURRENT OF books-overdue

Update a tuple in a cursor

UPDATE
  SET cursor-column1 = expression
  [,cursor-column2 = expression]...
  WHERE CURRENT OF cursor-name

A cursor-column here must be one of those defined by the SELECT component of the DECLARE cursor command and the cursor-name must be identical to that defined within the DECLARE command. An expression is equivalent to the right-hand side of an assignment statement in a high level programming language.

When the UPDATE command is executed only the current tuple is updated, provided of course the clause ENABLE UPDATES has been included in the command DECLARE cursor. The following statements extend the return-date of a book to 20-12-88 by updating the current tuple:

UPDATE
  SET return-date = '20-12-88'
  WHERE CURRENT OF books-overdue

TRANSACTION PROCESSING

A transaction is a sequence of operations upon record types and corresponding values producing a consistent and updated version of the database. The operations are logically related and perform a specific task, such as the updating of salary details of all employees by awarding, say, a 10% increase.

A transaction takes place at a specific point of time and has a defined beginning and end. When no errors or integrity violations occur, we can request the system to commit itself to the transactions which have taken place and to create a permanent version of the database. This is achieved with the COMMIT command. If an error occurs during a transaction, we can issue the command ROLLBACK which asks the DBMS to revert (rollback) to the previous state of the database.

Nested transactions are not normally allowed but an application program may contain one or more independent transactions.

The following statements outline the format of a transaction:

TRANSACTION transaction-name
  WHENEVER { ERROR I CONDITION } ROLLBACK

  statements

  COMMIT
END

The WHENEVER clause in effect activates a concurrent system process which 'keeps an eye' on all the operations performed on the tables and traps all system errors and integrity violations.

The 'condition' allows the user to specify the condition under which the ROLLBACK command is entered. In the following example the ROLLBACK is 'activated when a value under column 'salary' is found to be greater than 99,999:

WHENEVER salary> 99999 ROLLBACK

The 'statements' in the body of the transaction can in fact be any valid data manipulation statements such as INSERT, UPDATE, DELETE and SELECT.

Let us present another example transaction giving a 10% pay increase to all employees in department 'computer':

```
TRANSACTION transaction-name
   WHENEVER ERROR ROLLBACK
   UPDATE employees
      SET salary = salary + 10 * salary / 100
      WHERE department = 'computer'
   COMMIT
END
```

4.4 DATA STORAGE DESCRIPTION LANGUAGE (DSDL)

In Chapter 2 we discussed the 'internal schema' and the various levels of internal records. We argued for a single internal schema language offering all necessary facilities for mapping the logical schema onto appropriate storage structures effectively.

Whether a device/media control language (DMCL) becomes established or not, it should not affect the logical level, or restrict this in any way. The preservation of data independence (logical and physical) must be the guiding factor.

Although the primary aim of a DSDL is to translate the logical schema onto an internal equivalent [CODASYL, 1978], it could also be used to manipulate data on the actual devices without disturbing any logical views or indeed hampering their evolution. Moreover, the internal schema can be redefined, altered for tuning purposes and recompiled, without any alterations to the logical schema, subschemata, or application programs. It is through such an environment that data independence can truly materialise.

Depending on the internal data layer, appropriate DSDL commands can be used to carry out a number of tasks, such as the ones presented below:

1. Assign files to programs.
2. Assign devices and allocate space.
3. Specify communication buffers, permanent and transient.
4. Define physical units for input and output.
5. Define/isolate highly volatile or confidential data.
6. Specify storage structures (e.g chaining and tagging).
7. Specify addressing mechanisms (e.g hashing).
8. Define overflow areas and reorganisation criteria.

9.   Translate logical records into storage records.
10. Analyse storage records and define appopriate blocking factors and pages.
11. Identify virtual records and avoid duplication in stored values.
12. Specify storage boundaries for data items.
13. Specify the stored order of data items.
14. Create appropriate indexes for efficient data manipulation.

DSDL- and DMCL-related tasks can be classified under a number of headings depending on the type and level of their operation. We present the following categories:

Translation

The translation and mapping of logical records and data items to storage equivalent.

Inter-record

The specification of storage structures and relationships between records.

Intra-record

The specification of storage structures and relationships among data items in each separate storage record.

Resource allocation

The allocation of resources, including storage devices, record type and data item lengths, pages, blocks, etc.

Security

The specification of appropriate rules to safeguard against unauthorised manipulations.

Access

The declaration of appropriate addressing schemes and indexing for efficient storage and retrieval.

Reorganisation

The reorganisation of storage structures and stored values for reasons of database tuning, including data item order, overflow control, etc.

4.4.1 RDL Commands

Database software available today is rather weak in this area and very few actually provide a separate DSDL. Most vendors use their own techniques to create storage record types and access paths. Although the different types of storage structures that can be adopted are limited (e.g direct, indexed sequential and sequential), record linkage allows for innovation and independent development. In the following sections we present the most common features/facilities of existing software.

CREATE STORAGE STRUCTURE

This facility creates an appropriate storage structure for a table which has already been defined in the logical schema. The following is an example syntax for the definition of a storage structure:

```
CREATE STRUCTURE structure-name
    ON table-name (column-name1 [,column-name2]...)
    AS {BTREE I HASH I ISAM I HEAP}
    [VOLUME constant]
```

The AS clause enables the designer to choose one of four different file structures [Teorey & Fry, 1982] in order to store tuples of the corresponding table and therefore implement effectively manipulative operations which are of course application-dependent. The parameters of the AS clause correspond to the following:

BTREE	Create a balanced tree where each element represents the column(s) specified.
HASH	Create a hash file where the hash address of each tuple is calculated from the values of the specified columns.
ISAM	Create an indexed sequential access management system. This type of organisation offers a balance between direct and sequential access of tuples in tables.
HEAP	Create an ordinary (flat) file without any access structure (i.e without extra control fields, hash addresses, etc).

The VOLUME clause specifies the expected occurrences (tuples) under a table. This constant may be difficult to estimate, particularly where the organisation is introducing computing equipment for the first time, or where the number of real world objects to be stored in the structure varies a great deal. If the clause is omitted the volume will increase or decrease dynamically. This will obviously impose an overhead on the database especially in the case where new hash addresses have to be calculated.

Let us use an example to illustrate the command CREATE STRUCTURE. The following statements create a BTREE structure on table 'book' using its primary key (book-no) capable of representing up to 50,000 tuples:

CREATE STRUCTURE structure1
    ON book (book-no)
    AS BTREE
    VOLUME 50000

MAINTENANCE OF DATABASE STRUCTURES

Evidently, different applications impose different demands upon the storage
structure and therefore it becomes very difficult to find one which can satisfy them
all in an optimal manner. So, a DBMS must offer a choice of file structures in
order to implement different portions of the database utilising different storage
structures.

Moreover, after a structure has been set up it should be possible to modify this
in order to optimise access requests. To this end, it becomes necessary to collect
usage statistics and to store these under appropriate vendor-dependent and non-
transparent files.

Collect statistics

The following syntax enables the collection of statistics regarding the usage of a
table:

CREATE STATISTICS
    ON table-name (column-name1 [ALL | operations]
            [,column-name2 [ALL | operations]]...)

The entry 'operations' specifies the types of manipulative operations under
which the statistics are to be collected. The keywords here can be a combination of
INSERT, DELETE, UPDATE and SEARCH. When the ALL keyword is
specified then statistics under each of these will be collected. The following
example activates the collection of statistics for columns 'title' and 'author' where
they are processed with the SELECT command:

CREATE STATISTICS
    ON book (title SELECT, author SELECT)

Show performance statistics

The following command displays the performance stastistics of a table:

PERFORMANCE
    ON table-name

For example,

PERFORMANCE
ON book

Typical performance statistics may include:
(a) Current total records
(b) Percent utilisation of predefined volume space
(c) Percent utilisation of hash tables
(d) Average size of a collision chain in a hash table
(e) Number of insertions, deletions, updates, searches

Create index

Most relational systems use B-trees to implement indexes for efficient access and some use hashing as a means to retrieve tuples directly. It is common practice to create indexes on base tables (rather than on derived tables) using primary and secondary keys. Generally, an index can be created for any column which is used frequently within search/retrieval commands. The following syntax enables the creation of an index:

CREATE [UNIQUE] INDEX index-name
   ON table-name (column-name1 [ASC I DESC]
          I [,column-name2 [ASC I DESC]]...)

The keyword UNIQUE implies that all entries of the index will be unique and therefore duplicates will not be included. This is particularly useful when the primary key is indexed. If the schema column being indexed contains duplicate values, then the UNIQUE keyword may be omitted although this is not obligatory. For example, it may be necessary to hold duplicate index entries when there are duplicate author names under a column and users carry out frequent search requests which expect the retrieval of all such values. The following example creates an index on 'book' in ascending order of column author:

CREATE INDEX index1
   ON book (author ASC)

Drop index

Indexes take up extra storage space and when they are not utilised it becomes necessary to delete these from the database. The following command drops (deletes) an index.

DROP INDEX index-name

For example,

DROP INDEX index1

4.5 QUERY LANGUAGE

Strictly speaking, all necessary commands for the manipulation of data at all logical levels should form part of the data manipulation language (DML). Whether this is an independent language or an extension of a host language, is of no concern to the user in the present context.

However, there are cases when an even higher level language becomes necessary for quick and casual manipulations of data, primarily for the extraction of information rather than the transfer of masses of new data upon the database.

Query language systems [Gittins, 1986] offer this facility to the user who simply wants to manipulate a set of records without having to go through a DDL or DML. This can materialise under the following two modes of operation:

A.   DIRECT: The direct issue of very high level commands which manipulate appropriate files and retrieve records. For example, with RDL statements we can manipulate table (record type) SS-READER of Figure 3.28 and display the name and address of a reader with identification number 'R110'. (Both upper and lower case characters can be used to specify an attribute or table name.) The following statements illustrate this example:

SELECT name, address
  FROM ss-reader
  WHERE reader-no = 'R110'

B.   MACRO: A set of query language commands which form a 'macro', that is, commands which are interpreted by the DBMS following their activation by a single collective name and the supply of appropriate parameters (values) by the user.

Macros have been studied and researched extensively although not always with respect to database interrogation. We will assume here that the query language offers the commands MACRO and ENDMACRO to declare the beginning and end of a series of commands which are automatically stored on appropriate application files that form part of the user-interface. Thus, the issue of the statement: address, 'R110' could activate a macro (already defined by the user/programmer) to display the name and address of the reader with identification number 'R110'. The following statements define this where '%1' corresponds to the first parameter (value) supplied by the user, assuming that more than one parameter can be supplied to a macro:

MACRO address
  SELECT name, address
  FROM ss-reader
  WHERE reader-no = %1
ENDMACRO

When the user is connected with the query module online, it may prove necessary to impose certain restrictions on retrieval and update operations so that they do not impose excessive demands upon the system through long file searches or time consuming manipulative operations.

We envisage a DBMS environment where the volume of data to be retrieved is related to the number of online users (so that unacceptable waiting times are avoided) as well as to the contents of search requests. For example, in the following case the system (a preprocessor which analyses every query) could detect that the display of the 'edition' of all books is meaningless, and therefore terminate the retrieval after, say, 20 records:

SELECT edition
   FROM book

In many cases, query statements are more appropriately issued under traditional 'batch' jobs but with the same conditions of accessibility as may be the case under an online mode.

Query languages are generally self-contained and autonomous modules of the DBMS. The commands offered and their structural components can be classified as follows:

Definitional

Define application-dependent data types, domains, ranges and relationships (explicitly or implicitly). For example, create a virtual table/file (e.g CREATE VIEW my-books FROM holdings).

Declaratory

Declare the portions of the database required at any point of time. Declaratory statements must not be confused with definitional statements. For example, declare the subschema or view to be used in a transaction (e.g INVOKE view1 OF SCHEMA library).

Logical

Specify the logic for the retrieval of related records. For example, test the contents of records to see whether they refer to a female employee between the ages 25 and 30. This can be implemented as follows:

... WHERE sex = 'F' AND age < 30 AND age > 25

Manipulative

Manipulate the contents of tables/files and carry out specific operations. Example operations are select, update, insert, delete, assign a value to a variable. For example, update the address field (e.g SET address = '25 Carnoustie Grove').

Mathematical/Statistical

Specify simple mathematical functions and fields upon which these operate. Example functions are sum, average, count, maximum, minimum, sine, cosine. For example, find the sum of values under field 'salary' (e.g SUM (salary) FROM employees).

Informative

This class of commands enables the user to receive meta-information, that is, information which describes information proper in terms of available record types, attributes, types of attributes (e.g INTEGER, CHARACTER), sub-schemata or views, and others. For example, display the column names and associated data types under record type 'book' (e.g HELP COLUMNS FROM book).

4.5.1 RDL Commands

Recent developments established the query language as a common sublanguage for both user and programmer alike. Thus, we find a number of DBMSs today which offer the same commands (syntactically and lexically) for use within host languages, or as directly executable (interpreted) statements. Moreover, query-like statements exist for the definition of the logical schema as well as the subschemata (views) of an organisation. The reader may therefore assume that most of the statements we presented in Section 4.3 on the data manipulation language are equally available in a query language. The following tasks are frequently carried out under a query language mode:

(a)   Define a macro, that is, a stored command sequence
(b)   Execute a macro
(c)   Invoke a view
(d)   Invoke an application program
(e)   Carry out simple operations, such as SELECT, UPDATE INSERT and DELETE but on rather small sets of data
(f)   Seek information on what the database contains
(g)   Produce reports

4.6 QUERY BY EXAMPLE (QBE)

To expect 'infophobic' people to use the computer is one thing, to expect them to remember commands such as SELECT x FROM y WHERE i=j no matter how simple these are, necessitates not only the post of DBA but also the post of 'meta-information provider'. Research into man-machine communication is under way so that even friendlier interfaces can be established. An example here is the development of Query By Example (QBE) [Zloof, 1977, 1981; Sordi, 1984].

QBE offers a domain-dependent approach to man-machine communication where the user is presented with 'software forms' which have to be filled in before a query is satisfied. A software form can be visualised as a two-dimensional table of a record type the values of which are filled in during a session with the user. QBE can therefore be considered as a 'friendly interface' for database interrogation where the user is presented with appropriate information on pertinent application attributes.

The structure of a QBE interface to the database offers three basic levels of communication:

(a)   Simple operation/function commands, such as 'P' to print or display, 'D' to delete, 'I' to insert and 'U' to update.

(b)   Names of domains which are to be assigned values by the DBMS, in other words, attribute names.

(c)   Actual values of domains for use by the DBMS to interrogate the database.

4.6.1 Example Forms of QBE

In this section we present and discuss example forms of the QBE and corresponding commands. We use simple but realistic screen forms to illustrate the principles and also convert each QBE form to an equivalent set of statements in RDL.

Example 1

Let an example 'form' contain four attributes (Car-plate, Car-owner, Car-address, Car-tele) from table CAR, where the query implies find the name and address of owner with car registration 'PJO 155T':

CAR	Car-plate	Car-owner	Car-address	Car-tele
	PJO 155T	P	P	

The equivalent command in RDL is:

SELECT car-owner, car-address
    FROM car
    WHERE car-plate = 'PJO 155T'

Example 2

Another example of QBE, involving the insertion of a new record, is the following:

CAR	Car-plate	Car-owner	Car-address	Car-tele
I	SUG 929D	Ayres F H	2 Home View	561092

The equivalent command in RDL accomplishing the same task is:

INSERT
    INTO car
    VALUES ('SUG 929D', 'Ayres F H', '2 Home View', '561092')

Example 3

Let us consider another QBE example with the classical case of employee data
including: Payroll-code, Name, Date-of-birth, Salary and Department. Our aim
here is to illustrate how logical tests are presented on a QBE form by searching for
all employees who receive a salary greater than 15,000 (pounds or dollars):

EMPLOYEE	Code	Name	Date-of-birth	Salary	Dept
		P		>15000	P

The equivalent command in RDL is the following:

SELECT name, dept
    FROM employee
    WHERE salary > 15000

Example 4

Two or more tables (forms) can also be displayed on the screen under a multiple
window interface. Let us extend Example 3 above by retrieving all employees
(printing the Name, Salary and Overtime in ascending order of Name; 'AO' for
ascending and 'DO' for descending) in department 'comp' who receive a salary
greater than 15,000 and who have worked overtime greater than 10 hours:

EMPLOYEE	Code	Name	Date-of-birth	Salary	Dept
	0001	P.AO		P.>15000	'comp'

WORK-HOURS	Code	Standard	Overtime
	0001		P.>10

The following statements in RDL accomplish exactly the same task:

```
SELECT employee.name, employee.salary, work-hours.overtime
   FROM employee, work-hours
   WHERE employee.code = work-hours.code AND
            employee.salary> 15000 AND
            work-hours.overtime> 10 AND
            employee.dept = 'comp'
ORDER BY employee.name ASC
```

The equijoin is indicated by underlining two values in the two different tables. In this case, the equijoin is on attribute 'code'.

Example 5

Having presented a case involving the AND logical relational test (Example 4 above), we will proceed to show how the OR logical test can be represented on a QBE form. Let us use the same table, WORK-HOURS, to search for all employees who have either worked overtime greater than 5 hours or standard time greater than 37 hours or both. QBE resolves logical tests, generally, by ANDing values specified in the same row, and ORing values specified under different rows. The following example performs this task and displays values under attributes: Code (in ascending order), Standard, and Overtime:

WORK-HOURS	Code	Standard	Overtime
	P. AO	P.>37	
	P. AO		P.>5

The following statements in RDL accomplish exactly the same task:

```
SELECT code, standard, overtime
   FROM work-hours
   WHERE standard > 37 OR overtime > 5
   ORDER BY code ASC
```

4.7 DATA DICTIONARY

4.7.1 Aims and Objectives

A database is expected to evolve dynamically as the enterprise changes at both conceptual and logical levels. Proper and integrated control of the resources, including information and meta-information, is therefore a necessity rather than a desirable managerial aspect.

Managing a database can be a complex task and without proper control its advantages diminish as more application programs are developed, new data items are incorporated, and new record occurrences are inserted in the database. What appears to be necessary is a catalogue of all different entities and attributes, record types and data items, storage records and physical characteristics, applications and programs, and of course registered users. Such a catalogue is called the 'data dictionary' [Duyn, 1982].

Its primary objective is to hold and provide meta-information, that is, information about information. Data processing managers have come to recognise it as an essential part of the global information system, especially as the database has come to be recognised as a valuable and vital corporate resource of the whole enterprise.

The importance of data dictionaries has only recently been recognised and not all DBMSs offer software for creating and maintaining such a catalogue. We envisage an Information Resource Dictionary System (IRDS) which provides online reporting functions as well as DBA-related functions for maintaining its contents [Goldfine, 1984]. The variability of the services it provides can then be studied in connection with individual types of users [Kahn & Lumsden, 1983]. Before we look at each user in turn we will present an outline of what the dictionary can contain and how an IRDS can manipulate its contents.

The derivation of different 'views' from the same logical schema implies that different applications may have different logical views of the same portion of the database. Moreover, data items may be processed differently by application programs or indeed named differently. For example, the title of a book may be known as 'Book-title' in one application but as 'Title-of-book' in another. So, 'membership', 'functional' and 'descriptive' criteria can be used to design a dictionary containing vital characterisations of data.

Because the data item is considered to be the most elementary building block of logical record types, it is reasonable to use this as the basic occurrence entry in the dictionary as far as the logical schema, storage schema and subschemata are concerned. But we also envisage an appropriate section of the dictionary which refers to the conceptual level in order to record and document conceptual information at each stage of data analysis.

In order to discuss possible attributes which can characterise a dictionary entry, we find it necessary to introduce the term 'meta-item' corresponding to any meta-information or meta-attribute pertinent to a 'column' of a data dictionary entry. The general form of a dictionary base then becomes:

Entry no	Identifier	Meta-item-1	Meta-item-2	⋅ ⋅ ⋅
⋮	⋮	⋮	⋮	⋮

Thus, an IRDS can be employed to document data items and to provide information on each of these under a number of meta-items, such as:

1. Name
2. Description
3. Synonyms and homonyms
4. Logical record types

5. Subschema record types
6. Applications
7. Programs
8. Type (e.g CHAR, INTEGER)
9. Length (in bits or bytes)
10. Valid ranges (values)
11. Valid operations on values
12. Levels of accessibility
13. Update authority
14. Password levels
15. Frequency of use
16. Identifying properties and pertinent record types
17. Storage realms (e.g pages, files)
18. Conversion rules (e.g from bits to integer)
19. Coding schemes (e.g FT='Full-time')

Evidently, the dictionary can document other types of resources equally well using multi-entry types. It can, for example, document the subschema (e.g name, description, applications), the application program (e.g name, tasks performed, programmer, last update), the storage resources (e.g device name, description, capacity, database files, date of last service, service engineer), the users (e.g name, job title, department, duties, responsibilites).

On the basis of the above considerations, the IRDS can provide valuable feedback for the complete user community and generally aid the co-ordination of all database activities. Moreover, it will be able to cross-reference the entries in order to produce essential reports. Let us present an outline of IRDS-related functions and example reports for each user class.

At the data administration level, the IRDS - in conjunction with a communications facility (e.g electronic mail) - will be able to inform the user community of any changes to the database (definitional or functional). When a new entry or alteration of an existing entry is being contemplated, the DBA will be in a position to interrogate the dictionary in order to identify affected users, programs, subschemata, etc. The DBA will also be in a position to estimate the cost of a planned operation (e.g the introduction of a new subschema, application, etc). Moreover, the dictionary base can record the allocation of resources and usage statistics in order to aid performance analysis, tuning and restructuring tasks.

The applications analyst can use the IRDS to find out what data is available for existing applications, what data is missing, or how existing data can be redefined to meet the requirements of new applications. In other words, the IRDS base can be used as the basis for application modelling and step-wise refinement.

The applications programmer can use the IRDS to ensure data items are utilised correctly within the programs developed. The programmer can also find out the coding schemes available (e.g UG='Undergraduate', PG='Postgraduate'), the logical record types of a subschema, the data items of a logical record type, etc.

The user of an application can interrogate the dictionary to establish the format and type of input required by a process, or the nature and format of reports produced. Generally, the user can seek further clarification on types of information, commands, applications, etc.

In conclusion, it is of the utmost importance for the data dictionary to be kept up to date and accurate at all times. Although it will be available for interrogation by all types of users, only the DBA will be allowed to alter existing meta-items or other global characteristics of the organisation.

4.7.2 The Data Dictionary and the Database

Having discussed the aims and objectives of the data dictionary and IRDS, we are now in a position to investigate their co-existence with the database and DBMS. This section presents a scenario for their desirable co-existence and possible interface.

There are basically two modes for implementing an IRDS: (a) A stand-alone and independent software utility; (b) an IRDS integrated with the database, at one or more levels (conceptual, logical, internal). Clearly, an independent IRDS is equally useful to non-DBMS environments, and can be used to design a meta-information base which can of course be a database in its own right. However, an IRDS which is part of the DBMS software, integrated with the database itself, offers a powerful environment for documentation and database control.

An integrated DBMS-IRDS environment enables the automatic population of the IRDS-base through analyses of all types of data. Moreover, appropriate IRDS software which is compatible with DBMS software can be utilised to check the consistency and integrity of current and planned applications. Also, the correctness of translating application requirements to logical subschemata can be confirmed. Therefore, the IRDS-base must be built in such a way as to enable the above tasks to be carried out effectively.

Since the IRDS can be as informative as its contents permit, it is important to study carefully the different ways whereby the dictionary can be populated. We present the following four major areas through which the IRDS base can be populated:

(a) Directly, using an independent command language to feed in all meta-information.
(b) From analyses of the logical schema.
(c) From analyses of subschemata/views.
(d) From analyses of application programs.
(e) From analyses of valid query statements.

The analyses can be carried out automatically by accepting each unit as input (e.g the logical schema, each subschema, etc), scanning this in search of keywords and delimiters and transferring the output to the IRDS base. Clearly, automatic population of the dictionary base is only feasible when the IRDS is integrated with the DBMS.

In order to appreciate IRDS and DBMS integration, we will build an example data dictionary from the diagrammatic logical schema on Figure 3.27 by considering only the first three record types, namely, 'book', 'subject' and 'book-subject'.

Brief analysis of Figure 3.27 shows that the following meta-items can be created:

1. Name
2. Description

3.   Type (e.g Integer, String)
4.   Length
5.   Membership (i.e record type used)
6.   Identification status (e.g Primary, Secondary key)

An example data dictionary for our library schema is presented in Figure 4.1. Perhaps the reader can complete the dictionary to include information on the rest

DICTIONARY

Entry no.	Name	Description	Type	Length	Membership	Identification status
1	Book-no	Unique book identifier	String	7	BOOK, BOOK-SUBJECT	Key
2	Author	Surname and first names of author	String	40	BOOK	Data
3	Title	Title of a book	String	200	BOOK	Data
4	Publisher-code	Unique code for each publisher	String	10	BOOK	Key
5	Year	The year a book is published	Integer	4	BOOK	Data
6	Volume	The volume number of a book	Integer	2	BOOK	Data
7	Edition	The edition number of a book	Integer	2	BOOK	Data
8	Subject-code	Unique code for each subject	String	15	SUBJECT, BOOK-SUBJECT	Key
9	Description & keywords	Subject description and relevant keywords	String	200	SUBJECT	Data
10	Location in library	The physical location of a book	String	40	SUBJECT	Data

Figure 4.1   An example data dictionary based on Figure 3.27, defining the attributes in record type BOOK, SUBJECT and BOOK-SUBJECT.

of the record types of Figure 3.27; data items common to two or more record types (e.g Name, Address) must be dealt with appropriately so that synonyms and homonyms are included in the dictionary. Obviously, this requirement necessitates the adoption of appropriate meta-items.

Although each dictionary entry (see Figure 4.1) refers to a data item, by adopting further meta-items (e.g conceptual equivalent, view membership, storage equivalent, users, etc), we can construct a dictionary that contains information on each architectural level of the database. Cross-referencing of meta-item columns can then satisfy practically all retrieval requests.

Let us illustrate example queries for dictionary retrieval. The following data manipulation statements implement examples of dictionary retrieval in the same way as 'help' commands are used to provide meta-information for the user. Our aim here is to demonstrate that DML-like commands can be used effectively to perform various operations on the dictionary. We assume the existence of a single relational table called DICTIONARY as presented in Figure 4.1 corresponding to the IRDS base.

Example 1

Display the description of field 'author':

    SELECT description
      FROM DICTIONARY
      WHERE name = 'author'

Result:

Description
Unique book identifier

Example 2

Display full details on field 'title':

    SELECT *
      FROM DICTIONARY
      WHERE name = 'title'

Result:

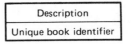

Name	Description	Type	Length	Membership	Id. status
Title	Title of book	String	200	Book	Data

Example 3

Display the field names of record type 'book':

    SELECT name
      FROM DICTIONARY
      WHERE membership = 'book'

Result:

Name
Book no
Author
Title
Publisher-code
Year
Volume
Edition

   In order to understand the mechanism whereby the co-existence of IRDS and
DBMS is established and maintained, we will discuss the scenario as presented on
Figure 4.2. The main objective here is to outline a methodology for, (a) the
population of the dictionary base and (b) its subsequent maintenance.
   The DBA cannot, by himself, determine the dictionary contents and must
therefore consult the applications analyst who in turn communicates with the
applications programmer. The IRDS is used and dictionary details are specified.
The IRDS communicates with database-dependent information (e.g logical
schema, subschemata, application or query programs) through the DBMS and the
physical database is updated/interrogated accordingly. Because the IRDS is
connected directly to the DBMS (see Figure 4.2), the dictionary base will be
maintained automatically - provided of course the creation of database-dependent information obeys the rules of the enterprise. Besides, the DBA is connected
directly to the DBMS and can therefore force a dictionary operation directly.

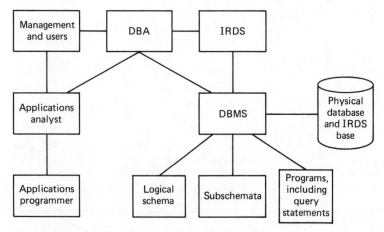

Figure 4.2   Setting up and maintaining the dictionary base.

4.8 AN OVERVIEW OF SOFTWARE INTEGRATION

The database approach to storing and retrieving information has opened a new horizon for the successful integration of a wide variety of information types and information environments. Moreover, complex and in many cases unrelated environments can be controlled uniformly and effectively. Consequently, the DBMS becomes a very complicated piece of software and it is only through a disciplined methodology that its structural units can be implemented.

The design of a DBMS cannot on the whole be isolated from the structural view the DBA wishes to adopt or indeed impose upon the enterprise. The overall structural picture of the database environment we propose evolves around the three major levels of logical schema, internal schema and subschema. However, these are considered part of the intra-enterprise realm and may not necessarily be adequate to describe inter-enterprise architectures (i.e structures and relationships between independent companies) and information types.

Teleprocessing, networking and distributed databases (i.e databases in different geographic locations) can be considered part of the inter-enterprise realm. These aspects cannot be ignored by the designers of DBMSs or indeed the management of the company that utilises these.

Connecting the database and the DBMS to other non-database software is also equally important. Examples here are, the word processing needs of the company, real time control applications, simulation of physical phenomena, etc. Appropriate interfaces to the database must therefore be made available as and where necessary. So, the more we expect from the DBMS, the more complex its software becomes. Furthermore, our demands change regularly and in many cases this affects existing 'static' information which cannot be updated without major restructuring and reorganisation.

In order to avoid major restructuring or inconvenience to the user community, management often opts for solutions which are not necessarily viable in the long term. A typical example is the purchase of a package which hooks on to the database and performs screen-based input and output operations. The danger here is that both the DBA and users may come to depend on the package heavily and, by default, hinder the evolution of the database itself.

We do not here condemn 'plug compatible' software but merely point out the hidden dangers which are not always easy to foresee. In any case, plug compatible software enables the enterprise to expand in a step-wise fashion, provided of course the DBMS itself is capable of accommodating new modules as and where necessary.

Management staff have to be very careful as there are numerous 'software modules' available in the market today, all sold under the umbrella of a DBMS, but without any overall co-ordination. What we are saying here is that some of these modules may not necessarily be fully controllable by a master module, that is, a single guardian software utility; the modules may exist as external 'parasitic' packages, each of course performing an honourable and well justified task.

We identify and present the following categories of database-related tools:

1. Database structure, design and implementation tools.
2. Application development, support and maintenance tools.

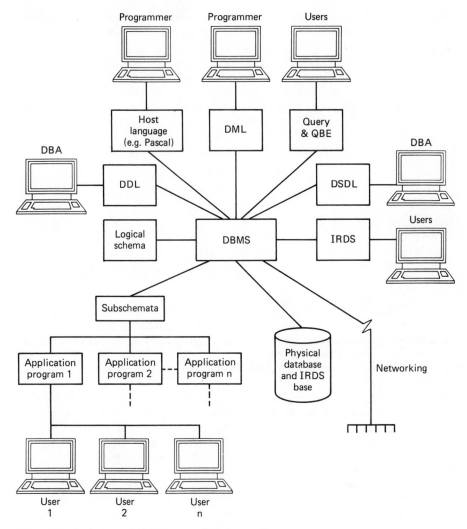

Figure 4.3 An integrated environment of database software.

3. Decision-support tools for users and management.
4. Performance evaluation, measurement and tuning tools.
5. Network and distributed database software tools.
6. User-friendly interfaces or connections to the database.
7. Interfaces to specialist packages external to the DBMS.

What we are arguing for is a modular software system which can be designed, implemented and used as such. Besides, where necessary, the modules must be able to interact and communicate at both intra- and inter-enterprise levels. The languages we presented earlier (e.g DDL, DML, query) are examples of software modules in the present context.

This requirement necessitates the adoption of common standards and protocols which are themselves defined and manipulated through meta-files, in more or less the same way as physical and logical independence is achieved. So, when standards themselves change, the database can evolve dynamically and without major reorganisation or inconvenience to the user community.

By introducing the DBMS as the 'standard language' to build and interface diverse environments, we achieve an integrated and consistent software architecture. Here, the software modules are the DDL, DML, query, QBE, DSDL, IRDS, and network access facilities. We envisage a DBMS which enables the declaration and invocation of software modules with a single statement, as for example:

```
MODULE module-name
    LANGUAGE {PASCAL | FORTRAN | COBOL | ADA}
    AUTHORISATION authorisation-identifier
    APPLICATION application-name1 [,application-name2]...
```

where application-name specifies the name of the application utilising a module. There is a strong relationship here between an application-name and a subschema or view name. Also, the concept of 'cursor' can play an important role when a module is interfaced with the database in order to offer a specific facility for the user community.

Figure 4.3 presents a complete and integrated environment of the major architectural components where the DBMS forms the heart of all activities. We must point out here that the Visual Display Unit (VDU) also represents other appropriate media for communicating with the database, examples of which are natural language sentences, speech synthesis and recognition, etc. Figure 4.3 shows quite clearly the different modes of storage and access of database information, as well as the types of languages and designated users, in the following manner:

DBA:	DDL, DSDL
Programmer:	Host language, DML
General user:	Application program, query & QBE, IRDS

An important issue for the designer of a DBMS becomes the definition and specification of each software module and the criteria whereby database tasks can be grouped together to form viable, independent and stable units. Lack of understanding of database principles is often to be blamed for the inadequacy and illogicality of many software utilities. Typical mistakes are: the merging of DDL and DSDL definitions into a single module, the merging of DDL and DML facilities, the lack of a common utility for logical schema and subschema design.

4.9 SUMMARY

In this chapter, we presented the architecture of high level database software from the logical point of view, and the various classes of commands necessary to: (a) create the logical schema and all subschemata, (b) manipulate record types, (c) implement and maintain appropriate physical structures and (d) interrogate the contents of a database directly, that is, without having to resort to programming. In order to illustrate the use of the various software commands, we adopted realistic examples which were implemented with the aid of a Relational Database Language (RDL).

We also discussed, in some detail, the data dictionary which provides an effective way to document the database in general, including the record types in use, applications and corresponding subschemata, software available, users, and the resources of the organisation as a whole.

The Data Description Language (DDL) enables the definition of all logical schemata and subschemata. The various types of commands we introduced enable the DBA to define the logical schema, create and maintain relational tables, create and maintain views or subschemata, grant and revoke permission to access tables, introduce and maintain integrity constraints.

The Data Manipulation Language (DML) offers a set of commands to store, retrieve, and manipulate record occurrences. The DML can be a stand-alone language or it can be used in conjunction with another high level programming language, such as Pascal, COBOL or FORTRAN. This high level language then becomes the *host* DBMS language. Within a DBMS there may be more than one host language.

The various types of commands we introduced enable us to search the contents of tables, join tables, perform simple mathematical functions (e.g average, sum, minimum, maximum), delete, insert and update tuples, and finally define and manipulate cursors.

The Data Storage Description Language (DSDL) provides a set of commands which aim to translate the logical schema into an internal equivalent, and to manipulate and maintain this without disturbing the logical subschemata in use. The classes of commands we introduced enable the creation and manipulation of storage structures, the collection of usage statistics for tuning and optimisation, and finally, the maintenance of appropriate indexes.

The query language provides a set of high level commands to interrogate the database directly. Although it was originally designed for the casual user, it is now widely accepted that it should be fully compatible (if not identical) with the DML.

Query By Example (QBE) offers a domain-dependent approach to interrogate the database. Here, the user is presented with software forms which have to be filled in before a query is satisfied. A software form can be visualised as a two dimensional table which is presented on the VDU containing adequate information to guide the user through the formulation of the query.

Finally, when the data dictionary is fully interfaced with the database it can form the basis for automatic documentation of all the resources of an enterprise including schema, subschema, application programs, users, devices, and others.

4.10 REFERENCES

ANSI, X3H2 Technical Committee on Databases, 'Relational Database Language', 1986.
CODASYL, Report of the CODASYL Data Description Language Committee, Pergamon Press, 1978.
Cosmadakis, S. & Papadimitriou, C. H., 'Updates of Relational Views', Proc. ACM SIGAT-SIGMOD Symposium on Principles of Database Systems, March 1983.
Date, C. J., 'An Introduction to Database Systems', Vol. II, Addison-Wesley, 1984.
Duyn, J. Van, 'Developing a Data Dictionary System', Prentice-Hall, 1982.
Furtado, A. L. & Casanova, M. A., 'Updating Relational Views', In: Query Processing in Database Systems, Kim W., Reiner D. & Batory D. (editors), Springer Verlag, New York, 1986.
Gittins, D., 'Query Language Systems', Edward Arnold, 1986.
Goldfine, A., 'Using the Information Resource Dictionary System Command Language', ISO TC97/SC21 N474, 1984.
Kahn, B. K. & Lumsden, E. W., 'A User-oriented Framework for Data Dictionary Systems', ACM SIGBDP, Vol. 15, No. 1, pp. 28-36, 1983.
Sordi, J. J., 'The Query Management Facility', IBM Systems J., Vol. 23, No. 2, pp. 126-150, 1984.
Teorey, T. J. & Fry, J. P., 'Design of Database Structures', Prentice-Hall, 1982.
Yannakoudakis, E. J. & Cheng, C. P., 'A Rigorous Approach to Data Type Specification', Computer Bulletin, Vol 3, Part 4, pp. 31-36, 1987.
Zloof, M. M., 'Query-By-Example: A Database Language', IBM Systems J., Vol. 16, No. 4, pp. 324-343, 1977.
Zloof, M. M., 'QBE/OBE: A Language for Office Business and Office Automation', Computer, pp. 13-22, May 1981.

5 COMMUNICATING WITH DATABASES IN NATURAL LANGUAGE

5.1 PROGRAMMING LANGUAGES

Research into man-machine communication has produced systems which allow the user to interrogate the database in natural language [Wallace, 1984]. Natural language systems are particularly useful for interrogating the database, rather than for designing the schema, subschemata, etc. They can thus be considered as alternatives to languages like DML, SQL and QBE, operating as front-end modules to these, or as stand-alone systems which retrieve data directly from the database [Sime & Coombs, 1983].

The database management system itself can produce natural language output from structured query languages. For example, given a set of SQL statements the DBMS can display their meaning in clear, unambiguous natural language [Luk & Kloster, 1986]. Translations and mappings from one language to another should also form part of the utility set of the DBMS [Grosz, 1983]. For example, algebra-based query specifications can be translated into iterative programs for efficient execution where the source level operates on sets of tuples and the generated programs manipulate tuples as their base objects [Freytag & Goodman, 1986].

Programming languages generally, are well suited for people who also have some knowledge of computer software architecture and elementary knowledge of data structures. Database languages including the DDL, DML, RDL and DSDL, have a specific syntax and lexicon which are not always easy to master and use effectively; these languages are not always based on the same syntax. Moreover, commands within the same language differ greatly depending on the user mode (e.g beginner, expert, etc) and user status (e.g ordinary user, DBA, etc).

Another problem with programming and database languages is that they expect the user or designer of a database to become familiar with dozens of commands, as well as the structure of the database itself. In most cases the user has to know the attributes that have been defined, the length and type of each of these, the relations, the views of an application, etc. The classical HELP command may of course be available to provide further meta-information, but this wastes time and computer resources.

There are basically two major categories of programming languages available today: (a) procedural, and (b) non-procedural. Procedural languages, such as Pascal, FORTRAN (FORmula TRANslation) and Ada, expect the programmer to specify exactly 'how' a specific task should be carried out. Non-procedural languages, such as LISP (LISt Processing) and PROLOG (PROgramming in LOGic) on the other hand, expect the programmer to specify 'what' tasks should be carried out by the system; the 'system' is defined here in the broadest possible sense and may incorporate software modules from the operating system, or even other procedural languages.

In this Chapter we discuss various 'user-friendly' interfaces and several techniques whereby a non-procedural language can be used to manipulate user queries. It is now widely accepted that non-procedural languages coupled with a reasoning ability, enhance the usability of databases [Welty & Stemple, 1981].

5.2 THE PROLOG PROGRAMMING LANGUAGE

In this section we will introduce the language PROLOG [Clocksin & Mellish, 1981; Bratko, 1986] which is based on first order predicate logic formulae and is particularly suited for natural language analyses. Moreover, the language can be interfaced with relational database management systems [Marque-Pucheu & Martin-Gallausiaux, 1984; Bocca, 1986], and can therefore form the basis for a simple man-machine interface.

Formulae in first order logic [Nilsson, 1981] contain various features that are not suitable for a computational language. Example features are the universal and existential quantifiers and a range of connectives. However, any formulae can be converted to one or more formulae in clausal form where there are no existential quantifiers and where all variables are universally quantified. One way to achieve this is to use the clausal form known as 'Horn clause', named after the logician Alfred Horn, which has the following form:

p1(x1), p2(x2),..., pn(xn) --> q(x)

A Horn clause, basically, consists of an antecedent section (i.e p1(x1), p2(x2), etc) and a consequent section (i.e q(x)) where the predicates p1(x1), p2(x2), etc, are joined by the comma (,) indicating a conjunction, and the consequent is monatomic. The Horn clause forms the basis of the PROLOG clause where the above takes the form:

q(x) :- p1(x1), p2(x2), ..., pn(xn).

In this form, q(x) becomes a conclusion or a fact, the predicates p1(x1), p2(x2), etc become a goal, and the complete clause becomes a rule which can otherwise be read out as:

q(x) IF p1(x1) AND p2(x2) AND ... pn(xn).

So, a Horn clause corresponds syntactically to a simple PROLOG rule or goal which does not involve negation or disjunction (i.e the OR operator). However, in PROLOG the antecedent section may consist of a single goal, or a conjunction of goals, or a disjunction of goals specified by the semicolon (;). Therefore, the above clause can also take the PROLOG form:

q(x) :- p1(x1); p2(x2); ... pn(xn).

which can be read out as:

q(x) IF p1(x1) OR p2(x2) OR ... pn(xn).

Furthermore, variables can be used as goals that can be satisfied when they actually fail by using the 'not' predicate. For example, if X2 fails, then not(X2) succeeds.

The first character of a variable in PROLOG must be either a capital letter or an underscore (—) followed by an arbitrary number of alphanumeric characters (i.e A-Z, a-z, 0-9), as well as the underscore character. Examples of permissible variable names are the following:

A
Xyz
Address
—symbol
One—to—one

A special type of variable is the underscore on its own which is used to signify the position of an argument within a clause rather than its value. When the underscore variable is used the corresponding values of the argument it represents are not retrieved by PROLOG. The underscore variable is otherwise referred to as an 'anonymous variable'.

A constant (value) of a clause must begin with a small letter or it can be any sequence of characters within single quotes. Quoted names serve two main purposes: (a) to store text as a unit rather than as individual characters, and (b) to denote constants which could otherwise be interpreted as variables. Generally, a value that contains only numeric characters is interpreted as a number. Examples of permissible constants are the following:

1821
'Mr Ayres'
'Dr'
'Athens'
'0274 561092'

The PROLOG user interacts with the language by providing logical formulae (i.e goals) and the system searches for proofs of the formulae. The user populates the database with a number of theorems (i.e clauses) which are then used to prove the goals entered. The full stop is used to signal the end of a goal or a clause. Clauses can be facts, such as mr—ayres is male (denoted by: male(mr—ayres).), or rules, such as X is the child of Y if Y is the parent of X (denoted by: child(X,Y) :- parent(Y,X).). Further examples of clauses and the meaning of each are presented below.

Facts and their meaning

librarian(mr—ayres).
> Mr Ayres is a Librarian

physicist(dr—huggill).
> Dr Huggill is a Physicist

manager(dr—stone).
> Dr Stone is a Manager

part—of(piston, engine).
> The piston is part of the engine

Rules and their meaning

mortal(X) :- human(X).
> X is mortal if X is human

mother(X,Y) :- female(X), parent(X,Y).
> X is the mother of Y if X is female
> and X is the parent of Y

loves(mary,X) :- loves(X,mary), male(X).
> Mary loves all men who love her

part—of(carburettor,X) :- car—engine(X).
> The carburettor is part of X if X is a car engine

Goals and their meaning

At the PROLOG prompt (in our case the symbols '?-') the user can provide a goal for the system to search for a solution, as is the case with the following.

?- librarian(mr—ayres).
> Is Mr Ayres a Librarian ?

?- part—of(piston, X).
> Is the piston part of any objects ?

?- human(X).
> Is there a human being ?

?- loves(X, mary).
> Does anybody love Mary ?

PROLOG can evaluate a query by answering with a YES or a NO or by actually listing the values of the goals that satisfy the query [Bancilhon & Ramakrishnan, 1986]. For example, if the PROLOG database contains the following facts:

librarian(mr—ayres).
programmer(dr—huggill).
programmer(dr—yannakoudakis).

then the query:

?- librarian(dr—yannakoudakis).

gives the answer NO. The query:

?- librarian(X).

produces the result:

X=mr—ayres

and therefore performs what is known as the 'instantiation' of a variable. Now, if we issue the query:

?- programmer(X).

then the result will be the first solution the system finds (i.e X=dr—huggill). If the first solution is satisfactory then we can press RETURN to exit the search, or we can force the system to search for a further solution by pressing ';' and RETURN. The process of ignoring a solution found and thereby uninstantiating a variable is called 'backtracking'.

Backtracking can also be achieved by using the standard PROLOG predicate 'fail' without getting stuck into an indefinite loop. In between each iteration we can use the predicate 'write' to transfer selected values/constants to the current output file or the display unit. For example, to list the names of all the programmers we can write:

?- programmer(X), write(X), fail.

and therefore produce the following output:

X=dr—huggill
X=dr—yannakoudakis

From the foregoing, it becomes clear that PROLOG can be used to set up factual databases and rules whereby these can be interrogated in simple sentences. Artificial intelligence programming techniques can then be used to scan the incoming 'unstructured' sentence and convert this into a set of structured query statements. Therefore, an essential feature of the programming language used must be its ability to manipulate strings and the general constructs of the human language, whether this is English, French, German, Greek, Arabic, etc.

5.3 NATURAL LANGUAGE SYSTEM ARCHITECTURE

The development of data models that capture the inherent characteristics of the enterprise at a very high level (conceptual), and the advent of data dictionary processors, have made it possible to design intelligent parsers (i.e systems which associate the phrases in a string of characters in a language with the component names of the grammar that generated the string) that are fully interfaced with both data model and data dictionary [Sparck-Jones & Wilks, 1985]. So, the DBA can now tailor the parser to individual applications much more easily than has been the case previously. What the vendor of a Natural Language Unit (NLU) must provide, is a common software module, that is, the interface builder.

The architecture of an NLU, regardless of whether this is a stand-alone system, or a plug-compatible piece of software that utilises DBMS utilities, comprises four basic modules [Wallace, 1984]. These are:

(a)   The parser that analyses the grammar of a sentence and identifies function
      words (e.g print, delete, etc) and content words (e.g 'Ayres', 'computer-
      department', etc).
(b)   The query generator that takes the output produced by the parser and
      converts this to a set of structured query language statements.
      Understandably, there will be cases where the parser or query generator
      fails to 'understand' the sentence and has therefore to interact with the
      user in order to collect more details.
(c)   The access software that actually isolates relevant values from the
      database and makes these available for display, or further processing.
(d)   The processing software that manipulates relevant record occurrences or
      tuples and performs the required tasks.

   Natural language systems can utilise the data dictionary in order to establish
application-dependent characteristics (e.g synonyms, homonyms, etc) before
they can analyse the incoming sentence effectively. In fact, the majority of NLUs
today use application-dependent characteristics which may not necessarily be
shared with other applications in the organisation. It is however possible to have
an application-independent parser, common to all subschemata supported by the
database; this is very difficult to implement and so the majority of current systems
provide software modules which enable the DBA to adapt the parser to individual
applications.
   For an application-independent parser to operate satisfactorily, it must
incorporate a number of facilities to 'understand', amongst others, a minimum set
of linguistic contructions [Bolc, 1980]. These are presented below, with appropriate examples:

1.   Binary questions; e.g IS Dr Stone the MANAGER of ULISS ?
2.   Commands; e.g DISPLAY the address of Dr Stone
3.   Negated questions; e.g Which employee does NOT live in Bradford
4.   Relative clauses; e.g Which are the employees that do NOT HAVE any
      children ?
5.   Adjectives; e.g Which PORTABLE machines are serviced by Mr Smith ?
6.   Sentences with generative attributes; e.g Which computers OF IBM use
      the 8086 chip ?
7.   Noun complements; e.g Where is the capital WITH population 13000000 ?
8.   AND relational operator; e.g Which employees work overtime AND earn
      more than 20000 pounds ?
9.   OR relational operators; e.g Which employees live in Cottingley OR
      Bingley ?
10.   Quantifiers; e.g HOW MANY employees have two children ?
11.   Comparisons; e.g Whose salary is GREATER THAN 20000 pounds ?
12.   From-to constructs; e.g Which employees went FROM Bradford
      TO London ?
13.   Time constructs; e.g Whose birthday is 15 January 1965 ?
14.   Simple calculations; e.g What is the AVERAGE salary in computing ?

   Another interesting feature of the NLU is the thesaurus of database attributes
and other characteristics which can be set up and maintained by the DBA.
Although the thesaurus can be global and can be set up in conjunction with the

design of the schema and subschemata, there will always be certain 'peculiar' applications that require individual attention and specialised dictionaries. However, an application-independent parser in the form of a core software module is feasible and can be expected from the vendors of the NLU.

A module that detects and corrects spelling errors is also desirable [Yannakoudakis, 1983; Yannakoudakis & Fawthrop, 1983a]. This can save the user from having to retype the entire request because of simple spelling errors. If a word cannot be identified or corrected using a simple dictionary (e.g English, French, Greek) and appropriate spelling rules [Yannakoudakis & Fawthrop, 1983b], then the user can retype the misspelled word without having to retype the complete original sentence/query.

There are clearly situations where certain words or strings that occur within the incoming sentence only make sense within a specific context. It becomes therefore necessary for the NLU to carry out context analyses, besides simple string analyses that can only process sentences in isolation. It is also necessary to link the current sentence with those that have already been submitted by the user, as well as the answers that have already been given by the system. Context analyses that associate facts, rules and goals achieved with the current sentence or query are based on a special class of techniques termed 'anaphora'. Examples of sentences involving preset values and past goals, and which can only be analysed effectively through anaphoric techniques are:

Can you tell me *today's* date please ?
(the system must be able to recognise the meaning of *today's*)

Display all programmers in department computing.

Which of *these* can program in Ada ?
(*these* refers to the programmers in the computing department)

What is the department of Dr Huggill ?

How many programmers does *it* employ ?
(*it* refers to the department of Dr Huggill)

In order to understand the processes behind a natural language system, we will use an example to illustrate the principles, assuming that the NLU utilises a relational database language such as SQL to retrieve data. Let the database contain information under the attributes: Name, Address, Telephone-no, Date-of-birth (all within relation 'Rel1'). A 'polite' NLU sentence or query may take the form:

Could you please give me the phone number of Mr Ayres ?

The major conceptual steps the NLU may follow are:

Step 1

Accept a sentence through the keyboard, or other device (e.g a disk file, or a voice recognition system).

Step 2

Use the data dictionary, a global and/or application thesaurus to identify: the function word 'give me' and convert this to the command SELECT, the attributes 'phone number' and the implied attribute 'name' and convert these to 'Telephone-no' and 'Name' respectively, and finally, the relation 'Rel1'.

Step 3

Create a standard communications buffer for general use within the NLU, as for example:

COMMAND: SELECT
ATTRIBUTES: Telephone-no
RELATIONS: Rel1
VALUES: Name = 'Ayres'

Step 4

Read the communications buffer and proceed to generate the SQL statement:

SELECT Telephone-no
    FROM Rel1
    WHERE Name LIKE '*Ayres*'

The introduction of the wildcard symbol '*' in the value 'Ayres' and the LIKE qualifier cater for incomplete values or cases where the initials are also stored under the same attribute. Clearly, when the values supplied by the user are complete (e.g when the primary key is given) and a single record occurrence can be retrieved, then the LIKE qualifier can be excluded from the RDL statements.

Step 5

Accept the output from step 4 and use this as input to a structured query language system, or as input to a DML program for further processing.

In the above example, we assumed that all the attributes which are necessary to answer a user query are available within a single relation. If the user requires information from two or more relations which are not specified explicitly, then the NLU must be able to identify (step 2 above) and employ all these relations (step 3 above) in order to satisfy the query.

Although the relational data model (see Section 3.5) provides a high level set-oriented interface, the user must be familiar with the logical structure of the database, including attribute lists and relations, before he can interrogate the database. For example, before the SELECT...FROM...WHERE command can be issued directly (see step 4 above) the user must have knowledge of the fact that relation 'Rel1' includes the attributes: Name, Address, Telephone-no and Date-of-birth. The procedure whereby knowledge of attributes, relations, keys, etc is utilised to access data is called 'logical navigation'.

Since the relational model fails to provide freedom from user-supplied navigation [Carlson & Kaplan, 1976], the NLU must provide the means to relieve the user of the requirement to master the logical structure of the database. In other words, the NLU must make it possible for the user to assume that the data of the entire database has been defined by a single relation called the 'universal relation' where attributes representing the same object in different relations are given the same name, and attributes representing different objects are given different names.

In order that the universal relation be accepted as a conceptual (not physical) tool, it is often necessary to view it as the natural join of all the relations in the database [Fagin, et al, 1982; Ullman, 1982; Korth, 1984], where null values must sometimes be used to pad out non-existent tuples. Another very important consideration, from the point of view of a systems designer, is the ability of the programming language used to 'interpret' the components of the user query or statement.

5.3.1 The Language Prolog and the Database

In this section we are going to describe how the non-procedural language PROLOG can be used to analyse a statement in a language, say English, and proceed to determine whether the statement is valid or not. We will also show how the insertion and retrieval of simple facts can be carried out using built-in PROLOG predicates. Before we do this we must present a clear definition of what constitutes a 'statement' and how this can be represented formally.

In most cases, the definition is generative, that is, it describes how a legitimate form (statement) can be generated. In order to be able to describe a language and its syntax, we need to utilise another language. The latter is usually referred to as 'meta-language'. (Compare this concept with 'meta-file', that is, a file that describes another file, as we have already discussed under Section 1.3.) In other words, we must have a well defined meta-language and grammar which comprises a set of rules that specify what sequences of strings are acceptable as statements of the language proper.

A meta-language describes the form or syntax of a language by a series of phrase definitions or meta-linguistic formulae. A well known meta-language is Backus Naur Form (BNF) where the name of each phrase is surrounded by pointed brackets, < and >, the symbol ::= implies 'defined to be', and the symbol 'l' separates optional forms of the phrase. For example, the definition of pence as a one or a two digit number becomes:

<pence> ::= <digit> | <digit> <digit>

The definition of a digit becomes:

<digit> ::= 0 | 1 | 2 | 3 | 4 | 5 | 6 | 7 | 8 | 9

PROLOG provides a suitable means to define the grammar of a language and can also be used to analyse any given statement in natural language [Mellish,

1985]. For example, to define a sentence as a 'noun—phrase' followed by a 'verb—phrase', in other words, a 'subject' followed by a 'predicate', we use the symbol --> to mean '...can take the form...', and write this as follows:

sentence --> noun—phrase, verb—phrase.

A noun—phrase can be defined as a 'determiner' followed by a 'noun' as follows:

noun—phrase --> determiner, noun.

A verb—phrase can be defined as a 'verb', or a 'verb' followed by a 'noun—phrase' using two separate formulae as follows:

verb—phrase --> verb.
verb—phrase --> verb, noun—phrase.

Actual values for nouns, verbs and determiners can be defined in PROLOG in a number of ways. Singular, plural and common phrases (e.g orange, oranges and the construct determiner(—) for the word 'the') can be represented adequately. Example cases are the following:

noun(singular) --> [orange].
noun(plural) --> [oranges].
noun(singular) --> [woman].
noun(plural) --> [women].
noun(singular) --> [man].
noun(plural) --> [men].
verb --> [eats].
verb --> [drives].
determiner(—) --> [the].
determiner --> [a].

A simple but complete program in PROLOG which can recognise a number of different English sentences is presented in Figure 5.1. The program reads in sentences from the default input stream using the predicate read(S), and displays information on the default output file (i.e VDU). The predicate 'nl', with no arguments, causes the start of a new line on the output. When the program is activated it prompts the user to type in a sentence in square brackets separating each word with a comma. What in fact happens is that PROLOG creates a 'list' (i.e an ordered sequence of elements that can have any length). A list can be either an 'empty' list written as [], or it can be a structure that has two components: the head and the tail. If the input to the program of Figure 5.1 is an empty list then the program terminates and prints the message 'End of session'; the predicate \= = can be read as 'not equal' and is used here to test whether the input (stored on S) is an empty list.

The program in Figure 5.1 can be described as a simple parser which contains appropriate definitions of grammatical forms and the necessary logic to scan an input list and determine whether it is a valid English sentence or not. The predicate 'phrase' is defined by: phrase(P, L) is true if list L can be parsed as a phrase of type P [Clocksin & Mellish, 1981]. Let us see how the program responds to certain user-input statements. In the following example session the symbols '?-' indicate that PROLOG is ready to accept a statement for analysis:

Type in your sentence..
In format [the,words]. or []. to exit.
?- [the,man,eats,an,apple].

Yes, this is a valid sentence.

Type in your sentence..
In format [the,words]. or []. to exit.
?- [the,man,eat,an,apple].

No, this is not a valid sentence.

Type in your sentence..
In format [the,words]. or []. to exit.
?- [the,men,eat,an,apple].

Yes, this is a valid sentence.

Type in your sentence..
In format [the,words]. or []. to exit.
?- [the,men,eats,an,apple].

No, this is not a valid sentence.

Type in your sentence..
In format [the,words]. or []. to exit.
?- [the,men,eat,a,green,apple].

Yes, this is a valid sentence.

Type in your sentence..
In format [the,words]. or []. to exit.
?- [the,men,eat,an,apple,slowly].

Yes, this is a valid sentence.

Type in your sentence..
In format [the,words]. or []. to exit.
?- [smith,sang,a,song].

Yes, this is a valid sentence.

Type in your sentence..
In format [the,words]. or []. to exit.
?- [smith,song,a,sang].

No, this is not a valid sentence.

Type in your sentence..
In format [the,words]. or []. to exit.
?- [smith,sang,a,song,to,the,sheep].

Yes, this is a valid sentence.

Type in your sentence..
In format [the,words]. or []. to exit.
?- [the,sheep,eat,a,pear].

Yes, this is a valid sentence.

Type in your sentence..
In format [the,words]. or []. to exit.
?- [the,sheep,eats,a,pear].

Yes, this is a valid sentence.

Type in your sentence..
In format [the,words]. or []. to exit.
?- [the,man,bought,the,red,apples,from,the,friend].

No, this is not a valid sentence.

Type in your sentence..
In format [the,words]. or []. to exit.
?- [the,man,bought,the,red,apples,from,smith].

Yes, this is a valid sentence.

Type in your sentence..
In format [the,words]. or []. to exit.
?- [the,men,sang,slowly,to,the,goat].

Yes, this is a valid sentence.

Type in your sentence..
In format [the,words]. or []. to exit.
?- [].
End of session

A PROLOG program can be viewed as a relational database in its own right; the relations are partly explicit (facts) and partly implicit (rules). Appropriate predicates of the language (i.e built-in commands or facilities) can make it possible to define and manipulate relations or tuples of tables. A number of predicates that can manipulate the database are presented below [Bratko, 1986].

see(F)

This predicate makes the file in F the current input file and therefore causes input to be switched from the previous input stream to F.

tell(F)

This predicate makes the file in F the current output file and therefore causes output to be directed to file F.

seen

This simply closes the current file specified by the predicate see(F).

told

This clears the buffer of the output file specified by the predicate tell(F) and closes the file.

read(T)

This causes the next term T to be read from the current input stream (file).

write(T)

This outputs term T on the current output file specified by the predicate tell(F).

assert(C)

This causes the clause in C to be added to the database.

asserta(C)

This causes the clause in C to be added at the begining of the database.

assertz(C)

This causes the clause in C to be added at the end of the database.

retract(C)

This deletes a clause that matches the one in C from the database.

We are now in a position to demonstrate how an interactive session with the PROLOG system can be used to insert, retrieve and delete tuples from the database. Let us assume that we have the following program about the weather:

cold :- low—temperature, cold—air.

warm :- high—temperature, warm—air.

terrible :- raining, foggy, windy.

sunshine :- not—cloudy, clear—sky.

mixed :- windy, sunshine, raining.

high—temperature.

warm—air.

The user may now proceed to interrogate the program (database) and insert or delete appropriate data about the weather as follows:

?- cold.
no

?- terrible.
no

?- warm.
yes

?- retract(high—temperature).
yes

?- assert(low—temperature).
yes

?- warm.
no

?- retract(warm—air).
yes

?- assert(sunshine).
yes

?- assert(raining).
yes

?- assert(windy).
yes

?- terrible.
no

?- mixed.
yes

?- retract(sunshine).
yes

?- mixed.
no

?- assert(foggy).
yes

?- cold.
no

?- terrible.
yes

Another typical example of a database is one that describes book suppliers using the record type 'suppliers' and the attributes 'key', 'name', 'class', and 'city'. It can contain, among others, the following PROLOG clauses:

suppliers(10, aristotle, logic, athens).
suppliers(20, socrates, philosophy, athens).
suppliers(30, euclid, geometry, salonica).
suppliers(40, plato, history, crete).

The query: 'Find the names of all suppliers in the city of Athens', can be transformed directly into the clause:

?- suppliers(—, N, —, athens), write(N), fail.

The query: 'Find the name and city of all suppliers who can supply books on philosophy', can be transformed into the clause:

?- suppliers(—, N, philosophy, C),
    write(N), write(C), fail.

The query: 'Find the names of suppliers of books on maths or geometry', can be translated into the PROLOG clause:

?- (suppliers(A, B, maths, D); suppliers(A, B, geometry, D)),
    write(B), fail.

Clearly, knowledge of the syntax of PROLOG is necessary before a user can formulate appropriate queries. Understandably, many potential users of the database may have difficulty with this syntax and it is therefore desirable to have a simple interface to such systems. Research in this area has established that PROLOG goals have a syntax which is very similar to Query By Example (QBE) [Neves et al, 1983]. Therefore QBE is a natural choice as an interface to PROLOG databases.

```
/* Definitions of grammatical forms of sentence */
/* and components thereof */
sentence-->
        sentence(X).

sentence(X)-->
        noun—phrase(X),verb—phrase(X).
sentence(X)-->
        noun—phrase(X),adverb,verb—phrase(X).
sentence(X)-->
        noun—phrase(X),verb—phrase(X),adverb.
sentence(X)-->
        noun—phrase(X),verb—phrase(X),preposition,
        noun—phrase(Y).
sentence(X)-->
        noun—phrase(X),adverb,verb—phrase(X),preposition,
        noun—phrase(Y).
sentence(X)-->
        noun—phrase(X),verb—phrase(X),adverb,preposition,
        noun—phrase(Y).

noun—phrase(X)-->
        determiner(X),noun(X).
noun—phrase(X)-->
        determiner(X),adjective,noun(X).
noun—phrase(X)-->
        proper—noun(X).
noun—phrase(X)-->
        adjective,proper—noun(X).

verb—phrase(X)-->
        verb(X).
verb—phrase(X)-->
        verb(X),noun—phrase(Y).
```

```
/* 'Dictionary' of words */
determiner(—)-->[the].
determiner(singular)-->[a].
determiner(singular)-->[an].
determiner(plural)-->[some].

preposition-->[to].
preposition-->[from].

noun(singular)-->[apple].
noun(plural)-->[apples].
noun(singular)-->[pear].
noun(plural)-->[pears].
noun(singular)-->[man].
noun(plural)-->[men].
noun(singular)-->[goat].
noun(plural)-->[goats].
noun(singular)-->[present].
noun(singular)-->[song].
noun(—)-->[sheep].

proper—noun(singular)-->[smith].

verb(—)-->[bought].
verb(—)-->[sang].
verb(singular)-->[eats].
verb(plural)-->[eat].
verb(singular)-->[sings].
verb(plural)-->[sing].

adverb-->[slowly].
adverb-->[quickly].

adjective-->[red].
adjective-->[green].

/* The logic of parsing */

parse:-
     write('Type in your sentence..'),nl,
     write('In format [the,words]. or []. to exit.'),nl,
     read(S),
     S \== [],
     ( (phrase(sentence,S),nl,nl,
        write('Yes, this is a valid sentence.'),nl,nl)
     ;
        (nl,nl,write('No, this is not a valid sentence.'),nl,nl)),
     parse.

parse:-
     write('End of session').
```

Figure 5.1. A PROLOG program to parse certain forms of an English sentence.

5.3.2 Conclusions and Further Research

The computer phobia that certain people appear to have, clearly hinders the acceptance of information systems generally, and the complexity of using computer-based systems does not help to alleviate their fears. Obviously, systems that enable the interrogation of databases in natural language are much preferred [Harris, 1983] to any other systems or languages, no matter how elegant these may be from the point of view of a computer scientist. For the casual database user or beginner, natural language front-ends open up a new horizon for man-machine communication.

In conclusion, natural language systems have a tremendous potential although more research is necessary to establish these as true alternatives to structured query languages. We identify the following four major areas for further research into natural language systems:

(a) Learning systems: Systems which learn the peculiarities of each application environment, following interactive sessions with the users. In other words, systems which evolve with time.
(b) Intelligent anaphoric systems: Systems which carry out context analyses and proceed to associate past sentences and goals achieved with current user requirements.
(c) Meta-information processors: Systems which differentiate between meta-information (e.g the type of an attribute) and information proper (e.g a value under an attribute). In other words, the front-end should be able to answer queries about the structure and the definitional aspects of the database itself, besides ordinary enquiries on values held under specific attributes.
(d) Networking systems: Systems which accept a user sentence, identify a relevant database from within a network, and proceed to satisfy the user requirements.

5.4 COMMUNICATING WITH DATABASES BY VOICE

Speech synthesis and recognition (otherwise referred to as voice I/O) occupies a privileged place within the realm of man-machine communication - a subject which has received a great deal of attention during the last five years. It was after the public at large started using microcomputers that the subject of 'user-friendly' interfaces for man-machine communication became absolutely vital to the design of any type of computer system. Although speech synthesis (i.e text to speech) has already proved to be a viable alternative to receiving information from the computer [Yannakoudakis & Hutton, 1987], further research is necessary with speech recognition systems and their interface to database systems.

We can confidently say that voice I/O is by far the most desirable means for communicating with databases and information systems in general. Other well established media of communication with the computer are the keyboard, touch-sensitive screen, the mouse, the joystick, image processing devices, etc. Of course voice is the most natural means of communication, but it is, at the same time, the most difficult to computerise effectively [Yannakoudakis & Hutton, 1987].

When the sound spectrograph was invented approximately forty years ago, phoneticians and linguists were confident that the mysteries of voice would be solved and the inherent characteristics of speech would at last be understood. Unfortunately this has not happened for a number of reasons [Yannakoudakis, 1985; De Mori, 1983]: (a) inadequate computer architectures, especially their slow speed, (b) noise and interference which are very difficult to tackle in an online mode, (c) accents of individuals and the characteristics of their vocal tracts, (d) the unpredictable manner in which words and sentences are formed.

Moreover, the sizeable vocabularies necessary to process human speech, make it necessary to look at alternative means of synthesising words from other subword elements, such as 'phonemes'. Phonemes are minimal units of speech which enable meanings to be distinguished (i.e they are minimal distinctive units). They are considered to be the building blocks of speech and can therefore be used to generate all phonetic variations of a language. Linguists recognise that the English language has approximately 40 phonemes out of which 24 are consonant phonemes and 16 are vowel phonemes. For denotational purposes, each phoneme is usually enclosed in slashes and can comprise one or more letters/symbols. Examples of phonemes and corresponding words are: /k/ as in COOL, /b/ as in RIB, /dz/ as in JUST.

Before speech can be processed intelligently, it becomes necessary to encode (digitise) the speech signals. There are two basic approaches to encoding, namely, waveform and source coding [Lee & Lochovsky, 1983; Yannakoudakis & Hutton, 1987]. A waveform coder usually operates at a speed of over 6.0 kilobits per second and can also be used to encode signals other than speech. A source coder ('vocoder') usually operates at speeds less than 6.0 kilobits per second and the techniques employed attempt to approximate the speech signals on the basis of a reference model for speech production. The lower the speed, the more complicated the coder becomes in order to achieve satisfactory speech reproduction. Also, the lower the speed, the less natural the 'voice' then sounds but, of course the costs of system design (e.g fewer logic gates/circuits), transmission and storage drop.

Finally, for a voice I/O system to operate satisfactorily it becomes absolutely vital to consider appropriate stressing and intonation techniques. This is particularly important with voice output systems. In most cases, stress on the correct syllable is achieved by means of rules which may exclude articles, conjunctions, prepositions, etc. Consider for example a rule that states: stress the first syllable of a word unless this is a prefix (contained in a predefined list), in which case the second syllable is stressed. Another example of a rule is one which states: if a word contains two or more consecutive and identical phonemes, then ignore all but one.

5.5 SPEECH SYNTHESIS

Voice output systems become operational via two major steps which are implemented through a set of rules and hence the approach is often referred to as 'synthesis-by-rule':

(A)   The transformation of a sequence of letters/symbols into a set of phonetic components and the extraction of information regarding the lexical and syntactical structure of the input. The end result of this step is the derivation of a set of new symbols or combinations of these which represent units of sound as well as boundaries between units (e.g words or sentences).

(B)   The matching of the phonetic symbols produced under (A) with those already stored in the computer memory and the subsequent linking of these in order to form a correct allophonic sequence. The latter is then coded and transmitted to the voice decoder.

The basic stages whereby text is converted to speech are:

(a)   Accept an incoming sentence or word from the database.
(b)   Normalise the input by dealing with abbreviations, synereses, numbers, foreign words, etc.
(c)   Identify morphemes, i.e distinguishable and meaningful linguistic forms which are different from others with similar sounds. This process is otherwise referred to as 'morpheme stripping' and can be implemented through rules or a dictionary look-up. However, not all speech synthesis systems employ morpheme strippers. A morpheme is not usually divided into other forms. For example, the word TYPICALLY consists of the morphemes TYPICAL and LY.
(d)   Perform letter-to-phoneme transformations using rules.
(e)   Apply stress assignment and intonation rules.
(f)   Perform phoneme-to-allophone transformations using rules.
(g)   Apply interpolation logic on the allophones generated with the aim to 'smooth' speech.
(h)   Generate appropriate speech parameters and pass these over to a speech synthesis device.

A text to speech system must also offer appropriate commands to speak a word, a sentence, or a line at a time. Provision must also be made to control the following:

(a)   Rate of speech, measured in words per minute.
(b)   Type of voice (e.g male, female, light male, light female).
(c)   Pitch level to determine the lightness or darkness of speech.
(d)   Prosody or pitch variation to emphasise more or less certain sections of the sentence.
(e)   Aspiration to control the puff of breath which accompanies the articulation of certain phonemes or allophones.
(f)   Loudness or volume of speech produced.

Although it is generally accepted that the English language has approximately 40 phonemes, a detailed analysis of their contextual variations can generate up to 1000 allophonic sounds. However, in practice approximately 200 allophones are enough to produce intelligible speech [O'Shaughnessy, 1983]. The rules for letter-to-phoneme transformations are of course easier to identify and implement in an ordinary high level programming language.

Let us use the phrase DIGITAL SPEECH to demonstrate the process for converting text to speech. The symbol '+' is used to denote the end of a morpheme, the symbol '#' is used to denote a short pause and the symbol '##' is used to denote an extended pause. Consecutive phonemes that obey the same rule are enclosed between slashes and each phoneme is separated from the next with a single space. The basic steps are:

1. Mark appropriate pauses:
   DIGITAL#SPEECH##
2. Identify morphemes or exception words:
   DIGIT+AL#SPEECH##
3. Apply letter-to-phoneme rules:
   /d/ih/jh/ih/t/+/ax l/#/s/p/iy/ch/##
4. Generate allophones for each phoneme, apply interpolation logic and generate speech parameters.

Although synthesis-by-rule is simple and attractive enough at the implementation stage, the resulting speech, while very intelligible, appears to be rather 'mechanical' and not very friendly because it lacks certain prosodic features (e.g rhythm and intonation). Further research is thus necessary, particularly at the stage where allophones are derived, in order to produce systems with more phonetic detail.

Another important topic worthy of mention is the so called 'speech synthesis from concept' [Young & Fallside, 1979]. That is, the construction of complete and accurate sentences using database attributes and corresponding values. For example, the following display:

Name	Title	Salary	Job name
Ayres F H	Mr	20000	Librarian

can and should also be converted to a meaningful sentence, and then to speech, on request. The above tuple can be converted to the sentence:

Mr Ayres is a Librarian with a salary of 20000 pounds

5.6 SPEECH RECOGNITION

In this section we discuss speech recognition systems (otherwise referred to as voice input systems) and the techniques used to digitise speech signals.

It can be argued that the problem areas we presented under Section 5.4 (i.e slow computers, noise and interference, accents of individuals, and the unpredictable manner in which sentences are formed) are enough to justify the lack of progress with the development of continuous speech recognition systems. It must be pointed out that although there exist a few continuous speech recognition devices, these operate on a rather small vocabulary which makes them unsuitable for general use.

The technology of voice input has concentrated on the design of speaker-dependent and isolated word recognition systems, and has in effect side-stepped the problem of segmenting continuous speech. Recently, we have seen a tremendous acceleration in research on voice systems in general, especially since surveys indicated that the market value of speech recognition systems will grow to over 1 billion dollars by the early 1990s.

Although speech recognition systems vary a great deal, they are all based on the same principles and outline logic. The basic idea is to 'train' the system to recognise a set of words, or units of speech, following repetitive pronunciation of each of these, and then to use the files containing the trained units (otherwise known as 'reference templates') in order to apply matching algorithms.

Speech signals appear to be very complex and unrevealing when they are looked at on the oscilloscope, that is, on a time domain. However, they are more readily understood and identifiable when they are analysed in the frequency domain where the amplitude of a signal is examined as a function of frequency. Spectrographs are ideal for this type of analysis and can reveal the spectral signature of each speech element.

Word recognition systems can adopt a number of strategies to identify and extract spectral information while at the same time minimising the processing time and the storage space necessary for the reference templates. A balance must be found between storage/processing costs and quality of speech. Let us discuss two commonly adopted approaches to determine the speech spectrum.

The simplest and cheapest method of converting a speech signal into a frequency domain is to count the number of times per second a signal changes algebraic sign; this can be achieved by means of a special circuit known as 'zero-crossing detector'. A more sophisticated variation of the zero-crossing detector technique uses filters to decompose the speech spectrum into a number of frequency bands (e.g 200-900 Hz, 800-2500 Hz, and 2000-3200 Hz). Counting the zero-crossings separately under each band can then approximate the corresponding formant frequencies.

An alternative approach is to digitise the signals and then to filter them. Now, digital processing of speech signals can eliminate filtering altogether. For example, a mathematical technique based on the so called Fast Fourier Transform series (FFT) can be used to compute directly the speech spectra, where the input signal is sampled at discrete time intervals and the values are represented digitally. It becomes necessary to have a sampling rate which is at least twice as large as the maximum frequency of the incoming analogue signal, as well as a fast processor which can cope with the volume of the required data.

Clearly, the number of bits per second necessary to represent speech is related to the range of the signals and it also affects the signal-to-noise ratio which is introduced by quantisation. For example, when sampling operates at 10 kHz and the quantisation at 11 bits, then the information rate is 110,000 bits per second. This rate is clearly much higher than the source rate which is approximately 50 bits per second. A voice recognition system must aim to eliminate this redundancy.

So, the basic steps of a speech recognition system are: (a) sampling and quantisation, (b) detection of start and end of incoming units of speech, (c) calculation of speech spectra, directly from digitisation, or indirectly through filters, (d) pitch contour evaluation, (e) segmentation, (f) word detection, either by applying 'bottom-up' techniques to associate phonemic features with the required lexicon, or 'top-down' techniques in order to identify complete units within the template database.

Although speaker-dependent and continuous speech recognition systems seem feasible and can become fully operational in the near future, alternative approaches must be explored with the aim to eliminate the need for extensive training of the system prior to its utilisation. A promising approach here appears to be the automatic speaker adaptation to the stored templates. The technique employs a set of representative sentences (approximately 20) which are spoken by the user in order to establish his/her unique pattern of phonemes. The system employs a set of speaker-independent templates, initially, and then alters these to adapt to specific user-templates.

The majority of current systems use what is called Dynamic Time Warping (DTW), a form of dynamic programming, which compensates for the non-linear time distortion that occurs in speech. DTW uses a matrix of 'distances' between the features of each incoming unit and those already stored on the trained templates of the voice bank, in an attempt to find the best match. DTW techniques are computationally intensive, require substantial storage space for rather small vocabularies, and are effective mainly for isolated word recognition systems.

A better technique is Hidden Markov Modelling (HMM) where several features from different trained variations of the stored templates are used. The technique employs a mathematical model to calculate transitional probabilities, that is, probabilities of going from one trained state to another, and proceeds to find the best overall match. HMM overcomes some of the limitations of DTW and can form the basis for the design of cheap and efficient speech boards.

5.7 AN INTEGRATED VIEW OF MAN-MACHINE INTERFACES

The widespread introduction of microcomputers into the home presages the first genuine revolution in education and training in over a century. With further advances in hardware, including voice chips, fast printers, high density storage devices, image processors, robots, turtles, optical fibre links, etc, there will be a tremendous need to communicate with knowledge bases. There will also be a shift from enterprise-based to home-based employment.

What we are proclaiming here is man-machine communication beyond the keyboard - an interface that has formed one of the great obstacles to the use of the computer, particularly by young children and novices.

In special education, as a general rule, the QWERTY keyboard has been substituted by a variety of concept keyboards. For certain kinds of operations, a Possum device allows letters of subjects - for example, using the Makaton system based on common symbols representing the basic English dictionary - to be utilised effectively by children with physical or mental disabilities. Such a system can be easily adapted for use by young children. For certain kinds of operations, such as controlling a robot or a turtle, again, the existing keyboard is largely inadequate.

The use of touch-sensitive screens provides a substantial opportunity, particularly when coupled to a pointer which reduces both the radiation exposure, and muscle fatigue. Systems already exist which can convert screens into touch-sensitive screens by putting an adaptor over the surface of the cathode ray tube. Such a system would allow the design of interactive environments in which the user could interrogate the database, let us say, the parts of a car engine, simply by pointing to the different parts on the screen. Whatever can be said for a touch-sensitive screen, can also be done with the light pen, or even more conveniently with a mouse. Both a mouse, and graphics tablets used for drawing and designing, allow moving items around.

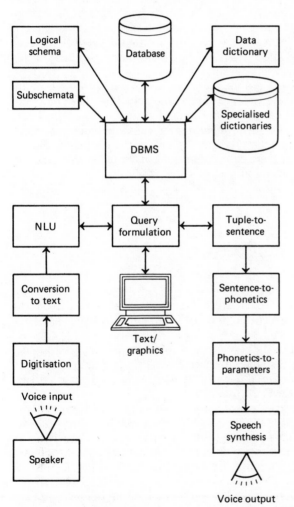

Figure 5.2 An integrated environment for speech synthesis/recognition and natural language communication.

The interfaces a DBMS can support for intelligent man-machine communication are absolutely vital for the user community as a whole. The acceptance or otherwise of the information system by the user community depends on these interfaces to a large extent. However, a detailed presentation of the various modes and devices for man-machine communication is beyond the scope of this book.

Having described the techniques for sentence analysis, and speech synthesis and recognition, we will proceed to integrate these with the DBMS. Our aim here is to place natural language communication with databases in the right perspective and to demonstrate that the three-level architecture, i.e logical schema, internal schema and subschemata, is capable of accommodating the NLU and speech devices.

Figure 5.2 shows an integrated environment including the DBMS, query formulation, logical schema, subschemata, database, data dictionary, NLU, and speech synthesis/recognition. The specialised dictionary may contain application-dependent terms and language constructs which enable the NLU to perform its tasks effectively. (Note the unidirectional flow of information between speech recognition (voice input) and the NLU, and between query formulation and speech synthesis from concept (voice output)).

In conclusion, a database can be populated and interrogated through multi-media interfaces which can evolve independent of the actual database model or DBMS in use. More specifically, application-dependent features of speech and natural language constructs can form separate interface-subschemata which supplement the database subschemata. It is only by making this distinction that we can manage effectively the ever-increasing complexity of a multi-media environment for man-machine communication.

5.8 SUMMARY

Research into man-machine communication has produced systems which allow the user to interrogate the database in natural language and therefore avoid the rigidity and the limitations of structured and 'artificial' languages such as DDL, DML and query.

The Natural Language Unit (NLU) is a piece of software that analyses a query or sentence written in natural language (e.g English, French) and proceeds to either transform this into a structured query statement, say, in RDL, or satisfies the query directly through its own built-in functions.

An interesting non-procedural language, particularly suited to natural sentence analyses, is PROLOG (PROgramming in LOGic) where the user interacts with the database by providing logical formulae (otherwise referred to as 'goals'). The PROLOG system then searches for proofs of the formulae. The user populates the database with a number of theorems (otherwise referred to as 'clauses') which are then used to prove the goals entered.

The architecture of an NLU, regardless of whether it is a stand-alone system or a plug-compatible piece of software that utilises DBMS facilities, comprises four basic modules:

(a) The parser that analyses the incoming sentence.
(b) The query generator that converts the output from the parser into query language functions.
(c) The access software that isolates relevant values from the database.
(d) The processing software that manipulates relevant values and performs the required tasks.

An alternative approach to communicating with the database is natural voice. Here, the *speech synthesis* module converts text to speech using database values (text and numeric data) by following a set of rules that decompose data into phonemes which are then fed into a speech synthesiser. The *speech recognition* module accepts incoming speech signals and compares these with those stored on a voice bank (i.e the bank of templates). When a match is found within a template of the voice bank, the corresponding command (usually held in textual form) is executed and the query is satisfied.

There are two approaches to speech recognition:

(a) Speaker-dependent recognition systems, where the speaker trains the system to recognise his/her own voice patterns.
(b) Speaker-independent recognition systems, where minimum training of the system is required before it can be used.

In the latter case, however, the size of the dictionary (i.e the number of recognised utterances) is very limited and further research is necessary in this area.

5.9 REFERENCES

Bancilhon, F. & Ramakrishnan, R., 'An Amateur's Introduction to Recursive Query Processing Strategies', ACM SIGMOD, Conference on Management of Data, Vol. 15, No. 2, pp. 16-52, 1986.

Bocca, J., 'On the Evaluation Strategy of EDUCE', ACM SIGMOD, Conference on Management of Data, Vol. 15. No. 2, pp. 368-378, 1986.

Bolc, L. (Editor), 'Natural Language Based Computer Systems', Hanser Verlag, 1980.

Bratko, I., 'PROLOG Programming for Artificial Intelligence', Addison-Wesley, 1986.

Carlson, C. R. & Kaplan, R. S., 'A Generalized Access Path Model and its Application to a Relational Database System', ACM SIGMOD, International Symposium on Management of Data, pp. 143-156, 1976.

Clocksin, W. F. & Mellish, C. S., 'Programming in PROLOG', Springer-Verlag, 1981.

De Mori, R., 'Computer Models of Speech Using Fuzzy Algorithms', Plenum Press, 1983.

Fagin, R., Mendelzon, A. O. & Ullman, J. D., 'A Simplified Universal Relation Assumption and its Properties', ACM TODS, Vol. 7, No. 3, pp. 343-360, 1982.

Freytag, J. C. & Goodman, N., 'Rule-Based Translation of Relational Queries into Iterative Programs', ACM SIGMOD, Conference on Management of Data, Vol. 15, No. 2, pp. 206-214, 1986.

Grosz, B. J., 'TEAM: A Transportable Natural Language Interface System', Proc. Conf. on Applied Natural Language Processing, Santa Monica, 1-3 February, 1983.

Harris, L. R., 'The Advantages of Natural Language Programming', In: Designing for Human-Computer Communication, Sime M. E. & Coombs M. J., Academic Press, pp. 73-86, 1983.

Korth, H., 'System/U: a Database System Based on the Universal Relation Assumption', ACM TODS, Vol. 9, No. 3, pp. 331-347, 1984.

Lee, D. L. & Lochovsky, F. H., 'Voice Response Systems', Computing Surveys, Vol. 15, No. 4, pp. 351-374, 1983.

Luk, W. S. & Kloster, S., 'ELFS: English Language From SQL', ACM TODS, Vol. 11, No. 4, pp. 447-472, 1986.

Marque-Pucheu, G., Martin-Gallausiaux, J. & Jomier, G., 'Interfacing PROLOG and Relational Database Management Systems', In: New Applications of Databases, Gardarin & Gelenbe (editors), Academic Press, London, 1984.

Mellish, C. S., 'Computer Interpretation of Natural Language Descriptions', Ellis Horwood, 1985.

Nilsson, N. J., 'Principles of Artificial Intelligence', Springer-Verlag, 1981.

Neves, J. C., Anderson, S. O. & Williams, M. H., 'A PROLOG Implementation of Query-By-Example', Proc. 7th International Computing Symposium, Nurnberg, pp. 318-332, 1983.

O'Shaughnessy, D., 'Automatic Speech Synthesis', IEEE Commun., Vol. 21, No. 9, pp. 26-34, 1983.

Sime, M. E. & Coombs M. J., 'Designing for Human-Computer Communication', Academic Press, 1983.

Sparck-Jones, K. & Wilks, Y., 'Automatic Natural Language Parsing', Ellis Horwood, 1985.

Ullman, J. D., 'The U. R. Strikes Back', Proc. ACM Symposium on the Principles of Database Systems, pp. 10-22, 1982.

Welty, C. & Stemple, D., 'Human Factors Comparison of a Procedural and a Non-procedural Query Language', ACM TODS, Vol. 6, No. 4, pp. 626-649, 1981.

Wallace M., 'Communicating with Databases in Natural Language', Ellis Horwood, 1984.

Yannakoudakis, E. J., 'Expert Spelling Error Analysis and Correction', Proc. 7th ASLIB Conference on Informatics, University of Cambridge, pp. 39-52, March 1983.

Yannakoudakis, E. J., 'Voice I/O: Problems and Perspectives', Computer Bulletin, Series III, Vol. 1, No. 3, pp. 10-12, 1985.

Yannakoudakis, E. J. & Fawthrop, D., 'An Intelligent Spelling Error Corrector', J. of Information Processing & Management, Vol. 19, No. 2, pp. 101-108, 1983a.

Yannakoudakis, E. J. & Fawthrop, D., 'The Rules of Spelling Errors', J. of Information Processing & Management, Vol. 19, No. 2, pp. 87-100, 1983b.

Yannakoudakis, E. J. & Hutton, P. J., 'Speech Synthesis and Recognition Systems', Ellis Horwood, 1987.

Young, S. J. & Fallside, F., 'Speech Synthesis from Concept: A Method for Speech Output from Information systems', J. Acoust. Soc. Amer., Vol. 66, No. 3, pp. 685-695, 1979.

6 DATABASE DESIGN METHODOLOGY

6.1 INTRODUCTION

Although systems analysis has provided a number of valid practical techniques for the determination of user functional requirements, it has failed, so far, to develop a complete and coherent methodology to integrate these techniques into an overall and objective cycle. Data analysis, on the other hand, has established a number of fundamental rules whereby attributes can be defined and interrelated to form viable entities [Housel et al, 1979; Yao et al, 1982]. Attribute and entity relationships can then be investigated further [Chen, 1976] to identify the inherent data structure (or model) of the enterprise.

At appropriate stages of database design, the DBA adopts certain axioms in order to analyse the inherent relationships among attributes. There are two important objectives here:

(a)   To ensure that the database can be manipulated without giving rise to any anomalies - this is the main aim of 'normalisation' [Codd, 1970, 1972].
(b)   To ensure that the logical schema is optimised and can evolve to meet new demands without major restructuring - this is the main aim of 'canonical synthesis'.

In the present chapter, we discuss database design from the global point of view, in terms of major stages and fundamental rules that can produce a normalised logical schema. The validation and integration of user views, that is, canonical synthesis, is discussed in Chapter 7. The overall methodology here is related to the three-level architecture we have adopted, that is, logical, external and internal.

6.2 TOP-DOWN AND BOTTOM-UP DESIGN

There are basically two approaches to database design: (a) top-down (i.e from conceptual entity to attribute), and (b) bottom-up (i.e from attribute to logical entity). The ultimate objective of each is to aid the design of the logical schema which reflects the organisation accurately [Olle & Sol, 1982]. After the logical structure has been designed, the DBA can consider storage and access criteria to cluster the entities, in order to produce an optimised internal schema.

Top-down

The top-down approach starts with the analysis of the organisation at the functional level, that is, the identification of all functions and processes to be supported by each application, and then assesses the entities required [Albano & de Antonellis, 1985; Atzeni & Batini, 1983] to perform specific objectives (see Figure 6.1). Functions reflect the activities of the enterprise and entities represent groups of attributes upon which the functions operate.

Relationships between entities are then analysed to represent 'real-world' associations, at both intra- and inter-application level. Example relationships are: Two or more pay rates per employee, two or more employees per department,

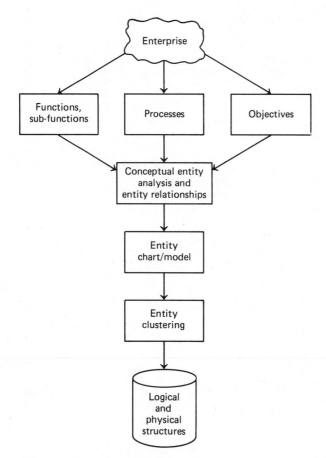

Figure 6.1 Top-down design.

one manager per department, etc. The assumption made here is that these associations can be expressed in a high level model of data.

The top-down approach has several weaknesses, one of which is that it does not go into sufficient detail at the intra-entity level, often missing, for example, some of the more complex composite keys. Another problem is the repeated breakdown of enterprise functions into smaller and smaller sub-functions. This makes it very difficult to maintain user interest in the design process. Although the users are not actually members of the design team, they are, nevertheless, expected to supply the necessary details that will help the designers clarify and refine the conceptual model of each application.

Emphasis is then placed on what the user or DBA has to say about individual applications, particularly regarding the identification of synonyms and homonyms. It is envisaged that an automated database design tool offers an interactive dialogue that aids the designer and guides him towards the solution.

The overall top-down design proceeds in an incremental manner, by incorporating new entities, establishing new relationships, and finally, resolving any conflicts which arise as a result of this gradual integration.

The result is a model of entities which is used as the blue-print for the design of the logical schema [Borgida et al, 1982]. Finally, storage and access requirements are considered and the entities are clustered to form viable physical units (e.g database files) which are defined by the internal schema.

Bottom-up

The bottom-up approach starts from individual attributes or data items and attempts to synthesise these, in order to form viable logical entities (see Figure 6.2). Following their definition and association with specific applications and corresponding views, different types of dependencies among attributes are investigated and dealt with accordingly [Housel et al, 1979; Yao et al, 1982]. Examples of dependencies are: (a) full functional, (b) simple functional, (c) transitive, and (d) multivalued. These are discussed later, not as part of a technique for bottom-up design, but rather, as dependence relationships for the creation of viable groups of attributes (i.e relations) which are free from anomalies arising as a result of manipulative operations.

Relationships are particularly significant as they are potential access paths [Carlson & Kaplan, 1976]. The chosen set of access paths will affect the efficiency of the database, as well as its ability to cope with future requirements, without major restructuring, to a considerable extent.

Clearly, the bottom-up approach aims to synthesise logical entities from attributes, although in practice it becomes very difficult to identify all possible attributes in all views. However, assuming that it is possible to gather all relevant information, this approach can actually produce the optimal logical structure.

6.3 MAJOR STAGES IN DATABASE DESIGN

The DBMS aims to define structures and to process data in a standardised manner, so that, communication between users and applications, programs and storage devices, is achieved through application-independent software modules or sublanguages. Clearly, a DBMS becomes a very complex piece of software with many utilities, tools and interfaces, the totality of which creates an information system offering a wide variety of facilities related to the usage of a computer.

Having accepted the three realms (i.e logical, external and internal) as the best possible way to study database design, we can proceed to look at the major steps necessary to set up and use a database.

Figure 2.2 shows an example of three applications, namely, APL1, APL2 and APL3, implemented with the aid of a DBMS. Each application has associated with it a program which communicates with a subschema. Each subschema is based on the logical schema of the organisation which, in turn, is mapped onto an internal schema.

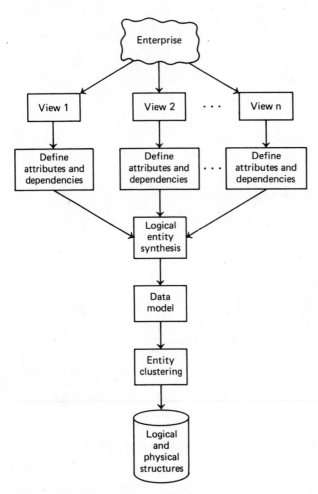

Figure 6.2 Bottom-up design.

In further functional analysis of the organisation, resultant schemata and subschemata, the major steps for database design, in no particular order, are:

1. Study the enterprise globally, identify all possible entities and relationships, and define the conceptual schema.
2. Study the conceptual schema and the DBMS available and derive the logical schema.
3. Determine storage, physical, usage and general retrieval requirements, and establish the internal schema.
4. Identify and analyse each application and pertinent requirements. Derive thereupon appropriate subschemata from the logical schema.
5. Develop the application programs using appropriate subschemata and data manipulation facilities.

It is important to emphasise here that, where appropriate, the above tasks can take place concurrently or incrementally. For example, if it becomes necessary to design, implement and use application software before the internal schema can actually be developed effectively, then these two steps can be carried out incrementally. Collection of vital usage statistics by the application software, or the data dictionary, as we shall see later, can then form the basis to tune and develop the internal schema further. We assume that a 'draft version' of the internal schema will be able to offer the necessary storage structures for the implementation of the necessary applications.

Figure 6.3 presents the flow of design information, starting with the conceptual analysis which must adopt the principles of 'conceptualisation' and 'self-sufficiency' as presented in Section 1.4. The design of appropriate subschemata refers to the logical schema, over and over again, but not to the information contained within the conceptual schema. Finally, the storage schema can be tuned and developed further on the basis of knowledge acquired from the usage of subschemata and applications in general.

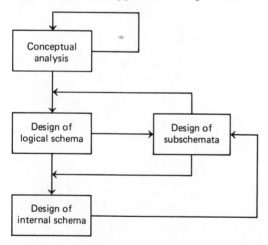

Figure 6.3 Major stages of information flow in database design.

6.4 SIX MAPPINGS

We are now in a position to describe the major stages in database design in terms of mappings which take place during the analysis, development, and implementation cycles. Figure 6.4 presents all six mappings involved, where the DBMS forms the sole tool for the creation and compilation of the logical and internal schemata.

Research into database management systems has yet to establish an integrated environment for the analysis of the enterprise, the creation of the conceptual schema, and its subsequent mapping to logical and internal schemata. However, data analysis tools and software to test the stability of database schemata, are available.

Evidently, different tools, techniques and therefore human skills for the setting up and manipulation of database structures under each of the six mappings, form a rather complex work environment. It becomes, therefore, necessary to consider various levels of database administration, such as Functional DBA, Consultant DBA, Applications DBA, Hardware DBA, and others. The tasks and responsibilities of each become obvious on the basis of the six mappings of Figure 6.4.

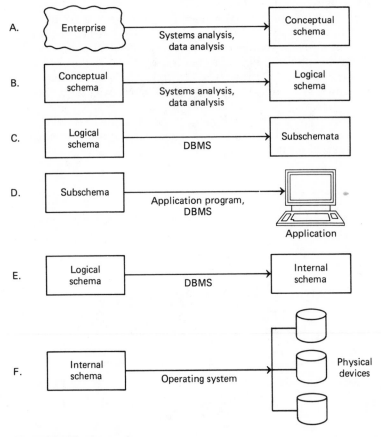

Figure 6.4 The six mappings.

Each mapping is now described briefly, not in any particular order, and as is the case with the five major steps in database design, certain mappings can take place concurrently or incrementally.

A. Enterprise-Conceptual schema

Mapping (A) involves the enterprise and its possible translation into a conceptual model, reflecting the inherent structures, entities, attributes, relationships, as well as processes required.

Traditional systems analysis techniques and data analysis exercises can help the database designer identify the inherent structure of the enterprise.

This mapping takes place without any reference to available DBMS software or indeed the computer technology in general. The ultimate objective is to identify and establish all the necessary information for mapping (B) to take over and build the logical schema.

B. Conceptual schema-Logical schema

Mapping (B) involves the conceptual schema and its translation to a logical schema. Strictly speaking, and provided the conceptual schema is complete and accurate, this mapping should be based on the conceptual schema alone and only on the information it provides. Exceptionally, the database designer may revert to a conceptual analysis step.

The logical schema is designed with a DBMS in mind and therefore represents computer structures, record types, data items, security considerations, etc, aiming to satisfy the demands of all applications.

C. Logical schema-Subschemata

Mapping (C) involves the logical schema and the derivation of subschemata thereupon. Because each application is unique, utilising only those sections of the logical schema necessary to satisfy its requirements, it makes sense to group these, application by application, in order to form what is otherwise referred to as the 'subschema' or 'view' of each application.

Moreover, subschemata offer a means of defining and isolating the operational realm of the user and therefore making it more difficult for the 'intruder' to access portions of the database which are of no concern to his application. Security is thus a major point in defence of the subschema.

Because only a subset of the logical schema is invoked and connected with an application at any point of time, data is actually input, output and manipulated much faster. Where more than one user accesses the same subschema at any point of time, it becomes possible to share the same data buffers and therefore avoid duplication, while resolving any deadlocks that may arise.

Evidently, there are applications and therefore subschemata which overlap, but this need not worry the database designer because the subschema can be considered as a 'virtual' subset of the logical schema.

D. Subschema-Application

Once the subschema of an application is defined, data can be stored, retrieved or manipulated accordingly. These tasks can materialise under two modes, depending on the requirements of the application or indeed the programmer:

(a) Query mode: Here the user activates a subschema and issues a series of commands which are part of the query language, Query By Example (QBE), or other stand-alone software interface.
(b) Mixed mode: Here the programmer prepares and compiles a program written in some host language, such as Pascal or FORTRAN, and invokes the subschema from his code. The program is then offered for general use.

E. Logical schema-Internal schema(ta)

This mapping aims to describe how data is actually stored on the physical devices, and basically attempts to translate the logical schema into its internal equivalent.

The transformations from logical to physical are not always one-to-one and major differences arise. For example, the physical order of data items can be different from the logical, a logical record can be split into two or more different physical records, common data items between different logical records may not necessarily be duplicated.

An appropriate DBMS language, such as the Data Storage Description Language (DSDL), can be used to create the internal schema, comprising definitions of stored record types, block lengths and distributions, security control, compression details, hashing of keys or other addressing schemes, such as, indexes, pointers, chains, etc.

F. Internal schema(ta)-Physical devices

Evidently, it is the operating system of the computer which performs the necessary formatting of the files on the physical devices so that they can expand or contract as required. Mapping (F) thus implies communication of database meta-information to the operating system.

This mapping is not very well defined and is indeed very controversial. The main point for discussion is how much storage detail should be included in the internal schema and what should be left to the operating system around which the DBMS is built. As we have already pointed out in Sections 2.1.1 and 2.2, the operating system and the DBMS should be considered as two interacting components of the overall information system, and not as a DBMS under the control of the operating system or vice versa. In any case, we can assume that DBMS functions and operating system functions are not distinguishable, as far as this mapping is concerned.

6.5 DECOMPOSITION AND NORMALISATION

Data analysis forms an essential part of database design [Howe, 1985]. The aim is to identify and define individual attributes and relationships among these, through a disciplined and methodical manner. Before the organisational structure (i.e the logical schema) is implemented on a specific DBMS, it becomes necessary to break down the universe of attributes into manageable units, the so called 'record types'. This process is called 'decomposition'. The process whereby each of these groups (i.e record types) is assessed in terms of stability, viability and freedom from insert, update and delete anomalies, is called 'normalisation' [Codd, 1970; Kent, 1983]. Decomposition is also used frequently as part of the normalisation process where a record type may be split into two or more record types. Another term frequently used while splitting relations is 'projection', that is, the isolation of one or more columns from a table.

Although the techniques of normalisation were developed with the relational model in mind, there is no reason whatsoever why these cannot be equally applied to non-relational database systems. We strongly recommend that normalisation be applied to all data, regardless of whether these are part of file-based systems, or database systems.

Before we look at the process of normalisation we will discuss the problems that may arise as a result of manipulating relations that are not normalised. In these cases, manipulation of relations may give rise to long and time consuming searches of the tables. There is also a possibility of deleting a tuple containing valuable information which may have to be re-input at a later stage. For example, take the case where publisher information is stored as part of book information. If a book is deleted (e.g when it is withdrawn from circulation) and if this is the only book which contains information on a specific publisher, then the details are lost.

Updating of tuples can also give rise to inconsistent states of the database. For example, if the address of each library user is stored with every book he borrows, and if there is a change of address, then all the corresponding borrower tuples must be updated accordingly, giving rise to duplicate effort, not to mention duplication of stored values. If the changes do not take place on the relevant borrower tuples, then the database will contain inconsistent information on the same reader(s).

Consider the case of an entity 'book' and the corresponding attributes:

Author-details, Title, Date, Edition, Publisher-details

Decomposition of this group may result in the following three groups:

Author-details
Book-details (Title, Date, Edition)
Publisher-details

If each of these is turned into a distinct and named group, then entity 'book' will be, in effect, represented by three different record types. Normalisation can now take over to determine whether each of these groups can stand alone, that is, whether each of these can be used to build a relational table. It becomes therefore necessary to consider the primary key of each, and how this can be used to bind the corresponding attributes together, by applying the rules of the relational model (see Section 3.5). As we shall see later, normalisation investigates the relationships in each group in more detail.

In the majority of applications today, systems analysts tend to look at the organisational needs in terms of a set of records, each of which refers to a conceptual information carrying entity. They subsequently proceed by attempting to find appropriate fields to describe each record. The weakness of this approach is that the 'record' then forms the basis of any subsequent processing cycle, and this in a way restricts the processing characteristics and capabilities of the fields themselves. It becomes, for example, more difficult to isolate fields for use as search identifiers, as and when required by each application.

An alternative approach starts with the examination of the fields themselves and attempts to identify natural groups, in terms of logical relationships within and between groups [Kouvatsos & Yannakoudakis, 1982]. The criteria whereby relationship types can be assessed fall under two distinct categories: (a) operational, and (b) definitional.

Operational criteria

By considering possible operations upon attributes, we can proceed to analyse these in conjunction with the corresponding relations. Examples of typical operations which must be analysed under the light of normalisation are: search, insert, delete, and modify tuples, or values generally.

In other words, we must consider the effect manipulative operations have upon the corresponding tuples and whether they still leave the database in a consistent state. For example, we must attempt to foresee and avoid a situation where a value under attribute 'Supplier status' is inserted under table 'Supplier-data' and where another table, say, 'Supplier-location' does not already hold the necessary details (e.g Name, Address, Telephone).

Identification criteria

The aim here is to investigate the identifying properties of individual attributes, and how these can be used to locate (isolate) the required tuples. These properties are heavily dependent on subjective information, which in most cases is quantitative in nature (e.g the length of each field, the type of each, etc). For example, if we decide that attribute 'Pay-code' is a primary key of three numeric bytes in length, then we can only hold and identify uniquely up to 999 customers (excluding pay-code zero).

Identification criteria are absolutely vital during the design of the schema, which will ultimately determine the viability of operations upon the database as a whole. It is therefore necessary to carry out a data analysis exercise, with the aim to assess the identifying properties of each and every attribute within the organisation. A good starting point, therefore, will be to establish what attributes can be used to identify tuples uniquely and what attributes or groups of these yield duplicates.

6.6 RELATIONSHIPS BETWEEN ATTRIBUTES

Normalisation deals, primarily, with three important types of relationships between pairs of attributes: functional dependence [Codd, 1970], transitive dependence [Codd, 1970], and multivalued dependence [Fagin, 1977; Delobel, 1978; Zaniolo & Melkanoff, 1981]. Each of these is discussed separately below.

Functional dependence

The concept refers to a relationship between two attributes, say, ATR1 and ATR2, on the basis of their associated values where, at any point of time, there exists only one logical value under ATR2 with a given value under ATR1. We say, ATR2 is functionally dependent on ATR1 using the notation:

ATR1----->ATR2

or ATR2 is not functionally dependent on ATR1 using the notation:

ATR1--/-->ATR2

In other words, for every value under ATR1 there is one and only one value, or factual information, under ATR2. Thus, a value under ATR1 must always occur with the same value under ATR2.

ATR1 can be a composite attribute in which case we talk of 'full functional dependence' using the notation:

ATR1co=====>ATR2

If ATR2 is not fully functionally dependent on ATR1co then the following notation is used:

ATR1co==/==>ATR2

It is of course possible for ATR1co to give 'partial dependence' on ATR2 when only a subset of ATR1co establishes functional dependence with ATR2.

Transitive dependence

This refers to a relationship among attributes in a relation where an attribute is functionally dependent on another through a third. This is particularly obvious when a non-key attribute is a fact (i.e provides functional dependence) about another non-key attribute. Let A, B and C be three different attributes. Transitive dependence is denoted as follows:

A----->B----->C

For example, consider the relation STYLE and associated table where 'S-number' is the primary key, 'Category' refers to a type of dress, and 'Location' holds the geographic area:

STYLE

S-number	Category	Location
s101	formal	Bradford
s102	casual	Leeds
s103	casual	Leeds
s104	formal	Bradford

Here, S-number----->Location and Location----->Category. Therefore, Category is transitively dependent on S-number through Location.

Multivalued dependence

This is a relationship among attributes in a relation where an attribute value has associated with it multiple values under another. In other words, an attribute multidetermines another. Let attribute A multidetermine attribute B. The notation we use is:

A---->>B

Multivalued dependence is particularly obvious with composite keys. Consider, for example, the relation KNOWLEDGE with the composite key 'Employee-code, Expertise, Language', where any given employee may have any number of corresponding types of expertise and be versed in any number of corresponding languages. Assume also that expertise and language are quite independent of each other, that is, no matter which employee is involved with a given job (expertise) the same language is used. Finally, a given type of expertise or language can be associated with any number of employees. Let the database table be as follows:

KNOWLEDGE

Employee-code	Expertise	Language
100	programmer	Greek
100	programmer	English
100	analyst	Greek
100	analyst	English
200	programmer	Greek
200	programmer	German
200	programmer	Italian

There are two multivalued dependencies in relation KNOWLEDGE:

Employee-code ---->> Expertise
Employee-code ---->> Language

that is, Expertise is a multivalued fact about Employee-code, and Language is a multivalued fact about Employee-code. It is clear that relation KNOWLEDGE contains a good deal of redundancy which in effect leads to certain update anomalies. As we will see later, for a relation to be in what is called 'fourth normal form' it must not involve any multivalued dependencies.

6.7 KEY ATTRIBUTES

These are attributes which are used during the processing of relations in order to identify unique as well as duplicate values within tables. One of the major tasks of the DBA is to identify key attributes and the type of dependency they provide within relations. As we saw in the previous section, the dependency can be full, transitive, or multivalued. The definition of each type of key attribute is presented below.

Key attribute

An attribute which is used to identify a record or clusters of records within a table or file. Its value is a symbolic rather than a physical address, and remains constant and independent of physical storage or reorganisational functions.

Depending on the actual physical database implementation, particularly the way inter-relation links are maintained, a key attribute can be physically present in one relation, but virtual in another. This may in fact be necessary if we wish to reduce key redundancy which is usually introduced when relations are linked together by means of common keys.

The value of a key can be a natural occurrence, such as 'computing', or it can be artificial, such as 'c101'. In the latter case, a coding system can be utilised to define each key domain as required.

Databases use a number of different types of keys, such as primary, secondary, single and composite. Throughout the following sections, we denote a key attribute with the symbol '#', as for example, Pay-code#.

Candidate key

A candidate key is an attribute or group of attributes which can be used to identify all tuples of a table uniquely. In this sense, it can be used to establish functional dependence relationships with other attributes. When the candidate key is a group of attributes, then it will have the property whereby the exclusion of one or more attributes from the group make it incapable of identifying each tuple uniquely. In other words, a candidate key does not contain any redundant attributes and, therefore, it forms a viable element that is a potential primary key.

Primary key

Each relation has one primary key capable of identifying uniquely all tuples within a table. It can be single or composite (i.e two or more attributes considered as one). The primary key is chosen rather subjectively one can say, from all candidate keys, and must be specified explicitly when the corresponding relation is defined.

Secondary key

This is a key attribute or group of key attributes the values of which can be repeated within two or more tuples. A secondary key is frequently used as an index to access other tuples from other relations.

Foreign key

Let the relations R1 and R2 be defined as follows:

R1(P1, S1)
R2(S1, S2)

where R1 uses P1 as the primary key and S1 as a secondary key, and R2 uses S1 as the primary key and S2 as a secondary key. Clearly, the values under attribute S1 in R1 can be duplicate, whereas the values under S1 in R2 must be unique. We say that S1 is the foreign key, as far as relation R1 is concerned. Perhaps an example will help clarify the concept better. If a relation comprises the attributes: Paycode, Name, Address, Telephone, Department-code, then clearly, values under attribute Department-code may be duplicate, assuming that a department has more than one employee. Here, the attribute Department-code is a foreign key because under another relation comprising the attributes: Department-code, Manager and Telephone, the attribute Department-code is the primary key.

Determinant

This is an attribute or group of attributes upon which some other attribute is fully functionally dependent.

Prime attribute

This is an attribute which participates in at least one candidate key.

Non-prime attribute

This is an attribute which does not participate in any candidate key.

6.8 THE FIVE NORMAL FORMS

Theoretical work on normalisation has established five normal forms, that is, states which can characterise a relation. So, we say that a relation is in first normal form (1NF), second normal form (2NF), etc. If a relation is in 5NF, then it is also in 4NF, 3NF, 2NF and 1NF. If a relation is in 4NF, then it is also in 3NF, 2NF and 1NF. If a relation is in 3NF, then it is also in 2NF and 1NF. Finally, if a relation is in 2NF, then it is also in 1NF.

The analyst carrying out the normalisation of attribute groups, must take extra care during the transition of a 1NF to a 5NF so that, where necessary, a low order relation can be reconstructed from one or more higher order relations. It is of course possible to end up with a relation which is impossible to decompose further either because the resulting groups of attributes cannot form viable relations, or because further decompositions will give rise to meaningless relations. We can now introduce the concept of *elementary relation* as follows:

> A relation which cannot be reduced (split) any further, without losing semantic information, is called an elementary relation (ER). An ER can of course be used in conjunction with others to produce a lower normal form relation.

6.8.1 First Normal Form (1NF)

A relation is in 1NF when it contains one or more attributes, each based on a single predefined domain, the values of which are atomic, and where repeating groups are not present. Also, a 1NF relation incorporates a primary key which can be single or composite, as long as it can identify each tuple uniquely [Codd, 1970].

It is interesting to note that what is an atomic value for one application, may not necessarily be so for another. A value is referred to as *atomic*, if the application does not deal with (process) parts of it. For example, the value 11/11/1983, corresponding to a birthdate, may not be atomic if the application is only interested in the 'Year' part.

The procedure for establishing a 1NF relation is primarily intuitive. Generally speaking, a 1NF relation cannot contain any attribute the values of which are based on more than one domain, but it is of course possible to have two or more attributes deriving their values from the same domain.

Example 1

Let a relation R1 with primary key AUTHOR-CODE# consist of the attributes:

R1(AUTHOR-CODE#, AUTHOR-NAME, TITLE, DATE, EDITION, PUBLISHER-NAME)

R1 does not have any repeating groups, and provided attribute AUTHOR-CODE# can identify each tuple uniquely, then R1 is in 1NF. Both attributes AUTHOR-NAME and PUBLISHER-NAME may derive their values from the same domain, say, NAMES of 30 bytes long. However, if AUTHOR-NAME is thought of as a composite attribute, comprising the surname and one or more first names, then R1 would not be in 1NF since AUTHOR-NAME would be a repeating group, having the following general form:

SURNAME FIRST-NAME-1,
        [,FIRST-NAME-2]...

Example 2

Let another relation R2 with primary key PERSONAL-CODE# consist of the attributes:

R2(PERSONAL-CODE#, NAME, ADDRESS, TELEPHONE, SALARY-
                    HISTORY:
                    DATE, SALARY,
                    JOB-TITLE)

Relation R2 clearly contains the repeating group: SALARY-HISTORY (DATE, SALARY, JOB-TITLE) through which all changes to the salary of an employee are recorded by date, salary and job title. To eliminate the repeating group from R2, we proceed to split the relation into:

R21(PERSONAL-CODE#, NAME, ADDRESS, TELEPHONE)
R22(PERSONAL-CODE#, DATE#, SALARY, JOB-TITLE)

where PERSONAL-CODE# becomes the primary key of R21, and relation R22 receives the composite primary key 'PERSONAL-CODE#, DATE#' which is capable of identifying each tuple in R22 uniquely. Both R21 and R22 are now in 1NF.

6.8.2 Second Normal Form (2NF)

A relation is in 2NF if it is in 1NF and every non-prime attribute is fully functionally dependent on each candidate key.

Example 1

Let us examine the following 1NF relation of publisher names and classified subjects under which they publish (as before, the symbol '#' indicates a key):

R1(PUB#, PUB-NAME, CLA#, CLA-NAME)

where PUB# and CLA# are the prime attributes and PUB-NAME and CLA-NAME are non-prime attributes. Notational representation of functional dependencies gives:

PUB# -----> PUB-NAME
CLA# --/--> PUB-NAME
PUB#, CLA# -----> PUB-NAME

PUB-NAME would be fully functionally dependent on 'PUB#, CLA#' if it were not for the fact that,

PUB# -----> PUB-NAME

Therefore,

PUB#, CLA# ==/==> PUB-NAME

Similarly,

PUB# --/--> CLA-NAME
CLA# -----> CLA-NAME
PUB#, CLA# -----> CLA-NAME

Therefore,

PUB#, CLA# ==/==> CLA-NAME because CLA# -----> CLA-NAME

Hence, R1 is not in 2NF because neither PUB-NAME nor CLA-NAME are fully functionally dependent on the key 'PUB#, CLA#'. If R1 is now split into the following three relations:

R2(PUB#, PUB-NAME)
R3(CLA#, CLA-NAME)
R4(PUB#, CLA#)

then, each will be in 2NF. R4 establishes a link between relations R2 and R3 by means of their primary keys. This is necessary because of the many-to-many relationship which is in effect implied by the environment; a publisher publishes under more than one class, and under a class there may be many different publishers. So, the three resultant relations are equivalent to the original R1 relation.

Example 2

Let us extend the original relation R1 by introducing the attributes publisher ADDRESS and VOLUME (the current total output of a publisher under each class), as follows:

R1(PUB#, PUB-NAME, ADDRESS, CLA#, CLA-NAME, VOLUME)

Following an analysis of the conceptual world, the analyst establishes that given the candidate key 'PUB#, CLA#', the following dependencies hold true:

PUB# -----> PUB-NAME
PUB# -----> ADDRESS
CLA# -----> CLA-NAME
PUB#,CLA# ==/==> PUB-NAME (because PUB# -----> PUB-NAME)
PUB#,CLA# ==/==> ADDRESS (because PUB# -----> ADDRESS)
PUB#,CLA# =====> VOLUME

Because not all the attributes are fully functionally dependent on the key 'PUB#, CLA#', relation R1 is not in second normal form. What we have to do now is separate all attributes which do not satisfy full functional dependence, namely, PUB-NAME and ADDRESS from the rest. The result is three relations, all in second normal form, as follows:

R2(PUB#, PUB-NAME, ADDRESS)
R3(PUB#, CLA#, VOLUME)
R4(CLA#, CLA-NAME)

6.8.3 Third Normal Form (3NF)

A relation is in 3NF if it is in 2NF and every non-prime attribute is non-transitively dependent on each candidate key. In other words, a relation is in 3NF if it is in 2NF and every non-prime attribute is fully functionally dependent on the primary key and at the same time not functionally dependent on any other non-prime attribute.

However, there are cases where two or more candidate keys have common or overlapping attributes, therefore giving rise to certain anomalies with manipulative operations, such as update and insert tuples. A 'strong 3NF' relation (otherwise referred to as a Boyce-Codd Normal Form (BCNF) after the names of the authors who identified this problem [Codd, 1972]), deals with overlapping attributes between candidate keys by introducing an extra rule stating that: A relation is in BCNF if it is in 3NF and every determinant is a candidate key.

Example 1

Let an organisation sub-contract work to computer programmers who undertake specific projects, each with a unique number. The following relation is enough to keep track of who is involved in what project and the expected time of completion:

R1(PROGRAMMER-CODE#, ADDRESS, TELEPHONE, PROJECT-CODE#, PROJECT-DESCRIPTION, START-DATE, FINISH-DATE)

Relation R1 is in 1NF because PROGRAMMER-CODE# can identify each tuple uniquely. The relation is also in 2NF because the primary key is not composite. However, the relation is not in 3NF because non-key attributes (START-DATE and FINISH-DATE) are functionally dependent on a non-key attribute (PROJECT-CODE#). Notationally,

PROJECT-CODE# -----> START-DATE
PROJECT-CODE# -----> FINISH-DATE

The actual transitive dependencies are:

PROGRAMMER-CODE# -----> PROJECT-CODE# -----> START-DATE
PROGRAMMER-CODE# -----> PROJECT-CODE# -----> FINISH-DATE

We can now express relation R1 in two 3NF relations as follows:

R11(PROGRAMMER-CODE#, ADDRESS, TELEPHONE, PROJECT-CODE#)
R12(PROJECT-CODE#,   PROJECT-DESCRIPTION,   START-DATE, FINISH-DATE)

Because each programmer is given a single project at a time, which is distinct from others in the same database (i.e PROGRAMMER-CODE#----->PROJECT-CODE#), there is no need for a linking or intersection relation between R11 and R12. Also, the BCNF criterion cannot be employed because there is only one candidate key.

Example 2

Consider the relations:

R2(PUB#, PUB-NAME, ADDRESS)
R3(PUB#, CLA#, DEWEY-NUMBER#, VOLUME)

Let us analyse each of these to see whether they conform with 3NF and BCNF requirements.
R2 uses PUB# as the candidate key and as the determinant because:

PUB# -----> PUB-NAME
PUB# -----> ADDRESS

Therefore, R2 is in 2NF and 3NF because it does not involve any transitive dependencies and the only determinant (PUB#) is also a candidate key.
In relation R3, the attribute VOLUME is fully functionally dependent on the candidate key 'PUB#, CLA#', in other words, to find out how many books a publisher has produced under a class, we must supply values under both PUB#

and CLA#. The attribute DEWEY-NUMBER# holds values of the well known Dewey Decimal Classification System (DDCS), a library system based on hierarchies that signify the class of an individual publication, as well as the depth of the hierarchy. If we assume that the values here are unique for each occurrence under CLA#, then attribute DEWEY-NUMBER# is a potential member of a candidate key. Also, values under DEWEY-NUMBER# can be used to access values under CLA#. Therefore, the following hold true:

CLA# -----> DEWEY-NUMBER#
DEWEY-NUMBER# -----> CLA#

The above considerations imply that relation R3 contains two candidate keys, namely, 'PUB#, CLA#' and 'PUB#, DEWEY-NUMBER#', with the obvious overlapping attribute PUB#. In other words, we have a case where the BCNF criterion must be adopted to investigate relation R3 further, as we explain below.

Under candidate key 'PUB#, CLA#' we have the following dependencies:

PUB#,CLA# ==/==> DEWEY-NUMBER# (because CLA# ----->
                                                DEWEY-NUMBER#)
PUB#,CLA# =====> VOLUME

Under the candidate key 'PUB#, DEWEY-NUMBER#' we have the following dependencies:

PUB#,DEWEY-NUMBER# ==/==> CLA# (because DEWEY-NUM-
                                                BER# -----> CLA#)
PUB#,DEWEY-NUMBER# =====> VOLUME

If we split relation R3 into:

R31(PUB#, CLA#, VOLUME)
R32(CLA#, DEWEY-NUMBER#)

then, R31 will be in 3NF because 'PUB#, CLA#' is the only determinant and primary key and also,

PUB#, CLA# =====> VOLUME

R32 is in 3NF and BCNF because it has the determinants CLA# and DEWEY-NUMBER#, both of which are candidate keys.

6.8.4 Fourth Normal Form (4NF)

A relation is in 4NF if it is in 3NF and if it does not contain any multivalued dependencies. In other words, a relation is in 4NF if it is in 3NF and, at the same time, it does not contain more than one independent fact about a real world object.

Example 1

Assume a database contains information on publishers, each identified by a unique code PUB#. A publisher may produce books under a number of different classification subjects (e.g Physics, Biology, Mathematics, etc), and an author may write books under more than one subject area. Let relation R1 contain three key attributes as follows:

R1(PUB#, CLA#, AUT#)

Assume also that the applications analyst has established the following:

The composite primary key: 'PUB#, CLA#, AUT#'
A single candidate key: 'PUB#, CLA#, AUT#'
Three prime attributes: PUB#, CLA#, AUT#
Non-prime attributes: None

To understand the relationships among these attributes, we present a set of record occurrences in Figure 6.5 showing three publishers, two classes and three authors. The table for this network is shown below.

R1

PUB#	CLA#	AUT#
P1	C1	A1
P1	C1	A3
P1	C2	A1
P1	C2	A2
P1	C2	A3
P2	C1	A1
P2	C1	A3
P3	C2	A1
P3	C2	A2
P3	C2	A3

Relation R1 is in 1NF, 2NF and 3NF because it does not violate any of the criteria we have discussed so far. However, there are storage problems because, clearly, a number of attribute values are duplicate. In other words, the multivalued dependence of AUT# on CLA#, that is,

CLA# ---->> AUT#

holds because the set of AUT# values that appears with a given CLA# value appears with every combination of this CLA# value and a given PUB# value. This can cause problems with insert, delete, and update operations. For example, if we wish to insert a new class under a publisher, then we must also have an author in order to create a valid tuple. So, R1 is not in 4NF. One way to eliminate multivalued dependence is to split R1 into two equivalent relations, say, R2 and R3, both in 4NF:

R2(PUB#, CLA#)
R3(CLA#, AUT#)

An alternative solution may appear to be the following:

R21(PUB#, CLA#)
R31(PUB#, AUT#)

which is not acceptable, as we demonstrate below.

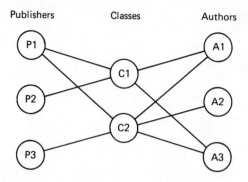

Figure 6.5 A network with three relations.

If we derive the tables R2, R3, R21 and R31 from the example of Figure 6.5, we can illustrate the effect a binding order has upon the cardinality of the corresponding table; R3 produces a cardinality of 5 and R31 a cardinality of 8 as shown below.

R2

PUB#	CLA#
P1	C1
P1	C2
P2	C1
P3	C2

R3

CLA#	AUT#
C1	A1
C1	A3
C2	A1
C2	A2
C2	A3

R21

PUB#	CLA#
P1	C1
P1	C2
P2	C1
P3	C2

R31

PUB#	AUT#
P1	A1
P1	A2
P1	A3
P2	A1
P2	A3
P3	A1
P3	A2
P3	A3

If we perform a join operation [Beeri et al, 1977] on relations R2 and R3 by means of their common key CLA#, using the RDL statements:

SELECT R2.PUB#, R2.CLA#, R3.AUT#
   FROM R2, R3
   WHERE R2.CLA# = R3.CLA#

we will create a table which is the same as the original (R1). However, if we perform a join operation on relations R21 and R31 by means of their common key PUB#, using the RDL statements:

SELECT R21.PUB#, R21.CLA#, R31.AUT#
   FROM R21, R31
   WHERE R21.PUB# = R31.PUB#

we will create a table, say R0, which contains the following tuples:

R0

PUB#	CLA#	AUT#
P1	C1	A1
P1	C1	A2	←———
P1	C1	A3
P1	C2	A1
P1	C2	A2
P1	C2	A3
P2	C1	A1
P2	C1	A3
P3	C2	A1
P3	C2	A2
P3	C2	A3

   Table R0 contains a new tuple <P1, C1, A2> (indicated by the arrow), which is not included in the original table R1. Therefore, the relations R21 and R31 cannot be accepted as fourth normal form relations.

Example 2

A clothing manufacturer wishes to process details of sewing machines by analysing the speed ranges (e.g 2000-3000 RPM, 3000-5000 RPM, etc) and type of cloth each can process. Let a relation R1 comprise the attributes:

R1(MACHINE-CODE#, SPEED#, CLOTH#)

with a composite primary key 'MACHINE-CODE#, SPEED#, CLOTH#', a single candidate key 'MACHINE-CODE#, SPEED#, CLOTH#', and three prime attributes, namely, MACHINE-CODE#, SPEED# and CLOTH#.

   Following a detailed study of the manufacturing procesess, the analyst establishes that a machine may operate at various predetermined speed ranges, and may also be capable of processing different types of cloth. In other words, there are two many-to-many relationships, one between MACHINE-CODE# and SPEED# and one between MACHINE-CODE# and CLOTH#. The multivalued dependencies therefore are:

MACHINE-CODE# ---->> SPEED#
MACHINE-CODE# ---->> CLOTH#

   Under fourth normal form, many-to-many relationships must not be represented within a single relation. So, by splitting R1 into:

R11(MACHINE-CODE#, SPEED#)
R12(MACHINE-CODE#, CLOTH#)

we derive two fourth normal form relations: R11 with a composite primary key

'MACHINE-CODE#, SPEED#', and R12 with a composite primary key 'MACHINE-CODE#, CLOTH#'.

6.8.5 Fifth Normal Form (5NF)

A relation is in 5NF if it is in 4NF and its corresponding table cannot be reconstructed from other tables each having fewer attributes than the original relation. The concept of 5NF deals with what is frequently referred to as 'join dependency' [Rissanen, 1979] because, usually, a join operation is used to reconstruct the original relation. So, the 5NF provides a framework for removing join dependencies, although 5NF relations are very rare and very difficult to discover.

It is worth noting also that, if a relation is split into two or more relations, each having the same primary key, then the original relation is in 5NF. As is the case with the 4NF, the 5NF also aims to reduce multivalued dependencies and therefore save storage, and at the same time eliminate anomalies with the operations insert, update, delete, etc.

Example 1

An organisation dealing with the distribution of books requires details on shops, publishing houses and classification of books. Let the relation R1 comprise the attributes:

R1(SHOP#, PUBLISHER#, CLASS#)

with a composite primary key: 'SHOP#, PUBLISHER#, CLASS#', a single candidate key: 'SHOP#, PUBLISHER#, CLASS#', and three key attributes: SHOP#, PUBLISHER# and CLASS#.

This relation can give us information on shops and corresponding classes, publishers and shops, and publishers and classes. Now, suppose that one of the requirements for the distribution of books is that, if a shop represents a publisher selling books under an approved class, then it sells these on behalf of the publisher. In other words, if the management of the shop opt to sell books under a given class, then they will sell the books published under this class for the publisher they represent. This rule implies that relation R1 involves join dependencies between SHOP# and PUBLISHER#, SHOP# and CLASS#, and PUBLISHER# and CLASS#.

We can now remove these join dependencies by splitting R1 into the following three 5NF relations:

R11(SHOP#, PUBLISHER#)
R12(SHOP#, CLASS#)
R13(PUBLISHER#, CLASS#)

We must point out here that if this rule was not in force (implying that if the management of the shop did not wish to sell books under a specific class (e.g sex), then they could opt not to sell books under this class for a company), then relation R1 would be in fifth normal form.

The reader may wonder whether the above three relations (R11, R12 and R13) will actually save any storage space, considering the fact that each attribute now appears twice in the resultant ensemble. The answer is 'yes', provided the cardinality of each table increases to a significant level. If this happens, as is most likely to be the case, then the values under the attributes SHOP#, PUBLISHER# and CLASS# will not be duplicated as much as they would have been in the original relation.

Example 2

A company specialising in the distribution of cars requires to hold details on representatives, manufacturers, and types of cars sold (e.g saloon, van, lorry, etc). Let a relation R1 comprise the attributes:

R1(REPRESENTATIVE#, MANUFACTURER#, TYPE#)

with a composite primary key: 'REPRESENTATIVE#, MANUFACTURER#, TYPE#', a single candidate key: 'REPRESENTATIVE#, MANUFAC-TURER#, TYPE#', and three key attributes: REPRESENTATIVE#, MAN-UFACTURER#, and TYPE#.

Now, assume that a certain rule is in force stating that, if somebody sells a certain type of car and represents the manufacturer of that car, then he sells that car for that manufacturer. As was the case with the previous example, the join dependencies are between REPRESENTATIVE# and MANUFACTURER#, REPRESENTATIVE# and TYPE#, and MANUFACTURER# and TYPE#.

The join dependencies can now be removed by splitting the original relation into the following three 5NF relations:

R11(REPRESENTATIVE#, MANUFACTURER#)
R12(REPRESENTATIVE#, TYPE#)
R13(MANUFACTURER#, TYPE#)

6.8.6 Conclusions

The process of normalisation provides a rigorous approach to establishing the inherent relationships among attributes by means of their identifying properties, and can lead to relations which are free from anomalies that may arise through manipulative operations (e.g insert, delete, update) on the corresponding tables. However, the analyst must be prepared to accept that there will always be the exceptional case where even a 3NF relation gives rise to certain anomalies.

Where an anomaly occurs, even after the relations have been normalised, then the analyst can resort to the corresponding entities to check whether two or more different entity types (or subsets of these) have been represented within a single relation. If they have, then this will most probably be the cause of the anomaly.

All the record types of the logical schema can and should be normalised according to the criteria of the five normal forms. Moreover, the record types of the subschemata (or views) must also be designed with similar criteria.

In summary, the different tasks that confront the analyst of the organisation while groups of attributes are normalised, can form part of a 'check list'. In what follows we present the major points covered during normalisation:

1. Types of keys (e.g primary, candidate, foreign)
2. Determinants
3. Name of each attribute
4. Name of each relation
5. Domain of each attribute
6. Repeating groups
7. Functional dependence
8. Transitive dependence
9. Multivalued dependence
10. Entity represented by each relation

Another aspect of database design, not receiving the attention it deserves, is the relations and tables that are created by the ordinary users, which in many cases are not even in 1NF. This is particularly obvious with facilities such as CREATE VIEW which can be applied on any tables that have not been 'locked' by the DBA. Anomalies can arise even where the resultant tables are virtual or transient. For example, the user may attempt to insert tuples on transient (temporary) unnormalised tables that have been created during an interactive session using the query language.

Clearly, we cannot expect the ordinary user of the database to be familiar with concepts such as functional or multivalued dependence, but we can expect an intelligent response by the DBMS that states categorically: Illegal operation... Hopefully, the response will not terminate there and the system will carry on to explain to the user the cause of the problem, and then proceed to offer alternative solutions.

6.9 SUMMARY

In this chapter, we introduced database design methodology from the global point of view, in terms of major stages and fundamental rules which ensure that the database can be manipulated without giving rise to any anomalies or inconsistent states.

There are basically two approaches to database design:

(a)   Top-down, that is, from conceptual entity to attribute.
(b)   Bottom-up, that is, from attribute to logical entity.

The ultimate objective of each of these is to aid the design of the logical schema which reflects the organisation accurately.

In further functional analysis of any organisation, resultant schemata and subschemata, the major steps in database design, in no particular order, are:

(a)   Define the conceptual schema.
(b)   Derive the logical schema from the conceptual schema.
(c)   Establish the internal schema and appropriate storage structures.
(d)   Derive appropriate subschemata from the logical schema to satisfy the applications of an organisation.

(e)   Develop application programs which manipulate the database.

Data analysis forms an essential part of database design. The aim is to identify and define individual attributes and relationships among these, through a disciplined and methodical manner and subsequently, to create clusters of attributes (the relations) which can be used as the building blocks of the logical schema.

The process whereby each relation is assessed in terms of stability, viability, and freedom from insert, update and delete anomalies, is called *normalisation*.

Normalisation of relations deals, primarily, with three important types of relationships between pairs of single or composite attributes: (a) Functional dependence, (b) Transitive dependence, and (c) Multivalued dependence.

Theoretical work on normalisation has establisehd five normal forms, that is, states which can characterise a relation. The First Normal Form (1NF) investigates the domains of the atrributes and eliminates repeating groups. The Second Normal Form (2NF) deals with functional dependence among attributes. The Third Normal Form (3NF) deals with transitive dependence. The Fourth Normal Form (4NF) and the Fifth Normal Form (5NF) deal with multivalued dependencies among the attributes.

6.10 REFERENCES

Aho, A. V., Beeri, C. & Ullman, J. D., 'The Theory of Joins in Relational Database', ACM TODS, Vol. 4, No. 3, pp. 297-314, 1979.

Albano, A., de Antonellis, V. & di Leva, A., 'Computer Aided Database Design: The DATAID Approach', In: Computer-Aided Database Design - The DATAID Project, Albano A., de Antonellis V. & di Leva A. (eds), North Holland, pp. 1-13, 1985.

Atzeni, P., Batini, P., Carboni, E., de Antonellis, V., Lenzerini, M., Villanelli, F. & Zonta, B., 'INCOD-DTE: A System for Interactive Conceptual Design of Data, Transactions and Events', In: Methodology and Tools for Database Design, Ceri S. (ed), North Holland, pp. 205-288, 1983.

Beeri, C., Fagin, R. & Howard, J. H., 'A Complete Axiomatization for Functional and Multivalued Dependencies', ACM SIGMOD International Symposium on Management of Data, pp. 47-61, 1977.

Borgida, A. T., Mylopoulos, J. & Wong, H. K. T., 'Methodological and Computer Aids for Interactive Information System Development', In: Automated Tools for Information Systems Design, Schneider H. J. & Wasserman A. I. (eds), North Holland, pp. 109-124, 1982.

Carlson, C. S. & Kaplan, R. S., 'A Generalised Access Path Model and Its Application to a Relational Database System', Proc. ACM SIGMOD International Symposium on Management of Data, pp. 143-156, 1976.

Chen, P. P., 'The Entity-Relationship Model: Toward a Unified View of Data', ACM TODS, Vol. 1, No. 1, pp. 9-36, 1976.

Codd, E. F., 'A Relational Model of Data for Large Shared Databases', CACM, Vol. 13, No. 6. pp. 377-387, 1970.

Codd, E. F., 'Further Normalisation of the Database Relational Model', In: Database Systems, R. Rustin (editor), Prentice-Hall, Englewood Cliffs, New Jersey, pp. 33-64, 1972.

Delobel, C., 'Normalisation and Hierarchical Dependencies in the Relational Data Model', ACM TODS, Vol. 3, No. 3, pp. 201-222, 1978.

Fagin, R., 'Multivalued Dependencies and a New Normal Form for Relational Databases', ACM TODS, Vol. 2, No. 3, pp. 262-278, 1977.

Housel, B. C., Waddle, V. E. & Yao, S. B., 'The Functional Dependency Model for Logical Database Design', Proc. of the 5th Conf. on Very Large Databases, pp. 194-208, 1979.

Howe, D. R., 'Data Analysis for Database Design', Edward Arnold, 1985.

Kent, W., 'A Simple Guide to Five Normal Forms in Relational Database Theory'. CACM, Vol. 26, No. 2, pp. 120-125, 1983.

Kouvatsos, D. D. & Yannakoudakis, E. J., 'A New Approach to the Design of Structured Bibliographic Records', Information Technology: Research and Development, Vol. 1, No. 4, pp. 285-300, 1982.

Olle, T. W., Sol, H. G. & Verrijn-Stuart, A. A., 'Information Systems Design Methodologies', IFIP WG 8.1 Working Conference, The Netherlands, North-Holland, May 1982.

Rissanen, J., 'Theory of Joins for Relational Databases: A Tutorial Survey', Proc. 7th Symposium on Mathematical Foundations of Computer Systems, Lecture Notes in Computer Systems, Vol. 64, Springer-Verlag, pp. 537-551, 1979.

Teorey, T. J. & Fry, J. P., 'Design of Database Structures', Prentice-Hall, 1982.

Yao, S. B., Waddel, V. E. & Housel, B. C., 'View Modeling and Integration Using the Functional Dependency Model', IEEE Transactions on Software Engineering, SE-8, 6, pp. 544-553, November 1982.

Zaniolo, C. & Melkanoff, M. A., 'On the Design of Relational Database Schemata', ACM TODS, Vol. 6, No. 1, pp. 1-47, 1981.

7 CANONICAL SYNTHESIS FOR DATABASE DESIGN

7.1 INTRODUCTION

Database design is a very costly and time consuming activity. A major objective is to design the logical schema which represents and reflects organisational requirements and is also extensible without major restructuring. Its architecture, therefore, must have the necessary structural properties which do not hinder its evolution in any way. Moreover, this 'minimal' structure should be independent of applications, software or hardware. Such a structure is otherwise referred to as 'canonical structure' [Martin, 1983], in other words, a stable and optimal structure.

During the past decade the use of database management systems has become increasingly important. A direct result of this has been the requirement for a reliable and consistent database design methodology. We have already discussed two major approaches to database design (see Chapter 6). These are: (a) Top-down (i.e from conceptual entity to attribute), and (b) Bottom-up (i.e from attribute to logical entity). They both aim to produce the global schema (data model) of the enterprise.

At first sight, the top-down approach [Albano et al, 1985; Atzeni et al, 1983] appears to be a simpler proposition than having to compose the data model from individual data elements, especially when this task is carried out manually. However, it can omit details that will, in turn, affect the final design. Although the bottom-up approach [Housel et al, 1979; Yao et al, 1982] requires a great deal of detailed information, it can produce a model which is based on data usage and is therefore more representative of the actual user environment.

Figure 7.1 shows the various levels of detail under both of these approaches in an attempt to place each in the correct perspective. We are not, in any way, claiming that one approach is better than the other, but we do claim that they can cohabit, and in many cases one can aid the operations of the other. One can complement the other by cross-checking and assessing the results it produces. It is the enterprise itself and the information available to the database analyst that will ultimately direct him to the correct approach.

In this chapter we are going to discuss canonical synthesis as an automated database design aid [Hubbard, 1978; Raver & Hubbard, 1977] whereby user views are analysed and interrelated in order to generate a canonical database structure. The emphasis is placed on user views since it is through these that the actual manipulation of the database takes place most of the time.

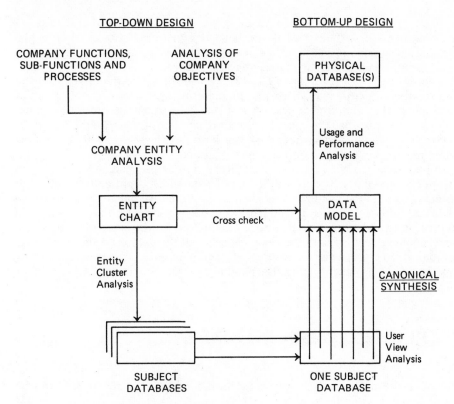

Figure 7.1 Top-down and bottom-up database design.

Database analysis and design, in the present context, can be split into four distinct stages:

1. Collection and formalisation of all the different user views of the existing or the proposed system.
2. Synthesis of the global data structure which can satisfy all the user requirements in an optimal fashion from the 'local views'.
3. Selection of a specific DBMS, and the translation of the optimal structure into a logical schema. In many cases the schema has to be constrained to the limitations of the DBMS in use.
4. Design and implementation of the physical structure. Often, optimisation at the physical level requires alterations in the logical design.

Typically, stages 1 and 2 are considered to be conceptual database design, stage 3 logical design, and stage 4 physical design.

Clearly, the overall process of database design is a costly, error-prone, and time-consuming activity. This is due to the size and complexity of even medium sized data processing environments. Besides, an excellent working knowledge of all the different user views is required for inconsistencies to be resolved and intelligent design decisions to be made.

A major problem arises when the design has to be altered, either because of enhancements or a failure in the original design work. Any changes in the database structure usually necessitate a complete schema re-compilation and appropriate amendments to all the applications affected.

Therefore, one of the aims of database design should be to derive analytical information and to establish corresponding structures which are as stable as possible so that undesirable side effects from subsequent alterations are minimised. Consequently, the need for an automated design aid [Hubbard, 1978, 1981; Bouzeghoub & Valduriez, 1984] which would at least cope with some of the more mechanical tasks, has long been recognised.

Martin [Martin, 1983] discusses canonical synthesis as a manual technique and defines a canonical schema as a 'model of data which represents the inherent structure of that data and hence is independent of individual applications of the data and also of the software and hardware mechanisms which are employed in representing and using the data'. So, by definition, for the database to be stable and capable of coping with the changing needs of the enterprise, it must have a canonical structure. This will ensure that there is minimal disturbance to existing application environments and corresponding software.

7.2 ELEMENT ASSOCIATIONS

In this section we are going to discuss the terminology necessary to understand the principles of canonical synthesis.

The most basic unit of information, in the present context, is called a *data element* or *data item*. It is an indivisible item of data which cannot be split and retain any meaning. Usually, it is a named property of an entity. The values given to a data element describe that property for every entity occurrence in which it appears. For example, the entity EMPLOYEE could have the data elements: NAME, ADDRESS, SOCIAL SECURITY NUMBER, PAYE NUMBER, SALARY, DATE OF BIRTH, EMPLOYEE NUMBER, SKILL LEVEL, NAME OF EACH CHILD, NAME OF SPOUSE, MARITAL STATUS, etc. For any particular entity there may be hundreds of possible data elements. Within any particular database there may be hundreds of entities and therefore thousands of data elements.

Data elements, on their own, are of little use. For example, the value of SALARY by itself, does not provide any meaningful information. However, when each EMPLOYEE NUMBER has *associated* with it one particular value for SALARY we then know how much each employee is earning at any point of time. Therefore, a database consists of data elements which have *associations* with each other. There are basically three different types of associations between elements:

(a)   *Type '1' Association*: A given occurrence of the 'from' element identifies one and only one occurrence of the 'to' element. The identification is unique and represents a functional dependency. For example, an EMPLOYEE NUMBER will identify only one value of SALARY and one value of NATIONAL INSURANCE NUMBER.

(b) *Type 'M' Association*: Here, a given occurrence of the 'from' element can identify zero, one, or many values of the 'to' element. The identification may not be unique and it represents a multivalued dependency. For example, an EMPLOYEE NUMBER may identify zero, one, or many CHILDREN.

(c) *Type 'C' Association*: Here, a given occurrence of the 'from' element may or may not identify a single value for the 'to' element. Therefore, if there is any identification, then it is unique. For example, an EMPLOYEE may or may not have a SPOUSE. If he does, then normally there will only be one SPOUSE (although in countries where polygyny or polyandry is allowed this may not be so). For our purposes of database design type 'C' associations will be treated as being a special case of type '1' association since there must always be the potential for a '1' association. (Type 'C' associations are not discussed separately here.)

Associations are in one direction only (going from an element to an element). A *mapping* is between a pair of elements and indicates the association in each direction. For example, there is a 1:M mapping between EMPLOYEE NUMBER and DEPARTMENT NUMBER, that is, each employee will belong to only one department, but each department may have many employees. We often use diagrams to represent the known relationships between sets of data elements. For example,

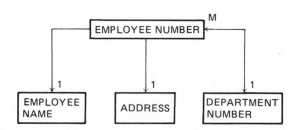

Here, the absence of associations going from ADDRESS to EMPLOYEE NUMBER and from EMPLOYEE NAME to EMPLOYEE NUMBER does not mean that they may not exist. It means that we are not interested in them. If forced to put in both the missing associations they would both be of type 'M' as several employees may share the same address (in the case of employees living in the same house) and also, several may have the same name (if the company is very large or if father and son join the same firm and they both have the same name). Therefore, the four possible mappings are 1:1, 1:M, M:1, and M:M. We will see later that there are special problems related to M:M mappings.

There may of course be more than one association between two data elements. When this occurs, the associations must be *named* in order to distinguish between them. For example, a person will usually have a HOME address and a WORK address. This can be presented as follows:

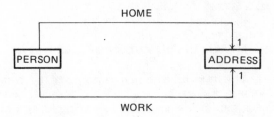

Because there are two links between the same two data elements (i.e PERSON and ADDRESS) the links are labelled. Such situations can be avoided by introducing an extra data item, as is the case in the following diagram:

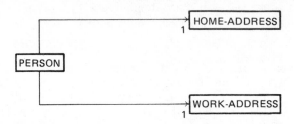

Type 'M' associations may go from both elements HOME-ADDRESS and WORK-ADDRESS to PERSON in order to show who lives at a particular address, and who works at a particular address.

7.2.1 Keys, Attributes, and Data Element Groups

Although most of the terms used here have already been defined with the relational model in mind (see Sections 3.5.1 and 6.6), they will be re-interpreted here with respect to the actual element associations we discussed earlier.

A *key* is an element which is able to identify uniquely other data elements. That is, a key has one or more type '1' associations leaving it. It is possible to have more than one data element whose values identify uniquely the set of properties of an entity. These are called *candidate Keys*. Usually one of the candidate keys is chosen as the *primary key*, that is, the data element whose values will be used to identify uniquely all record occurrences under an entity.

For example, both EMPLOYEE NUMBER and NATIONAL INSURANCE NUMBER are able to identify uniquely the properties of the entity EMPLOYEE like NAME, ADDRESS, TELEPHONE NUMBER, etc. It is worth noting that, unfortunately, most organisations prefer to use their own local primary keys which are often not related to keys in other organisations, even though the same record occurrence (e.g same person) may be held on their database.

An *attribute* is any element which is not in the primary key. Each attribute is identified by the primary key for that set of entity properties.

A *secondary key* is any attribute with one or more type 'M' associations leaving it. In other words, a secondary key is able to identify non-uniquely sets of other data elements.

A *data element group* is the combination of primary key and the attributes which it identifies. In other words, the complete set of properties for an entity.

There are certain data elements which cannot be identified by only one other data element. These require a primary key which consists of more than one data element. This type of key is referred to as a *concatenated key*. The following diagram shows an example of a concatenated key:

In order to ascertain what GRADE a STUDENT has for a particular COURSE, we need both the STUDENT element and the COURSE element before we are able to identify the GRADE achieved.

Of course the concatenated key may consist of many individual elements all of which are required for the identification of one or more attributes, as for example:

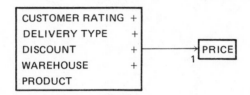

The concept *entity* is difficult to define precisely, but what we can confidently say is that it is something about which we need to hold certain information. Often, it is something real like an employee, a department, or a piece of equipment. However, it can also be something insubstantial like an aeroplane flight path, an invoice, or the status of a production line.

A common 'mistake' is to assume that an entity instance is equivalent to a data element group instance (e.g when a particular employee is identified by that employee's data group consisting of EMPLOYEE NUMBER, NAME, ADDRESS, etc). Generally, this is a safe assumption however, there are cases when the properties of an entity may be spread across several data element groups and mixed in with the properties of several other entities. This occurs when data elements are grouped by 'how they are used' rather than by 'how they appear to be related'.

To further understand the concept entity and the logical relationships that may exist between data element groups, we will present a realistic example. Consider the classical case of customers, orders, employees, departments, and projects. A customer may have issued a number of orders, each of which may in turn comprise a number of items (the order line). An employee may be involved with a number of projects, and a project may require an input from a number of employees. Also, a project may aim to produce one or more products each of which may in turn require a number of assembly components. The latter may also be manufactured under a number of different processes.

All the above descriptive detail makes it very difficult to follow and understand the relationships among the data element groups. The so called *entity-relationship* model offers the means to present the relationships in a clear diagrammatic manner. Figure 7.2 presents all the entities and relationships we discussed above. Through such a diagram it becomes possible, not only to understand the organisational structure, but also to detect any inconsistent associations (see Section 7.3.1).

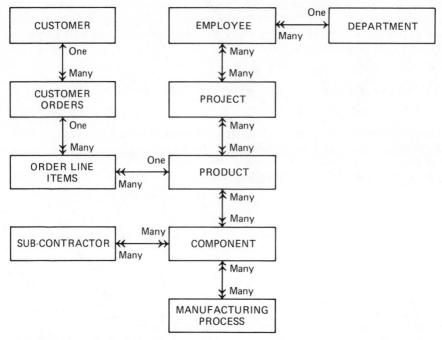

Figure 7.2   An example entity chart.

7.3 READYING THE VIEWS FOR CANONICAL SYNTHESIS

As views are being compiled, it is possible to make mistakes and for inconsistencies to occur between different user views. Also, for the process of canonical synthesis, the data in the views must have been checked previously to make sure everything is correct. There are various validation checks [Baldissera et al, 1979] the views must be subjected to before synthesis can take place. In this section we are going to discuss the major points which must be investigated by the database analyst prior to the utilisation of a canonical synthesis algorithm.

Even something as simple as ensuring that each of the data element names has only one possible meaning (i.e that there are no *homonyms*) and that no two data elements are being used to represent the same piece of information (i.e there are no *synonyms*) is no easy task. Homonyms and synonyms do appear frequently as for example, when different departments adopt individualised terms to suit their specific applications. Also, in many cases, we find it very difficult to establish common (global) terms between applications.

So, it becomes necessary to go through each potential data element, one at a time, deciding on a global (database-wide) name for it, along with its precise definition and the reasons it is required. This, plus any other information which is required on the data elements (e.g where they originate, where they are printed, security access levels, etc), should be entered into a *data dictionary* which allows everyone to keep track of all the data elements within a database. The data dictionary can also be used to check against the user views to ensure no unknown data elements are used.

7.3.1 Inconsistent Associations

Inconsistent associations appear where there is more than one different association type between the same two data elements. The following is an example of a direct inconsistent association between EMPLOYEE NUMBER and HISTORY involving both type '1' and type 'M' links:

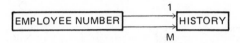

Such direct inconsistent associations are easily detected using a checking routine of some sort. Usually, the inconsistencies result from associations originating from two quite separate user views. In any automated system it should be possible to trace the exact origin of such conflicting associations.

There are however other inconsistent associations which are much more difficult to detect. These are indirect inconsistent associations which should also be detected and reported to the analyst. The following are example cases of indirect inconsistent associations:

Case 1

Case 2

Case 3

Case 4

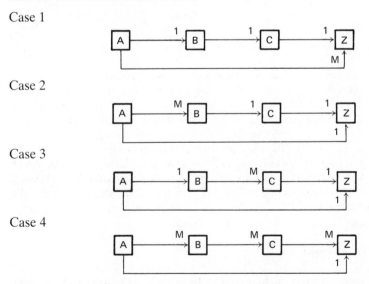

Case 1 above is generally recognised as inconsistent. However, case 2 and its variants 3 and 4 have not yet been recognised as such. This appears to be due to the problem of ascertaining the equivalence of paths of associations containing one or more type 'M' links.

Following on from the above, we can give a global definition for an inconsistency:

> Any two or more paths of dependencies which have the same source and destination data elements but which infer different resultant dependencies, are inconsistent.

This definition, whilst it is comprehensive, does not take into account the semantics of more complex situations. Our experience suggests that each case requires individual attention by an informed analyst as to whether its semantics are being violated in any way.

Finally, the diagrammatic representation of the general form of an inconsistent association is presented below (note that the symbol '/' is read out as OR):

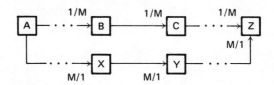

7.3.2 Illegal Associations

There are several types of association which are effectively illegal. We discuss the following three:

(A) Reverse Associations Between Keys

Since a large proportion of the canonical processing algorithm works on the associations between the keys within the database structure, the omission of the specification of a reverse association between two keys is considered to be an error condition. That is, the mappings of 1:0, 0:1, M:0, and 0:M which exist between two data elements found to be keys after all the user views have been merged together (see Section 7.4.1 for details), are considered to be in error.

However, rather than specifying all such reverse associations (a task which could be tedious for the analyst), it is acceptable to assume that all missing reverse associations are treated as being of type '1' or type 'M', depending on the preference of the analyst.

(B) Peculiar Associations

There is a set of associations which appear to be nonsensical. Although type 'M' links going from attributes to keys are indicators of secondary keys, type 'M' links which point to attributes from either keys or other attributes would seem to serve no purpose. Such links usually do not affect the processing of the schema but they should still be considered as undesirable. Thus, one solution would be to report them as errors, but since they seldom affect the processing of the views, they may simply be deleted from the generated final schema design, rather than hold up the processing of the views. Alternatively, an option may be offered to the analyst to promote to key status the attributes that have type 'M' links entering them.

(C) Associations Between Concatenated Elements

There are certain types of association which appear between concatenated data elements that can create some difficulties in the design process. If both of the elements in question are keys then there is no problem, provided the following rules are observed:

1.   If one of the keys is a subset of the other, then only a 1:M mapping is allowed to go from the larger key to the smaller.
2.   When the keys have one or more components in common but neither is a subset of the other, then there must be an M:M mapping between them.

However, if one or both of the concatenated elements are considered to be attributes rather than keys, then complex arrangements can be developed, as explained below.

(a)   If one of the elements is a subset of the other but the subset is not a key, then only a 0:M mapping is allowed to go from the large concatenation to the small. Having a type '1' association going in the reverse direction would violate second normal form (2NF) since not all of the large concatenated key is required to identify the attribute subset.
(b)   If the larger concatenation is the attribute and the subset is a key, then the addition of a 1:M mapping from the large concatenation to the small becomes quite legal but it does of course change the large concatenation to being classed as a key since it will then identify another element with a type '1' link.
(c)   Should both concatenated elements be attributes, then the logical implications are unacceptable. Again, a 1:M link is implied but as the type '1' link will change the larger element into a key with the subset as its attribute, again second normal form is violated. Therefore, a 0:M link has to be settled for.
(d)   Category (b) above also creates some complications in that altering the status of a concatenation to a key can invalidate 0:M links to that element from concatenations which have it as a subset. This problem will require that concatenated elements be dealt with smallest first in order to prevent such a situation occurring.

Instead of having a special algorithm to deal with such complications, a far better approach to process concatenated elements and their links to each other is to impose a rule that states: ALL SUBSETS OF KEYS MUST THEMSELVES BE KEYS.

Moreover, as the only reason for the existence of concatenated elements is that there will be (at some point of time) intersection data for them to identify, then another rule can be imposed stating: ALL CONCATENATED ELEMENTS MUST BE KEYS.

These two rules, effectively, deal with all the problems and 1:M mappings can be made between any concatenation and its subsets. The rules should be considered part of the process of normalisation of the user views to conform to third normal form (3NF) criteria.

7.3.3 Normalisation of the Views

In the previous sections we discussed definite errors which can occur as a result of conceptual differences between various users, or indeed as a result of an oversight by the database analyst. Almost all such errors can and should be detected by appropriate software because they cause logical conflicts in the design.

There is however a class of mistakes which are very difficult (if not impossible) for software to detect. These can occur when the user interprets or represents incorrectly his own view of the data. This is mainly to do with data element 'groupings' which form records, segments, tuples, etc, as users see them. Thus, once the views are normalised, the resultant data structures will be most clear and unambiguous and canonical synthesis can then take over to process these further.

There are three major normal forms (or testing phases in the present context) the views must go through in order to obtain the correct representation of the data and therefore enable the design of the 'best' possible database structure. These are the first, second and third normal forms as we have already discussed in Section 6.8. The fourth and fifth normal forms may seem rather esoteric but we must point out that it is desirable to have user views up to the fourth normal form before canonical synthesis can be applied. As a minimum requirement for canonical synthesis, user views must be in third normal form.

We will now present some further examples of normalisation using appropriate views which are analysed according to first, second and third normal form criteria. To further understand the relationships among the elements of views, we present, in diagrammatic form, all the dependencies of attributes on simple as well as concatenated keys.

7.3.3.1 FIRST NORMAL FORM (1NF)

For a view to be in first normal form, all data elements must be single valued (i.e the values of any one data element must originate from only one domain). Also, there must not be any repeating attributes. The following view violates first normal form:

EMPLOYEE NUMBER	EMPLOYEE NAME	PAYE	ADDRESS	SALARY	SKILL CODE	RATING
(KEY)						

Here, each employee may have any number of skills and a specific rating under each. Although this structure is permitted in ordinary data processing applications, there are several problems with it. For example, RATING is dependent on both EMPLOYEE NUMBER and SKILL CODE even though the primary key is

EMPLOYEE NUMBER. A number of questions arise as a result of this: Do we implement variable length records with the consequent increase in complexity, or do we use fixed length records and only allow for a certain number of repetitions in which case we will always have to deal with overflow or be wasting a large amount of disk space with unfilled fields ?

The solution is to split such a view into the two simple views it actually represents, as follows:

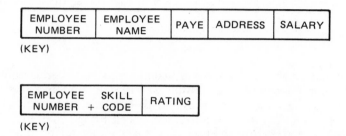

The second view has a concatenated key consisting of both the EMPLOYEE NUMBER and the SKILL CODE along with the attribute RATING. This particular solution is relevant mainly to relational databases. A solution for CODASYL (network) or other database structures, is to use pointer lists, as indicated below:

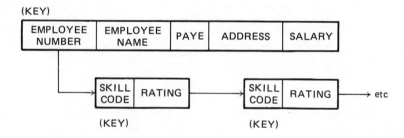

7.3.3.2 SECOND NORMAL FORM (2NF)

For a view to be in 2NF, it must be in 1NF and every attribute must be functionally dependent on the entire key of the view. This applies mainly to views with concatenated keys in that the analyst must ensure that all attributes are dependent on the whole key not just a subset of it. Let us discuss 2NF with the following example:

PART CODE + SUPPLIER CODE	SUPPLIER NAME	SUPPLIER DISCOUNT	PRICE

(KEY)

This may seem like a perfectly valid view. However, when examining all functional dependencies (denoting these with unidirectional arrows which imply that the element being pointed to is functionally dependent on the element the arrow derives from), we establish the following relationships:

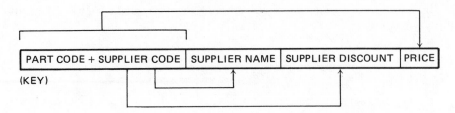

It is clear that the above view is not in second normal form because only PRICE is dependent on the complete key, while SUPPLIER NAME and SUPPLIER DISCOUNT are dependent only on SUPPLIER CODE.

The solution is to split the view into two: one consisting of SUPPLIER CODE (as primary key) and the attendant supplier information, and the other consisting of the concatenated primary key PART CODE + SUPPLIER CODE and the attribute PRICE. This is presented diagrammatically as follows:

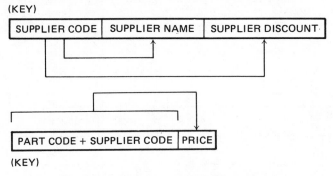

The above two views result in far less storage space being used because there will be only one copy of supplier name and discount rather than duplicate copies for each of the parts that are held by a supplier. Also, the new arrangement removes the danger of 'losing' a supplier who does not have any parts (say, for a short time only). Of course this makes all subsequent deletion and update operations on the supplier attributes far quicker because there is only one copy to alter or delete each time.

7.3.3.3 THIRD NORMAL FORM (3NF)

For a view to be in 3NF it must be in 2NF and every attribute must be non-transitively dependent on all candidate keys. Transitive dependence appears when an attribute is dependent on another attribute and through it on the primary key. For example, with data elements EMPLOYEE, DEPARTMENT and LOCATION and where an EMPLOYEE must be at the LOCATION of his DEPARTMENT, we derive the following diagram:

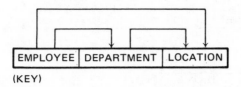

(KEY)

Transforming this into 3NF by removing transitive dependence, we obtain the following two views:

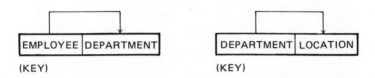

(KEY)   (KEY)

Let us discuss another example with the following elements:

CONTAINER NUMBER	SHIPPING AGENT	DELIVERY HANDLING	VESSEL NUMBER	DATE OF ARRIVAL

(KEY)

Here, the view is not in 3NF because DATE OF ARRIVAL (a non-key attribute) is dependent on VESSEL NUMBER which is, in turn, dependent on the primary key CONTAINER NUMBER. If this view is not analysed further it can lead to the following problems:

(a)   If the vessel is not carrying any cargo (i.e when there are no containers on board) then the date of arrival of the vessel cannot be recorded.
(b)   If at any point before the vessel sails the number of containers drops to zero (due to cancellations or failure to turn up), all tuples containing the date of arrival will have been deleted and so the information would be lost.
(c)   If the date of arrival has to be altered, then every container tuple will have to have its date of arrival (the value) altered.
(d)   If the view is left as it is, then it will be using valuable disk space which could be more usefully employed to hold other information. Efficient use of the available disk space is always a necessity for database management systems, and so it is always important to avoid duplicate information where possible.

All the above problems can be eliminated by splitting the original view into the following two equivalent:

CONTAINER NUMBER	SHIPPING AGENT	DELIVERY HANDLING	VESSEL NUMBER

(KEY)

VESSEL NUMBER	DATE OF ARRIVAL

(KEY)

7.3.4 Deviation from Third Normal Form

There are cases where, due to computer performance, speed of retrieval, multiple view elements, special user requirements, etc, it becomes necessary to deviate from strict third normal form. However, such deviations *must* be well thought out and should be implemented only when there is a definite need to do so.

The most common reason to deviate from 3NF is the case that involves long views containing many attributes a few of which are being continually accessed (say for on-line enquiries) while the rest are required for batch runs only a few times a day/week/month. Take for example the following view:

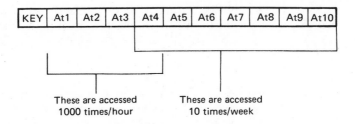

KEY	At1	At2	At3	At4	At5	At6	At7	At8	At9	At10

These are accessed
1000 times/hour

These are accessed
10 times/week

In this example, particularly where the fields (at the internal schema level) are accessed only 10 times/week and where these are very large (e.g when they contain detailed textual data, addresses, etc), there is a definite case for splitting the record in two. This will enable faster access on the more frequently accessed fields and therefore optimise disk input/output.

With the aid of a DBMS, the above considerations can of course be implemented at the internal schema level so that the 'ordinary' users can still see a single record being handled as and where appropriate.

The process of normalisation always leads to far more record types than were specified originally. This, surprisingly, has the effect of reducing the amount of data which is stored because it cuts down on the repetition of information usually contained within data structures that are not normalised.

7.4 THE CANONICAL SYNTHESIS ALGORITHM

The canonical synthesis algorithm we have adopted and implemented successfully, can now be presented clearly under the following stages:

1. Merge all 3NF user views; here, all the views are accumulated together to
    form the first version of the schema.
2. Scan the schema and identify all key and non-key elements.
3. Establish appropriate bonds between the components of concatenated
    keys.
4. Search for isolated attributes, that is, elements which only have type 'M'
    associations going into and out of them; these are then 'promoted' to
    special key status.
5. Scan the resultant schema looking for peculiar links; these are type 'M'
    links coming into attributes from either other attributes or keys. If any are
    found, they are reported and are either deleted from the schema or are
    promoted to key status.
6. Find all one-way associations and turn these into type '1' links, type 'M'
    links or terminate the algorithm following intervention by the analyst; for
    details of this stage see Section 7.3.2.
7. Scan all known keys (including isolated attributes), and look for M:M
    mappings between two keys. If any M:M mappings are found, then there
    should exist a concatenated key for each, composed of the two original
    keys with 1:M links to them. If such a concatenated key does not already
    exist, then create one automatically.
8. Having dealt with the mappings between keys, report all 1:1 mappings
    between keys along with any common attributes.
9. Scan the resultant schema looking for redundant links; redundant links of
    type '1' are removed from the schema whereas type 'M' are only marked
    as being possible redundancies.
10. Search for attributes which can be identified by more than one key, in
    other words, intersecting attributes; if any are found, then they are either
    (a) assigned to belong to the first key linked to them by redirecting all the
    other key links to their chosen owner key, (b) duplicated for each of the
    keys, or (c) promoted to key status.
11. If any intersecting attributes are found at this stage, then perform again
    the process of removing redundant links (stage 9 above) as new
    redundancies may have been created from the previous stages.
12. The schema is now complete and can be presented in the form of a graph
    and can also be described by the software automatically.

The above algorithm can be applied in a single pass, putting all the user views
through the synthesis in one go. However, it is much more instructive if views are
added in groups or individually and appropriate reports are produced in each
pass. This enables a far better understanding of how the resultant structure is
generated. Moreover, recursive processing allows further analysis on views which
affect dramatically the database structure.

Having presented the canonical synthesis algorithm, we will proceed to discuss
auxiliary software features that can be implemented in order to design an

integrated system which will facilitate the designer even further. The following three features can lead to an indispensable software engineering tool for database design:

(a)   Interactive manipulation of the generated schema.
(b)   The ability to constrain the schema to a particular DBMS's limitations.
(c)   The ability to generate the appropriate Data Description Language (DDL) statements to implement the designed schema on the target DBMS.

In the following sections we discuss the major stages of the canonical synthesis algorithm, in more detail. We adopt capital letters to denote elements of views as well as keys which are indicated accordingly. Further details of the results that can be expected under each of these stages are presented in the Appendix. This discusses a hospital database for a regional health authority including information under the entities: Patients, General Practitioners, Hospitals, Consultants and Drug Suppliers.

7.4.1 Merging of the Views

This process integrates [Biskup & Convent, 1986] the information contained in all the user views ignoring repetitions of identical associations between data elements [Elmasri & Navathe, 1984]. For example, merging the following views 1 and 2 produces the resultant data structure represented in 3:

View 1 (NEW)

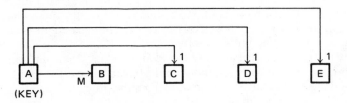

View 2 (NEW)

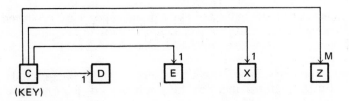

View 3 = View 1 + View 2

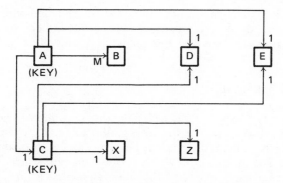

As each new view is read in, only those data elements and associations which have not appeared before are added to the schema. At this stage, the schema will look very messy but the later stages (notably, the removal of redundancies) will tidy it up.

User views usually consist of more than one key plus its associations and are accumulated in a step-wise fashion giving the basic starting schema structure for the canonical synthesis algorithm to refine further. The following diagram illustrates the result of adding yet another view (view 4) to view 3 above:

View 4 (NEW)

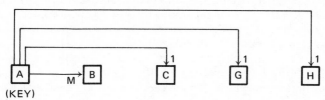

View 5 = View 3 + View 4

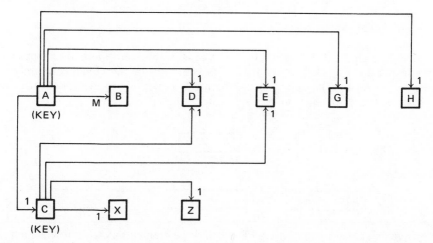

It is very important to emphasise, at this stage, that while views are merged together, no other processing of these should be carried out because it can make the designed schema dependent on the order in which the views are encountered. Such a dependence is extremely undesirable for a design methodology seeking to produce consistent results. This point appears to have been overlooked by a number of algorithms that have been implemented commercially.

7.4.2 Keys and Attributes

Although the user views specify which elements are keys and which are attributes, it would not be sensible to rely on the users getting this right. Therefore, in order to determine which elements are actually keys, it is necessary to look through the current schema and mark as keys all those elements which have type '1' associations leaving them. All the other data elements, as far as this stage is concerned, can be considered as attributes. In the following example, A, D, and F are the key elements:

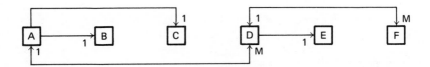

Element F does not have any attributes but because it has a type '1' link leaving it and going to the key data element D, then F must also be considered a key. If the association from F to D is undefined, then F would be considered as an isolated attribute (isolated attributes are discussed in Section 7.4.7).

The process of determining the keys automatically frees the analyst from having to specify these correctly. Providing all the relationships are correct, then the algorithm can determine which elements are actually keys and which only appear to be keys.

7.4.3 Concatenated Keys

Those data elements which are found to be concatenated (these are always keys) are a special case. This is because it is possible for the individual components of the key to exist in the database as separate keys with their own set of attributes. Consider the following four views:

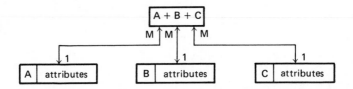

Given a concatenated key A+B+C and the elements A, B, and C which also exist as individual keys, then there must be 1:M links between the components and the concatenation, as shown in the above diagram. So, when such links are not specified they must be created automatically by the algorithm.

Now, if the concatenated key is already pointed to with a 1:M link which originates from a key that is a subset of itself, then only the unmatched individual elements should have the 1:M link created by the algorithm.

Let us look at another example where the concatenated key A+B+C already has a 1:M link with the key A+B and also, the concatenated key A+B involves further links with the individual keys A and B. The following diagram illustrates this:

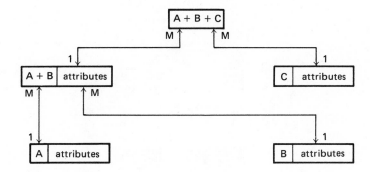

7.4.3.1 Problems with Concatenated Attributes

If any of the components of a concatenated key already exist as attributes rather than as keys, then a number of problems can be encountered. We discuss two cases:

(a)   Because the component is an attribute, then only the type 'M' link going from the component to the concatenation is legal because the type '1' link going from the concatenated key to the component violates second normal form. If such an association does exist, it must be reported and possibly deleted from the schema.

(b)   The second case states that if a component of a concatenated key has not been specified as a key it must be turned into one (i.e it must be given special key status). This is a reasonable stance to take as dealing with non-key components of concatenated keys can lead to complex data structures. However, the possibility of such elements occurring in an actual database environment is very small.

7.4.4 Dealing with M:M Associations

An M:M mapping between two key data elements gives cause for concern when designing a schema in two major areas:

(a)   The implementation of an M:M structure within a database (at the physical level) is not easy. For 1:M associations it is possible to use chains or tables of pointers, or a structure where the 'children' follow on from the 'parent'. These relatively simple solutions are of little use when we deal with M:M structures.

(b)   The second problem, as far as we are concerned, is that whenever an M:M
      mapping occurs then eventually there will be a need to store intersection
      data. So, if there is no intersection key we must create one. The latter
      actually alters the structure of the database schema. The following
      diagram illustrates the alterations in the design, that is, the way an M:M
      mapping is dealt with:

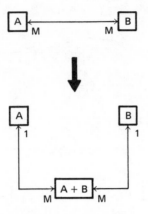

In order to keep the data structure as stable as possible, future needs for
intersection data must be anticipated. Therefore, an intersection key of A+B
must be created along with 1:M mappings between the individual keys A and B
and the concatenation. This enables the M:M link to be deleted since it can be
deduced from the two 1:M links.

There is of course the possibility that A and B are themselves already
concatenated. Furthermore, A and B may contain common (overlapping)
components. So, a case where the key A+B+D, say, has an M:M mapping with
A+C+D+E should lead to the creation of the key A+B+C+D+E. If a
concatenated key has an M:M mapping with a subset of itself, then this must be
considered as an error condition.

7.4.5 Dealing with 1:1 Associations

Let us discuss the case of a 1:1 mapping between two key elements. This usually
takes the form of a 1:1 link between two candidate keys for a set of attributes as
illustrated in the following example:

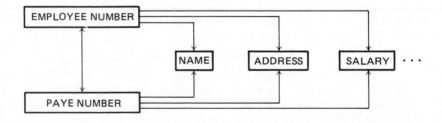

The above case shows two keys (EMPLOYEE NUMBER and Pay As You Earn (PAYE) NUMBER which identify the same attributes, but we could also have a case where one identifies a subset of the other. A decision must then be made by the analyst as to which of the candidate keys will be the primary key. It is usual for the non-primary key to be designated as a secondary index.

The following diagrams present the complete range of possible situations that can occur. Each key is denoted by the capital letter 'K' followed by a number and each attribute is denoted by the capital letter 'A' followed by a number.

Case 1: One of the keys indentifies attributes which are a subset of another key

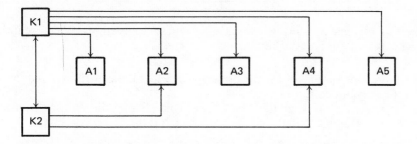

Case 2: One of the keys indentifies no attributes at all

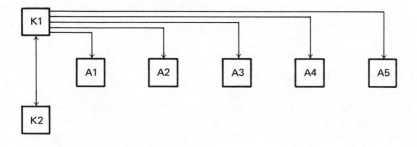

Case 3: Each key identifies its own unique set of attributes

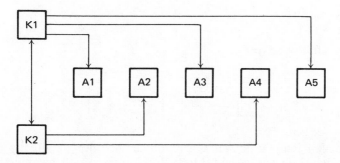

Case 4: Each key identifies its own attributes as well as others which are also identified by other keys

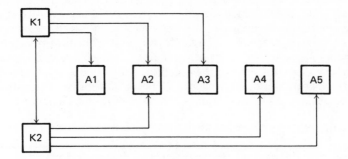

There are several possible ways of dealing with such situations. We present the following two major approaches:

(a)   Choose one of the keys as the primary key with all the attributes and the other key under it.
(b)   Allow the keys to keep the attributes which only they identify and transfer the intersecting attributes to the key which has the 'strongest' link.

In the interests of stability the keys should be kept separate. Only when one of the keys is very rarely used and all its attributes are directly identified by the other key should combining of the keys be considered.

Complete identities rarely occur and they should always be checked out most carefully by the analyst.

7.4.6 Removal of Redundancies

As we discussed in Section 7.4.1, associations can become redundant when their dependency is implied by two or more other associations. Loops can also be classed as a special category of redundancies and must be detected and dealt with accordingly. Redundant associations are discussed below.

(A) Redundant Type '1' Associations

Consider the following case:

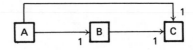

Here, the link going from A to C is redundant because it is already implied by the links going from A to B and B to C. It is important for the analyst to check carefully that such redundant links are semantically the same as the alternative path discovered. Study the following realistic case:

In the above example the removal of the link between EMPLOYEE and LOCATION can only be made when all the employees of a department are always located at the same place as the department itself. In some companies this would be the case and therefore the link could be deleted but in others the employees would require their own location field.

(B) Redundant Type 'M' Associations

So far only redundant type '1' associations have been considered. There is also a possibility of redundant type 'M' associations appearing. Indeed, when dealing with M:M associations between keys the 'M' associations are considered to be redundant when a path consisting of an 'M' association followed by a '1' association is created. The following case illustrates this:

Case 1

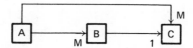

In the above case, the type 'M' link from A to C can be considered redundant in certain situations (e.g when dealing with M:M mappings). However, there are other related situations which also constitute possible redundancies and appear to depend upon the individual semantics of each case. We present two cases of this as follows:

Case 2

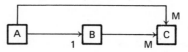

Case 3

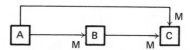

Thus, all redundancies detected by the algorithm must be checked by the analyst in order to make sure that there is no semantic conflict.

Following on from the previous three examples (case 1, case 2 and case 3) we can proceed to define the general case of a redundancy as follows:

> Any paths (two or more) of dependencies having the same source
> and destination data elements and which infer the same resultant
> dependency indicate a possible redundancy.

The diagrammatic form of the general redundancy can then be shown as follows (reading the symbol '/' as OR):

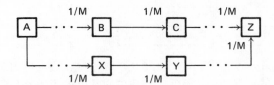

Any software that attempts to implement the removal of redundancies must at least be able to cope with the following logic (a subset of the general case): When there is a path of length 1 and one or more paths of length greater than 1 each with the same source and destination elements (implying the same relationship), then the direct relationship is considered to be redundant.

Whilst the removal of redundancies reduces the size and complexity of the schema, there remain two important questions to be considered:

(a)   Will the use of an alternative longer path give rise to unacceptable program execution times for any application programs ?
(b)   Are the alternative paths completely semantically equivalent to the direct path ? It is of course possible to obtain the same information from the alternative path 99% of the time and only find out much later that there is a slight semantic difference.

(C) Dealing with Loops

Loops can make the structuring of the data into parent-child relationships (mainly for hierarchic and network databases) a very difficult problem to tackle. It is therefore essential that all loops are detected and reported by the canonical synthesis algorithm. The analyst can then assess the problem and break the loop at some point. The algorithm should also be able to find the weakest link in a loop and therefore indicate a possible break point. Finally, care is required when loops are searched for, since the algorithm can report a loop as many times as there are relationships built in a loop.

The following example shows four elements, A, B, C and D with a loop going from A to B to C to D to A:

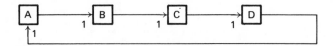

7.4.6.1 PROGRAMMING CONSIDERATIONS

A redundancy checking routine can consume a large amount of processing time and so various programming considerations need to be observed. It is estimated that between 10% and 99% of processing time can be taken up just to search for redundant links, the exact percentage depending on the size and complexity of the schema and the efficiency of the search algorithm.

The most likely solutions to finding redundant associations will necessarily be recursive in nature. Also, because the structure being dealt with is a network, then potentially every association could be marked as redundant.

In practice, the following considerations can reduce to a considerable degree the number of paths that have to be searched:

(a)   For a redundancy to appear, the starting element must have at least two type '1' links leaving it (i.e one link being redundant and the other forming the start of an alternative path to get to the same destination element).

(b)   The destination element must have at least two type '1' links entering it (i.e one coming directly from the starting element and the other forming a possible last link in an alternative path).

(c)   Our experience with the implementation and testing of a canonical synthesis algorithm using realistic databases, suggests that alternative paths are rarely longer than three or four links in length. Also, any redundancies which are implied by long alternative paths would be very time consuming to track down. Therefore, the programmer has a choice to either limit the depth of search to four of five paths, or to report (not delete) redundancies implied by alternative paths over a certain length since imposing limitations on the algorithm is highly undesirable.

(d)   Any implementation of the algorithm must take care not to allow the scanning of a circular path of links 'ad infinitum'. All loops found should be reported once and subsequently avoided by the search routine.

The above considerations relate only to the removal of redundant type '1' links. Redundant type 'M' links can be detected by adopting one of the following two classes of a search technique:

(a)   A restricted search that considers a type 'M' link followed by any number of type '1' links to be a valid alternative to a direct 'M' link. This has the advantage of execution times in line with that of searching for redundant type '1' links, but can miss equivalent paths which are not of this form.

(b)   An unrestricted search that considers paths which contain at least one type 'M' link as a possible alternative form of linking. While this approach can discover all possible alternative paths, it detects, primarily, large numbers of semantically null alternative paths at a cost (i.e processing time).

7.4.7 Isolated and Intersecting Attributes

An isolated attribute is that data element which does not have a type '1' link either leaving or entering it, although it will have 'M' type links to and/or from it. This means that, strictly speaking, an isolated element cannot be classified as a key nor as an attribute. There are three possible ways of dealing with isolated elements:

(a)   Quite often, when the maximum number of repetitions is known or when the DBMS itself allows the definition of repeating groups, then appropriate logical and physical structures can be implemented.

(b)   Rather than deal with variable length records or have a restriction on the number of repetitions, the view can be implemented as a lone key record.

(c)   Finally, an isolated attribute can be considered an error and reported as such.

Regardless of which of the above approaches is adopted, a decision must be made as to whether or not the attribute is to be included in the final design. Ideally, the analyst should be informed (under an online mode) and the choice should be offered to deal with each case on its own merit.

Let us now discuss intersecting attributes and how these can be processed. An intersecting attribute is that element which appears to be identified by more than one key. Usually, this is caused when several keys have been given an identically named attribute which actually means different things. The following diagram illustrates this:

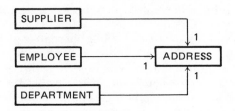

In this case there should have been separately named attributes for the address of each entity (i.e SUPPLIER-ADDRESS, EMPLOYEE-ADDRESS and DEPARTMENT-ADDRESS). The data dictionary is of course a means to control this type of situation and should be used in conjunction with the complete range of routines for canonical synthesis.

There are in fact three possible ways of dealing with such a problem:

(a)   Duplicate versions of the attribute can be created such that each key
       points to its own copy of that attribute. Thus, the previous diagram can be
       transformed into the following:

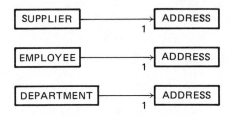

       Here, it is accepted that attribute ADDRESS may belong to several
       entities and so, rather than create a unique attribute for each, the element
       is triplicated. For this particular example there are no complications as a
       result of duplication but in a database which handles multiple addresses
       for a single entity (e.g insurance companies holding multiple addresses for
       each entity) this type of duplication can be dangerous.
(b)   The attribute is assumed to belong to one of the keys and the links to it
       from the other keys are redirected to point to that key. In other words, the
       links are redirected to an owner key. Thus, the new solution appears as
       follows:

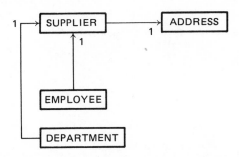

For this solution to be valid all the departments and employees for a particular supplier must be at the same address. Also, all employees and departments must belong to the particular supplier they identify. Such a solution may also create new redundancies as it could alter the structure of the schema. Moreover, the following two major questions must be addressed:

(i)   Which key should be chosen as the owner ? A decision here must be made on some concrete grounds; the analyst can either assign the attribute to that key which requires it the most, or he can choose an arrangement that creates the least structural impact following the re-routing.

(ii) Given that re-routing is bound to cause structural alterations, then is such an effect desirable at all ?

(c)   The element can be treated as a lone key with no attributes as is the case with isolated attributes.

7.5 FURTHER INVESTIGATIONS ON CANONICAL SYNTHESIS

An intelligent canonical synthesis system must give the analyst the option of altering the parameters as and where appropriate. Example 'parameters' here are direct relationships between elements with the same name, the stage(s) at which the routine to remove redundancies is invoked (e.g after the re-routing of links, when an intersecting attribute is detected, etc), the order in which 'identities' are processed, and others.

Ideally, the analyst must interact with the system, checking on its results and groupings in progress, and must also be able to alter certain parameters and therefore derive different schemata. These can then be compared and assessed at a number of levels: global, view, element, associations, etc.

It becomes therefore necessary to implement certain measures which quantify logical equivalence, or otherwise, between different schemata. To this end, two different types of measures can be considered: symmetric and asymmetric similarity measures.

Let 'A' denote the number of matches between schema 1 and schema 2, 'B' the number of occurrences in schema 2 only, 'C' the number of occurrences in schema 1 only. The following measures can then be adopted:

Symmetric Measures

(1) $\dfrac{A}{A + C}$

(2) $\dfrac{A}{A + B}$

Asymmetric Measures

(3) $\dfrac{A}{A + B + C}$

(4) $\dfrac{2A}{2A + B + C}$

(5) $\dfrac{A}{A + 2(B + C)}$

When there is a possibility of one schema being a subset of the other, then symmetric measures are appropriate.

Another important consideration is the 'hierarchic' level at which each element appears. This means that we must match direct and indirect associations between data elements with the same name and level under every root key that has a path going into each of these. In other words, for two data elements to be identical they must both have the same name, be at the same level and have the same associations.

As well as the need to compare generated schemata on the basis of logical equivalence criteria, there is useful information to be obtained by comparing user views against each other. Such a comparison can also differentiate between essential (main) and secondary views.

There is usually substantial redundancy in the user views as information is repeated many times over in various applications (i.e there is a large number of common elements between different views). So, logical comparison of views against each other should allow those views which are complete, or almost complete subsets of others to be ignored or processed differently. The problem is particularly serious where database administrators allow ordinary users to create their own permanent views.

Another aspect of canonical synthesis is the need for each association between elements to have a measure of importance. This would be particularly relevant when dealing with redundant links, intersecting attributes and identities. Weights would enable much more intelligent decisions to be made although their introduction must be balanced against the amount of information that needs to be entered into the design process. Ideally, canonical synthesis should be possible with whatever reasonable information is available, and should only require extra detail for final refinements.

There appear to be two main approaches to entering weights of any sort, whether they are association weights, frequency of access of individual elements/ views, transaction processing details, and others:

(a)   To include additional information along with the specification of the data elements and their relationships.
(b)   To keep additional quantitative information completely separate from that of the data elements and their associations.

Either way, quantitative information can be entered through a separate language that allows the dynamic aspects of a proposed structure to be modelled in the light of different loads put on it and therefore enables intelligent restructuring of the schema.

Taking canonical synthesis to its logical conclusion, an automated database designer will have sufficient information to suggest the following:

(1)   The 'best' access paths to retrieve the desired information.
(2)   Predictions on performance times for any given set of retrievals, provided the average access times of the target DBMS are known.
(3)   Predictions on the effect of the addition of new user views or growth in file sizes on the existing design.
(4)   Possible physical arrangements of the logical groupings generated indicating the critical access paths. However, this type of information can only be considered as part of the preliminary physical database design.

7.6 SUMMARY

An important objective during the database design process is the creation of the logical schema which represents and reflects the organisational requirements and is also extensible without major restructuring. The architecture of the schema must have the necessary structural properties which do not hinder its evolution. A 'minimal' structure which is independent of applications, software and hardware is otherwise referred to as *canonical structure*, in other words, a stable and optimal structure.

In this chapter, we discussed canonical synthesis as an algorithmic approach to data analysis and logical schema design. We also integrated canonical synthesis into the bottom-up design and discussed the level at which it relates to top-down design.

The actual canonical synthesis algorithm we presented investigates three types of associations between data elements:

(a)   Type '1' associations where a given occurrence of the 'from' element identifies one and only one occurrence of the 'to' element.
(b)   Type 'M' associations where a given occurrence of the 'from' element can identify zero, one, or many values of the 'to' element.
(c)   Type '0' (zero) where the association between elements is of no interest to the analyst.

The major steps of the canonical synthesis process deal with the following issues: (a) Merging of the user views, (b) Distinction between keys and ordinary attributes, (c) Concatenated keys, (d) One-to-one (1:1) associations, (e) Many-to-Many (M:M) associations, and (f) Removal of redundancies.

The Appendix of the book contains a complete set of reports produced by the canonical synthesis algorithm we have implemented in the language Pascal. The algorithm has been applied to a hospital database and the reader can see the result of each of the above steps.

7.7 REFERENCES

Albano, A., de Antonellis, V. & di Leva, A., 'Computer Aided Database Design: The DATAID Approach', In: Computer-Aided Database Design - The DATAID Project, Albano A., de Antonellis V. & di Leva A. (eds), North Holland, pp. 1-13, 1985.

Atzeni, P., Batini, P., Carboni, E., de Antonellis, V., Lenzerini, M., Villanelli, F. & Zonta, B., 'INCOD-DTE: A System for Interactive Conceptual Design of Data, Transactions and Events', In: Methodology and Tools for Database Design, Ceri S. (ed), North Holland, pp. 205-288, 1983.

Baldissera, C., Ceri, S., Pelagatti, G. & Bracchi, G., 'Interactive Specification and Formal Verification of User's Views in Database Design', Proc. 5th Int. Conf. on Very Large Databases, pp. 262-272, 1979.

Bernstein, P. A., 'Synthesizing Third Normal Form Relations from Functional Dependencies', ACM TODS, Vol. 1, No. 4, pp. 277-298, 1976.

Biskup, J. & Convent, B., 'A Formal View Integration Method', ACM SIGMOD, Conference on Management of Data, Vol. 15, No. 2, pp. 398-407, 1986.

Bouzeghoub, M. & Valduriez, P., 'New Tools for Logical Database Design', In: Database Design Update, Baker G. J. & Holloway S. (eds), BCS Database Specialist Group Publication, pp. 131-141, 1984.

Elmasri, R. & Navathe, R., 'Object Integration in Logical Database Design', Proc. of the IEEE Conf. on Data Engineering, Los Angeles, pp 426-433, April 1984.

Ganguli, D., 'Information Management Using a Relational Database', In: Database Design Update, Baker G. J. & Holloway S. (eds), BCS Database Specialist Group Publication, pp. 97-130, 1984.

Housel, B. C., Waddle, V. E. & Yao, S. B., 'The Functional Dependency Model for Logical Database Design', Proc. of the 5th Conf. on Very Large Databases, pp. 194-208, 1979.

Hubbard, G. U., 'Techniques for Automated Logical Database Design', Proc. of the New York University Symposium on Database Design, pp. 219-227, May 1978.

Hubbard, G. U., 'Computer-Assisted Database Design', Van Nostrand Reinhold, 1981.

Martin, J., 'Managing the Database Environment', Prentice-Hall, 1983.

Raver, N. & Hubbard, G. U., 'Automated Logical Database Design', IBM Systems Journal, Vol. 16, No. 3, pp. 287-312, October 1977.

Yao, S. B., Waddel, V. E. & Housel, B. C., 'View Modeling and Integration Using the Functional Dependency Model', IEEE Transactions on Software Engineering, Vol. SE-8, No. 6, pp. 544-553, November 1982.

8 RELATIONAL ARCHITECTURE

8.1 INTRODUCTION

In Chapter 3, we introduced the relational model and its peculiar terminology which is based on known mathematical concepts, particularly the theory of matrices. In Chapter 4, we adopted a Relational Database Language (RDL) in order to discuss high level database software - RDL has now been proposed by the International Standards Organisation (ISO) as the industry standard for the design of relational databases. The aim of this chapter is to present the relational architecture [Codd, 1970, 1972] independent of any available software (e.g SEQUEL [Chamberlin et al, 1976], INGRESS [Stonebraker et al, 1976], and RDL [ANSI, 1986]), standards, modules, commands, etc. The emphasis here is on set-theoretic manipulation of relational tables, and also how trees and networks can be represented adequately, within the framework of the relational architecture.

The difficulty with diagrammatic representation of tree and network linkages between records [Bachman, 1969] and the limitations of record-based systems [Kent, 1979] in general, is that they can be very confusing and indeed quite unnecessary in many cases. Take, for example, the case where a relation (RELATION-1) is linked to another (RELATION-2) as shown in Figure 8.1. Because 'Key1' is common to both relations, implying that RELATION-2 can be accessed from RELATION-1, then another link (regardless of whether this is

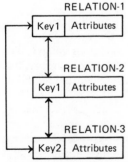

Figure 8.1 An example of 'linked' relations.

logical or physical) from RELATION-1 to RELATION-2 is quite unnecessary. Single-arrow links are particularly vulnerable to redundancy and extra care must be taken when the schema is established.

Generally, a logical link from one relation to another does not need to be physically implemented, provided such a link can be established with the use of existing pointers or keys. The relational approach to database design capitalises on this simple fact and attempts to simplify record relationships by combining *key-attributes* with *data-attributes* to form tuples or records. Each tuple then forms a unique entry in a table. Also, relations that contain only key attributes are eligible.

8.2 DOMAINS AND ATTRIBUTES

It is of the utmost importance that each tuple be identified/isolated uniquely from others in a relational table. Usually, the primary key performs this task, eventhough there may be a number of alternative attributes (i.e non-primary key attributes) within a given table which can also form the basis for unique identification; we know these as 'candidate keys'. Since duplicate tuples are not allowed, then, in the worst case, the combination of all the attributes in a relation can be used for unique identification of tuples. In practice, it is not necessary to involve all the attributes of a relation to identify tuples uniquely.

An alternative way to identify tuples, although not necessarily uniquely, is to use foreign keys (see Section 6.7). It is therefore important for the user that navigates through the relational database by using keys which form the logical access paths, to know whether a key is likely to yield duplicate data or not.

So, the logical linkage (bond) of entities is established through attributes which are common between relations, provided of course the domains of these attributes are equivalent. Although the concept *domain* does not have a physical equivalent, it can be argued that it is ultimately determined by the definition of each attribute.

A basic requirement of the relational model is that each attribute must receive values from a single pre-specified domain of a given type (e.g 'character', 'integer', 'real', etc). For example, the domain: BOOK-NUMBER N(5) is the complete range of integer values between 00000 and 99999. It is therefore important that relational schema declarations include, as a minimum, relations, attributes, domains, as well as keys.

Clearly, the complete ranges of values an attribute may take cannot be determined at the stage of logical schema design since there is always the possibility for a new application to demand a new set of values or ranges. We must, therefore, be prepared to recompile the logical schema when necessary, after we have re-examined the information provided by the conceptual model of the enterprise.

The type of a domain an attribute can use may also vary at the subschema level and conversions should be carried out by the DBMS in an automatic manner. Example conversions are from a decimal number to a binary, from a 30 byte to a 10 byte long character, etc. Also, domain values may be codified appropriately. An example of a coded set of values is presented below where the domain 'Day' is defined as a set of integer numbers 1 to 7 corresponding to the first three letters of each day of the week:

DOMAIN Day N(1) CODED FROM
   (1='MON', 2='TUE', 3='WED', 4='THU',
   5='FRI', 6='SAT, 7='SUN')

In this example, the statement CODED FROM defines a set of allowable values by compressing data, but can equally be used to expand data, as is the case with the following example:

DOMAIN Month A(3) CODED FROM
   ('JAN'=1, 'FEB'=2, 'MAR'=3, ...)

where the numbers 1 to 12 are translated to the first three letters of the months of the year.

Let us now see how domains are employed to define relational schemata using the example of Figure 8.2. This presents a number of declarations written in a pseudo-DDL for a library schema with the following notation:

N(n)   :   A numeric string of n digits long
A(n)   :   An alphabetic string of n letters long, including space
X(n)   :   A character string of n bytes long, including letters, numbers,
          symbols, etc
:   A key attribute
/   :   A continuation line

The schema in Figure 8.2 presents the definition of each domain/range, independent of the relations BOOK, SUBJECT, READER, BORROWER, and PUBLISHER. After the domains have been defined, the constituent parts (attributes) of each relation are specified including those domains which become key attributes. The primary key of each relation is as follows:

Relation	Primary key
BOOK	Book-no#
SUBJECT	Subject-no#
READER	Reader-no#
BORROWER	Book-no#, Reader-no#
PUBLISHER	Publisher-no#

The relation BORROWER requires a combination of keys (Book-no#, Reader-no#) for unique identification of tuples because if the attribute Book-no# is not included, then duplicate tuples may occur when the same reader takes out a number of books on the same date.

```
SCHEMA      NAME IS Library
DOMAIN      Book-no                      N(10)
DOMAIN      Author                       A(20)
DOMAIN      Title                        X(100)
DOMAIN      Publisher-name               X(40)
DOMAIN      Year                         N(4)
DOMAIN      Edition                      N(2)
DOMAIN      Subject-no                   N(20)
DOMAIN      Subject-description          X(100)
DOMAIN      Location                     X(30)
DOMAIN      Reader-no                    N(10)
DOMAIN      Reader-name                  A(20)
DOMAIN      Reader-address               X(100)
DOMAIN      Publisher-no                 N(10)
DOMAIN      Sex                          A(1)
            / CODED FROM (M='Male', F='Female')
DOMAIN      Status                       N(1)
            / CODED FROM (1='Undergraduate', 2='Post-graduate',
            /                3='Lecturer', 4='Professor',
            /                5='Technician', 6='Administrator')
DOMAIN      Date                         N(6)
RELATION    BOOK (Book-no#, Author, Title, Publisher-no#,
            /      Year, Edition, Subject-no#)
RELATION    SUBJECT (Subject-no#, Subject-description, Location)
RELATION    READER (Reader-no#, Reader-name, Reader-address,
            /        Sex, Status)
RELATION    BORROWER (Book-no#, Reader-no#, Date)
RELATION    PUBLISHER (Publisher-no#, Publisher-name, Location)
END
```

Figure 8.2.   An example of a relational schema.

8.3 MANIPULATION OF RELATIONAL TABLES

In many organisations, it is after a DBMS has been installed that the user community (including managers, analysts and programmers) start to improvise and explore other functions which can be implemented under the umbrella of database software. The successful implementation of an application usually leads and directs another. This is part of the transitional stage which builds up the confidence of all the staff involved.

The step-wise refinement and step-wise integration of user views has received much appraisal by the user community and this fact cannot be overlooked by the designers or vendors of the DBMS. Product demand, supply, marketing, economics and general trends may well affect the stability of an organisation, its expansion or contraction. It is, therefore, rather difficult to predict precisely what will be the future needs and requirements of users.

New relations, new attributes, new procedures, or new hardware may become necessary, and expansion in one form or another is bound to be considered by the management of a 'healthy' organisation. The logical schema should thus be expanded or contracted dynamically, in order to reflect these changes. It is therefore important that any existing software is not altered or at least not altered substantially.

Clearly, the DBMS must provide a number of utilities (commands) which manipulate relations and their corresponding tables [Hall, 1984]. Considering the linear structure of the relations themselves and the tabular form of the corresponding tables, it becomes possible to introduce traditional set-theoretic and relational algebra concepts [Merrett, 1978] in order to enable the formal specification of manipulative operations (e.g union, intersection, difference etc) [Hitchcock, 1974].

Some of these set-theoretic operations expect the relations involved to be compatible before they can be manipulated. The relations and their corresponding tables are said to be *compatible* when they fulfil both of the following:

(a)   They have the same degree, that is, the same number of attributes;
(b)   Their corresponding attributes are defined on the same or equivalent domains.

It is of course possible to have relations which contain different attribute names and yet are fully compatible. Take for example the following two compatible relations, DEPARTMENT and DIVISION, used in two different applications, 'Finance' and 'Planning' respectively:

DEPARTMENT (Dept-code#, Description, Location)
SECTION (Code#, Description, Location)

where the attributes 'Dept-code#' and 'Code#' are based on the same domains; the differing names simply match the requirements of the individual applications.

In many cases, it becomes necessary to split a table into two or more sections for reasons of efficiency at the physical level of data manipulation. For example, if certain columns of a table are more frequently referenced than others, then it makes sense to arrange the data structures in such a way as to allow fast access to these columns (e.g through direct physical links, indexes etc) skipping the rest all together.

A table, in the present context, is defined as a set of tuples each of which conforms with the specification of a relation; a tuple may be rightly considered synonymous to a record for our purposes here. A number of operations can thus be performed on the tuples in a 'vertical' or 'horizontal' manner, resulting in a new table which contains only those tuples and columns that have been selected from the source tables. The parameters of the operations which carry out the searches will of course include user defined values as search identifiers. To understand the operations we present in the following sections, we assume that the tables are scanned in a top-down manner until the end of a table is reached.

The operations we discuss, using pseudo-commands, are: union, intersection, difference, selection, projection, join, and division [Codd, 1972]. Throughout the discussion of these operations, attribute names are denoted by the letters 'At' followed by a number and all table values are denoted by the letter 'V' followed by a number.

8.3.1 Union

Two or more compatible tables can unite to form a new table where all unique tuples are put together. The operation can thus be used to insert a new tuple within a table by supplying a second table of cardinality one.

Let two tables from relations R1 and R2 be as follows:

R1

At1	At2	At3
V10	V20	V30
V11	V21	V31
V12	V21	V31
V13	V22	V32

R2

At1	At2	At3
V10	V20	V30
V12	V21	V31
V13	V22	V33

The statement:

UNION: R3 = R1 ∪ R2

produces the following table:

R3

At1	At2	At3
V10	V20	V30
V11	V21	V31
V12	V21	V31
V13	V22	V32
V13	V22	V33

8.3.2 Intersection

Two or more compatible tables can intersect to form a new table which contains tuples common to all the tables involved. The end result is therefore a new table containing all overlapping tuples.

We must be very careful here to distinguish between intersecting relations and intersecting tables. In the case of intersecting relations, we imply that relations are linked together by means of keys - as we have already described under the network model (see Chapter 3) - where a many-to-many (M:M) relationship is split into two one-to-many (1:M) relationships which in turn, necessitate the creation of a new 'intersecting relation'. The INTERSECTION operation we discuss here deals with the intersection of tables in terms of set-theoretic operations upon the tuples themselves. For example, if we use the same tables from R1 and R2, then the statement:

INTERSECTION: R3 = R1 ∩ R2

produces the following table:

R3	At1	At2	At3
	V10	V20	V30
	V12	V21	V31

8.3.3 Difference

The difference between two compatible tables R1 and R2 (in that order) will be that set of tuples which belong to R1 but not to R2. For example, if we use the same tables as before, then the statement:

DIFFERENCE: R3 = R1 - R2

produces the following table:

R3	At1	At2	At3
	V11	V21	V31
	V13	V22	V32

However, the difference R2 - R1 and therefore the statement:

DIFFERENCE: R3 = R2 - R1

produces the following table:

R3	At1	At2	At3
	V13	V22	V33

Clearly, this operation can be used to delete one or more tuples from a table.

8.3.4 Selection

This operation enables the retrieval of selected rows and/or columns from a given table on the basis of logical conditional selection operators such as 'equal', 'greater-than', 'and', 'or'. The end result is a table with cardinality n (n<=m where m is the cardinality of the original table). For example, given a table from relation R4, a selection request can state: 'select all those tuples which have a value 'V1' under attribute At2'. Let relation R4 form the following table:

R4	At1	At2	At3
	V11	V1	V31
	V12	V1	V31
	V12	V2	V32
	V13	V1	V33
	V14	V3	V34

The statement:

SELECTION: R3 FROM R4(At2) = 'V1'

produces the following table:

R2	At1	At2	At3
	V11	V1	V31
	V12	V1	V31
	V13	V1	V33

The statement:

SELECTION: R3 FROM R4(At1) = 'V12'
                    AND (R4(At3) = 'V31' OR R4(At3) = 'V32')

produces the following table:

R3	At1	At2	At3
	V12	V1	V31
	V12	V2	V32

The resultant table contains all the attributes of the original table R4; when an attribute is not specified within the SELECTION statement, then any values it may contain are acceptable. Finally, as we have already seen in Chapter 4, the selection statement can search two or more tables in order to derive another.

8.3.5 Projection

This operation enables us to construct a new table by extracting complete columns under specific attributes regardless of their values. In other words, the projection operation partitions a table in a vertical manner. Let us use the same table (R4) we used to illustrate the selection operation. The statement:

PROJECT: R3 FROM R4(At3)

produces the following table:

R3	At3
	V31
	V31
	V32
	V33
	V34

When the column(s) projected is not the primary key, then we may have duplicate tuples in the resultant table. It is therefore desirable to have a facility to suppress the selection of duplicate tuples, as for example, the statement:

PROJECTION: R3 FROM R4(At3) DUPLICATES NOT ALLOWED

which produces the following table with unique tuples:

R3	At3
	V31
	V32
	V33
	V34

The table produced by the projection operation can then be reordered and subsequently processed as required. Also, the table may have the attributes in a different order. For example, the statement:

PROJECTION: R3 = R4(At3, At2)

produces the table:

R3	At3	At2
	V31	V1
	V31	V1
	V32	V2
	V33	V1
	V34	V3

8.3.6 Join

This operation selects tuples from different tables, using standard operators such as 'equal', 'greater-than', 'less-than', etc, and proceeds to concatenate these to form a new table. The operators, otherwise referred to as *theta* operators, are applied to specific attributes (usually keys) which share a common domain (i.e they are compatible). So, we refer to each type of theta join as 'equijoin', 'greater-than-join', 'less-than-join', etc.

Depending on which attributes are actually selected for inclusion in the resultant table, the join operation can be classed as 'natural join' (when the resultant table does not contain identical attributes), or 'semijoin' (when the resultant table contains tuples only from one of the tables used).

Let two relations R1 and R2 form the following tables where the attributes AT4 and AT6 are to be used for an equijoin:

	At1	At2	At3	At4	At5
R1	V11	V21	V31	V41	V51
(1)	V12	V22	V32	V42	V52
(2)	V13	V23	V31	V43	V53
(3)	V14	V23	V31	V43	V53
	V15	V24	V33	V44	V54
	V15	V25	V34	V45	V55

	At6	At7	At8
R2			
(2) (3)	V43	V31	V80
(1)	V42	V32	V81
	V60	V70	V82
	V61	V71	V82

The statement:

JOIN: R3 FROM R1(At4) = R2(At6)

produces the following table:

	At1	At2	At3	At4	At5	At6	At7	At8
R3								
(1)	V12	V22	V32	V42	V52	V42	V32	V81
(2)	V13	V23	V31	V43	V53	V43	V31	V80
(3)	V14	V23	V31	V43	V53	V43	V31	V80

In the above tables, the numbers in brackets indicate the tuples which were selected successfully because they satisfied the criterion:

R1(At4) = R2(At6)

We must emphasise here that when attributes are used as the basis of joining tables together, then it makes sense to ensure, where possible, that they are homogeneous. For example, the attributes concerned can be examined to establish whether they are of the same type (domain) or not, since it is illogical to attempt to join two tables through two incompatible attributes; for example, one numeric and one alphabetic. We would of course expect the DML software to point out any inconsistencies during compilation or run-time.

8.3.7 Division

The simplest form of the division operation involves a binary relation (a relation with two attributes) used as the dividend, and a unary relation (a relation with one attribute) used as the divisor. Let the attributes be At1, At2 and At3, where R1(At1, At2) and R2(At3). Also, let At2 be the attribute in R1 which may contain values also found in At3. The new relation R3 (derived from a division) will contain attribute At1 and all those tuples (duplicates not allowed) which have all the values entered under At3. Let two tables R1 and R2 contain the following tuples:

R1	At1	At2
	V11	V21
	V12	V31
	V12	V32
	V12	V33
	V15	V22
	V16	V23
	V17	V32
	V17	V33
	V17	V31

R2	At3
	V31
	V32
	V33

The statement:

DIVISION: R3(At1) = R1(At2) / R2(At3)

produces the following table:

R3	At1
	V12
	V17

8.4 SUBSCHEMA DEFINITIONS

Within an organisation, it is frequently necessary to view the same portion of the logical schema in different ways, perhaps as many as there are applications and therefore subschemata. For example, if a relation contains four attributes, then in one application it may be necessary to use all four of them, and in another only the first two. Similarly, an application may rename one or more attributes (i.e change the names that appear in the logical schema) without affecting other applications that may already use the same attributes. Moreover, the resulting table itself may be processed differently from application to application or from session to session. These manipulative functions should be carried out with the aid of appropriate DBMS commands.

We must stress here that, although re-definitions of existing schema attributes and structures are eligible at the subschema, the definition of completely new attributes, relations, etc, should not be permissible. That is, the schema should contain enough attributes, relations, domains, etc, so as to satisfy each and every application in an organisation.

In certain applications, it will appear as though the introduction of a new attribute or relation is unavoidable, but the user community must resist this or else it will have to ensure, beyond any doubt, that no redundancy will be introduced within the schema or any of the existing subschemata. An efficient method of ensuring that redundancy is kept to a minimum (if not eliminated altogether) is to maintain an up to date data dictionary through a powerful Data Dictionary Processor (DDP) which allows sophisticated interrogation and cross-referrencing of the various attributes in isolation or in clusters (i.e relations, subschemata, etc).

If the attribute names within the derived relations are important, or new names are indeed desirable, then it should be possible to define these within each of the operations of UNION, INTERSECTION, DIFFERENCE, SELECTION, PROJECTION, JOIN and DIVISION. Example statements that introduce new attribute names within a derived table (R3) are presented below:

UNION: R3(At1newname, At2newname, At3newname) = R1 $\cup$ R2
INTERSECTION: R3(At1newname, At2newname, At3newname) = R1 $\cap$ R2
DIFFERENCE: R3(At1newname, At2newname, At3newname) = R1 - R2

Although the order of the attributes within relations is not significant, when each relation is declared in the schema, the attributes are usually defined one after the other. We can therefore assume that when a relation is being manipulated and the order of the attributes is not specified, then these will appear in the order they have been declared in the first place.

Thus, if we wish to alter the names of the attributes and/or their order selectively, then we can introduce a delimiter, say, the symbol '%' followed by a number which signifies their order within the derived relation. For example, the statement:

UNION: R3(Atr1newname, %1, Atr3newname) = R1 $\cup$ R2

will create a new table (R3) with three attributes, two of which bear new names and one remains the same as that used within the first of the two relations that are united. Let us look at another example of two relations: R20(At1, At2, At3, At4) and R30(At11, At22, At3, At44). The statement:

INTERSECTION: R3(%2, %1, Atr3newname, %2) = R20 $\cap$ R30

creates the relation:

R3(At11,At2, Atr3newname, At44)

Generally, if the resultant relation introduces new attributes from existing ones, then we will expect the DBMS to insert the former automatically in the schema or data dictionary, and to define their domains from the corresponding domains of the original attributes. Of course, if the relation is to become permanent, then the DBA will have to authorise the updating of the associated meta-files. It all depends on the complexity of the organisation as a whole, and the communication set-up between programmers, analysts and management.

8.5 REPRESENTING TREES

Although, at first sight, the relational form of a table does not seem to be capable of representing trees and networks, it does in fact handle these structures in a very simple and indirect manner. The relational model offers a dynamic environment whereby these structures can be set up from one process to another, without restricting the user to the pre-defined schema declarations, as is the case with the CODASYL approach which is discussed in Chapter 9.

Let us see how a relational table can accommodate a tree structure. Let the relation BOOK of a library schema contain the following attributes:

BOOK (Book-no#, Title, Subtitle, Author, Publisher, Date)

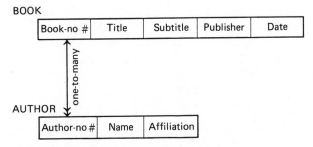

Figure 8.3   An example relational-like tree.

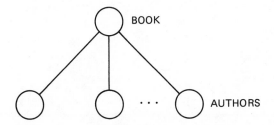

Figure 8.4   The corresponding tree of Figure 8.3.

The general case will of course involve one or more repeating groups which are not allowed in the relational architecture. Let the repeating group here be with attribute 'Author' corresponding to 'Author-no#', 'Name' and 'Affiliation', when we have two or more co-authors of a book; the diagrammatic representation of this indicates a one-to-many link as presented in Figure 8.3. This structure is of course a tree, the general representation of which is presented in Figure 8.4. Figure 8.3 shows two relations which can now be re-written as follows, eliminating the need for a one-to-many link:

BOOK (Book-no#, Title, Subtitle, Publisher, Date)
AUTHOR (Book-no#, Author-no#, Name, Affiliation)

Attribute 'Book-no#' is repeated within relation R2 in order to establish unique identification in conjunction with attribute 'Author-no#' for all the tuples of the corresponding table. In further analysis of the above relations we establish that BOOK has Book-no# as primary key and the relation is normalised. However, relation AUTHOR violates second normal form because the attributes 'Name' and 'Affiliation' are functionally dependent on 'Author-no#', that is, a subset of the primary key 'Book-no#, Author-no#'. This anomaly is resolved by re-defining the relations as follows:

BOOK (Book-no#, Title, Subtitle, Publisher, Date)
AUTHOR (Author-no#, Name, Affiliation)
BOOK-AUTHOR (Book-no#, Author-no#)

where BOOK-AUTHOR forms the intersection relation of BOOK and AUTHOR.

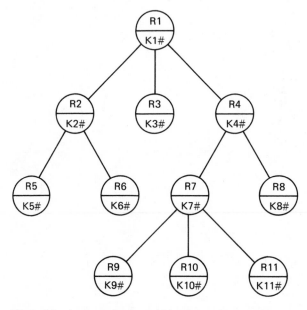

Figure 8.5   An example of a multi-level tree with 11 relations.

For the general case of relational representation of trees, the primary key of the 'parent' relation must be included within the 'child' relation in order to identify all tuples uniquely. Let R1, R2,...,R11 be the relations and K1#, K2#,...,K11# be their corresponding primary keys as shown in Figure 8.5. Also, assume that each relation contains a number of data attributes from the set ATTOTAL1, ATTOTAL2,...,ATTOTAL11. The relational definition of this environment is as follows:

R1 (K1#, ATTOTAL1)
R2 (K1#, K2#, ATTOTAL2)
R3 (K1#, K3#, ATTOTAL3)
R4 (K1#, K4#, ATTOTAL4)
R5 (K1#, K2#, K5#, ATTOTAL5)
R6 (K1#, K2#, K6#, ATTOTAL6)
R7 (K1#, K4#, K7#, ATTOTAL7)
R8 (K1#, K4#, K8#, ATTOTAL8)
R9 (K1#, K4#, K7#, K9#, ATTOTAL9)
R10(K1#, K4#, K7#, K10#, ATTOTAL10)
R11(K1#, K4#, K7#, K11#, ATTOTAL11)

Clearly, a number of attributes and associated values appear duplicated in the above relations, introducing a certain degree of redundancy. However, this redundancy may not exist at the physical level but only be part of the external view of the programmer or user, since efficient physical structures can reduce duplication substantially. Besides, in practical data processing applications the number of key attributes is much less than the number of data attributes.

8.5.1 From Table to Tree

It is as easy to establish relations from trees as to create trees from relational tables. We can, therefore, talk of definition trees and occurrence trees. Consider the relations SCHOOL, TECHNICAL-STAFF and their linking type SCHOOL-TECHNICAL as shown in Figure 8.6. Let their corresponding tables be as follows:

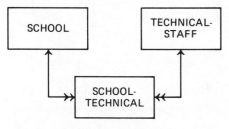

Figure 8.6   Two relations and their intersection.

SCHOOL

Name	Details · · ·
Astronomy	· · ·
Biotechnology	· · ·
Computing	· · ·

TECHNICAL-STAFF

Name	Details · · ·
Albert	· · ·
Charles	· · ·
Emmanuel	· · ·
John	· · ·

SCHOOL-TECHNICAL

School-name	Staff
Astronomy	Albert
Astronomy	Charles
Astronomy	John
Biotechnology	Albert
Biotechnology	Charles
Biotechnology	Emmanuel
Computing	Charles

We can now proceed to create trees from these tables by using 'School-name' as the most binding attribute (see Figure 8.7) or by using 'Staff' as the most binding attribute (see Figure 8.8). The concept *binding attribute* is, in many cases, closely related to the concept of primary or identifying key.

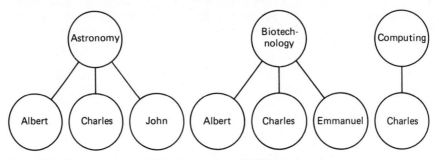

Figure 8.7   Occurrence trees with binding attribute 'SCHOOL-Name'.

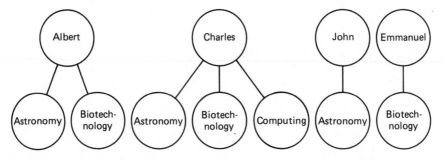

Figure 8.8   Occurrence trees with binding attribute 'TECHNICAL-STAFF-Name'.

Let us study another example with the following table called CATALOGUE, disregarding the primary key:

CATALOGUE

Author	Title	Publisher	Date	Edition
Knuth	The art of computing: Vol I	Addison	1968	1
Knuth	The art of computing: Vol I	Addison	1970	2
Knuth	The art of computing: Vol II	Addison	1972	1
Knuth	The art of computing: Vol II	Addison	1975	2

If we accept the binding order:

Author--> Publisher--> Title--> Date--> Edition

then, the above table accommodates the tree presented in Figure 8.9. However, if we accept the binding order:

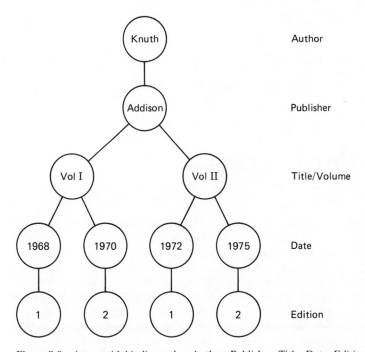

Figure 8.9   A tree with binding order: Author, Publisher, Title, Date, Edition.

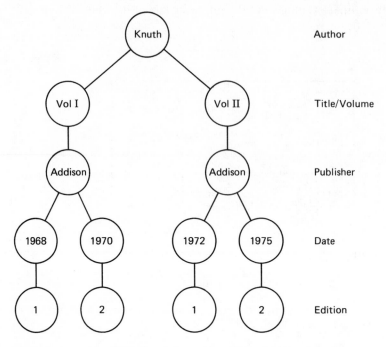

Figure 8.10   A tree with binding order: Author, Title, Publisher, Date, Edition.

Author--> Title--> Publisher--> Date--> Edition

then an alternative tree is created as shown in Figure 8.10.

8.6 REPRESENTING NETWORKS

The general form of a network contains many-to-many relationships which can of course be transformed into a series of tree structures. Let us discuss an example network as shown in Figure 8.11, where a publisher employs many authors and where an author may work for a number of different publishers. This can be decomposed into three relations, namely, PUBLISHER, AUTHOR and PUB-AUTH as shown in Figure 8.12, where the new relation PUB-AUTH forms the link between the two, and, at the same time, eliminates redundancy by allowing common information to be shared by both relations. This common information can, for example, be three books published by publisher A, written by the same author X, who has also written two books for publisher B.

Figure 8.11   A two-relation network.

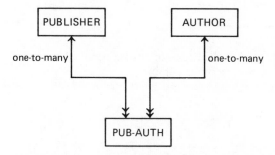

Figure 8.12   The composition of the network in Figure 8.11 into two one-to-many relationships.

Let us look at an example table with two publishers and another with four authors as follows:

PUBLISHER

Publisher-code#	Publisher-name	Publisher-location
500	Addison	London
600	Wiley	New York

AUTHOR

Author-code#	Author-name	Affiliation	Date-of-birth
F100	Feller W	Princeton Univ.	1940
K120	Knuth D	Stanford Univ.	1945
R400	Rao S	Kanpur Institute	1938
W050	Wirth N	ETH Zurich	1942

The primary key of PUBLISHER is 'Publisher-code#' and the primary key of AUTHOR is 'Author-code#'.

We are now in a position to associate publishers with authors through a linking relation, say, AUTHOR-PUBLISHER which contains two key attributes: the primary key of AUTHOR, and the primary key of PUBLISHER. The following table implies that, the authors K120 and W050 have written books for publisher 500, the authors F100 and R400 have written books for publisher 600, and author W050 has also written a book for publisher 600:

AUTHOR-PUBLISHER

Publisher-code#	Author-code#
500	K120
500	W050
600	F100
600	R400
600	W050

Both relations PUBLISHER and AUTHOR can of course be combined into one but the amount of duplication could be unacceptable.

8.7 SUMMARY

The tabular form of relational tables coupled by the strict definition of relations, enables the formal specification of manipulative operations, within the framework of the relational architecture. In this chapter, we introduced the basic characteristics of relational tables (including keys, domains and ranges), and proceeded to discuss the operations: UNION, INTERSECTION, DIFFERENCE, SELECTION, PROJECTION, JOIN, and DIVISION. These were discussed independent of any DBMS software or standard, using high-level pseudo-commands and example parameters.

Before we apply some of the above operations, it becomes necessary to ensure that the tables under manipulation are compatible. Two tables are said to be compatible when they fulfil both of the following:

(a)   They have the same number of attributes (columns)
(b)   The domains of the attributes are equivalent.

The operations UNION, INTERSECTION and DIFFERENCE, can only be applied to compatible tables.

Although the relational approach to database design does not enable the explicit definition of trees and networks, these structures can occur by implicit definition of intersecting relations and appropriate tuples. We presented practical examples, based on library information systems, illustrating clearly how trees and networks can occur naturally.

8.8 REFERENCES

ANSI, X3H2 Technical Committee on Databases, 'Relational Database Language', 1986.

Bachman, C. W., 'Data Structure Diagrams', Database, Vol 1, No. 2, pp. 4-10, 1969.

Chamberlin, D. D., et al., 'SEQUEL 2: A Unified Approach to Data Definition, Manipulation, and Control', IBM J. Research and Development, Vol. 20, No. 6, pp. 560-575, 1976.

Codd, E. F., 'A Relational Model of Data for Large Shared Databases', CACM, Vol. 13, No. 6. pp. 377-387, 1970.

Codd, E. F., 'Relational Completeness of Database Sublanguages', In: Database systems, Rustin R. (editor), Prentice-Hall, pp. 33-64, 1972.

Hall, P. A. V., 'Relational Algebras, Logic, and Functional Programming', Proc. ACM SIGMOD Conf. on Management of Data, June 1984.

Hall, P. A. V., Hitchcock, P. & Todd, S. J. P., 'An Algebra of Relations for Machine Computation', Conference Record, 2nd ACM Symposium on Principles of Programming Languages, 1975.

Hitchcock, P., 'Fundamental Operations on Relations', IMB UKSC-0051, May 1974.

Kent, W., 'Limitations of Record-based Information Models', ACM TODS, Vol. 4, No. 1, pp. 107-131, 1979.

Merrett, T. H., 'The Extended Relational Algebra: A Basis for Query Languages', In: Databases: Improving Usability and Responsiveness, Shneiderman B. (editor), Academic Press, 1978.

Stonebraker, M., Wong, E., Kreps, P. & Held, G., 'The Design and Implementation of INGRESS', ACM TODS, Vol. 1, No. 3, pp. 189-222, 1976.

9 A NETWORK DATABASE LANGUAGE

9.1 INTRODUCTION

In Chapter 3, we discussed three major data models whereby the relationships of the data elements within an organisation can be captured and represented effectively. These are the hierarchic, the network, and the relational models. DBMSs today are often classified according to the type of data model which can be defined using a Data Definition Language (DDL) and then processed by an appropriate Data Manipulation Language (DML).

Data models bind data elements together in order to reflect the real-world objects and the way these are interrelated. Historically, a data element has always been defined in terms of a named record type that contains a number of data items, each associated with a specific data type (e.g integer, real, character, etc). Thus, all the data items of an organisation are grouped into named multiple record types.

Let us use an example to illustrate a named group that represents a record type called 'Product' with five data items: 'Product-code' of type NUMERIC (4 decimal digits); 'Description' of type CHARACTER or string (20 bytes); 'Colour' of type CHARACTER (8 bytes); 'Weight' of type REAL (i.e an approximate numerical value with a precision that is defined by the implementor of the DMBS); 'Price' of type REAL. The following are typical Network Database Language (NDL) statements that may appear within a schema DDL to define record type 'Product':

```
RECORD Product
    UNIQUE Product-code
    ITEM Product-code      NUMERIC 4
    ITEM Description       CHARACTER 20
    ITEM Colour            CHARACTER 8
    ITEM Weight            REAL
    ITEM Price             REAL
```

The UNIQUE statement defines the database key (i.e the primary key) of a record type informing the DBMS that the values of the named data item (e.g Product-code) must be unique. In other words, duplicate values are not allowed and these will be detected automatically by the DBMS during the manipulation of record occurrences.

Now, a multi-type data model consists of multiple, related record types offering greater flexibility than a single-type data model, and therefore enabling greater precision in modelling the organisation and its real-world objects. Here, each record type, such as the one presented above, is also assumed to have an independent existence.

Both the relational model, exemplified by the Relational Database Language (RDL) we discussed in Chapter 4, and the CODASYL (Conference On DAta SYstems Languages) proposal [Taylor & Frank, 1976; CODASYL, 1978; ANSI, 1986], are multi-type data models. Although the CODASYL committee proposed a COBOL-like syntax (over fifteen years ago) for defining and manipulating databases, rather than a data model as such, it is often referred to as the 'CODASYL model' because it has formed the basis for the implementation of many simple network DBMSs. It has also formed the basis for most of the database concepts and terminology, including schema, subschema, and data manipulation languages.

In the hierarchic data model, a dependent record type is assumed to have no independent existence apart from its parent record type (i.e the record type above it). For example, a job-history-details record type could not exist in the database without being a dependant of a personal-details record type. If we wish to have an occurrence of a job-history-details record type, then we will be forced to create a 'dummy' occurrence of the personal-details record type. If we wish to delete an occurrence of job-history-details, then we must also delete the corresponding occurrence of personal-details, and vice versa.

We have singled out for discussion two different approaches to database architecture, the relational and the network, because they are frequently debated and compared [Sibley, 1976]. There have been attempts to interface heterogeneous database structures [Spaccapietra et al, 1982] and to adopt a common vehicle (e.g PROLOG) for efficient access to both network and relational databases [Gray, 1985] although the industrial user community appears to be in favour of a single model at a time. In this chapter, we are going to discuss the network architecture using the well established CODASYL system and appropriate Network Database Language (NDL) commands. (An example of an alternative network specification data language has been presented by Deheneffe and Hennebert [Deheneffe & Hennebert, 1976].)

The CODASYL proposal is basically a simple network model where each record type may be used to define a series of inter-connected hierarchical data structures. Also, multi-path hierarchical structures may be created at the intra-record level by defining data aggregates with the OCCURS clause (as is the case with the COBOL programming language). The CODASYL committee was in fact formed originally in order to investigate possible extensions to COBOL so that it could support multiple record type or database oriented data processing.

The database committee of the American National Standards Institute (ANSI) has proposed a revision of the CODASYL specifications giving particular attention to a schema, subschema and data manipulation languages [ANSI, 1986] (these are discussed later). Before we describe the network architecture using example commands from the ANSI proposal, we define the following data types which can be used to specify the domain of each data item [Yannakoudakis & Cheng, 1987]:

CHARACTER n: Where n specifies the maximum number of bytes to be used.

INTEGER: For signed or unsigned integer values with a precision defined by the implementor of the DBMS. The precision usually depends on the word-length of the computer in use.

FIXED n m: For exact numeric values with a given precision (greater than or equal to n unsigned where n > 0), and scale (equal to m signed).

NUMERIC n m: For exact numeric values with a given precision (equal to n unsigned), and scale (equal to m signed).

FLOAT n: For approximate numeric values with precision greater than or equal to n unsigned.

REAL: For approximate numeric values with a precision defined by the implementor of the DBMS. As is the case with type INTEGER, the precision here depends on the word-length of the computer in use.

DOUBLE PRECISION: For approximate numeric values that are greater than or equal to the precision of type REAL.

In many applications, it is useful to have a facility to specify a default value for a data item. To this end, the DEFAULT clause in NDL can be used after the specification of a data item (i.e its name, data type, and whether it is subscripted or not). For example, to distinguish between values under data item 'Weight' that signify a weight of, say, zero kilos and values that have not yet been determined, we can specify a default value of -1 as follows:

ITEM Weight REAL DEFAULT -1

The default value of type CHARACTER can be specified with a string in double quotes (" "). For example, to specify a default value as 'unknown' for data item 'Address' we can write:

ITEM Address CHARACTER 60 DEFAULT "unknown"

Finally, the notation we adopt in this chapter to illustrate the network database commands is as follows:

(a)   Square brackets ([]) indicate optional elements.
(b)   Braces ({ }) indicate a list of elements, entries, subentries, etc.
(c)   Three full stops (...) immediately after a list of elements or a single
        element indicate that this can be repeated one or more times.
(d)   A vertical line (|) can be read as OR and separates alternative elements in
        a list.

9.2 LOGICAL RELATIONSHIPS AND SET TYPES

As we discussed in Chapter 3, the relational model establishes all the relationships implicitly through attributes which are common between relations or files, provided of course the common attributes are defined on common (equivalent) domains. In other words, a *foreign key* binds record types together and through it, both hierarchic and network structures can be derived from the corresponding relational tables (see Chapter 8). A foreign key is an ordinary data item in a record type but an identifier (i.e a key) in another.

The CODASYL approach, on the other hand, utilises the concept *set* to define inter-record relationships which are all strictly one-to-many. Each set type is named and must have one record type declared as its *owner* and one or more record types declared as its *member* record types. Each occurrence of a set is expected to contain one occurrence under the owner record type and zero, one, or more occurrences under each of its member record types. When an occurrence under any record type is stored (e.g connected or inserted) in the database, it belongs to at most one set occurrence of each set type in which it is a member record type.

There are three different categories of sets:

(a)   Singular sets where the owner record type is a special 'imaginary' record type, the SYSTEM. The SYSTEM record type has no components (i.e data items) and is not subject to any integrity constraints. The main purpose of a singular set type is to arrange all the record occurrences within the set into sorted sequence for efficient processing.

(b)   Recursive sets where the same record type is both an owner and a member record type. This category allows the clustering of record occurrences, logically, at the intra-file level.

(c)   Ordinary sets where two or more ordinary record types are involved in the definition of a set type.

(a) A singular set

```
SET ADDR-SORT
   OWNER SYSTEM
   ORDER SORTED
   MEMBER ADDRESS
      KEY ASCENDING POSTAL-CODE
```

(b) A recursive set

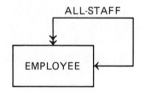

```
SET ALL-STAFF
   OWNER EMPLOYEE
   ORDER · · ·
   MEMBER EMPLOYEE
      KEY · · ·
```

Figure 9.1   Example set types.

(c) An ordinary set (two record types)

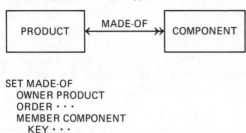

SET MADE-OF
   OWNER PRODUCT
   ORDER · · ·
   MEMBER COMPONENT
      KEY · · ·

(d) An ordinary set (three record types)

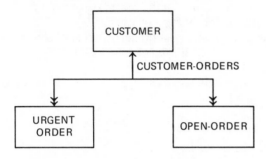

SET CUSTOMER-ORDERS
   OWNER CUSTOMER
   ORDER · · ·
   MEMBER URGENT-ORDER
      KEY · · ·
   MEMBER OPEN-ORDER
      KEY · · ·

Figure 9.1   (continued).

Let us discuss some example set types using appropriate record types. Figure 9.1(a) shows a set type called ADDR-SORT which maintains a list of addresses sorted in ascending order of postal code. This is a singular set with a single member record type (i.e ADDRESS). The clauses SET, OWNER, ORDER, MEMBER, and KEY define a set type.

Figure 9.1(b) shows a recursive set type called ALL-STAFF which maintains a list of all the employees of an organisation. This type of relationship groups employees together when several employees form departments of the same organisation. An appropriate data item within record type EMPLOYEE can of course be used to codify the departments and process these further. For example, data item DEPARTMENT may contain the value 'FI' for Finance, 'CO' for Computing, 'QU' for Quality Control, etc. It becomes then the responsibility of the user or programmer to isolate and process individual departments.

Figure 9.1(c) shows an ordinary set type called MADE-OF where record type PRODUCT is the owner and record type COMPONENT is the only member.

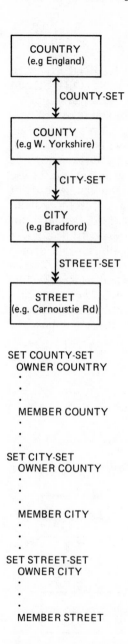

SET COUNTY-SET
 OWNER COUNTRY
 .
 .
 .
 MEMBER COUNTY
 .
 .
 .
SET CITY-SET
 OWNER COUNTY
 .
 .
 .
 MEMBER CITY
 .
 .
 .
SET STREET-SET
 OWNER CITY
 .
 .
 .
 MEMBER STREET

Figure 9.2   A multi-level hierarchy.

This relationship enables an organisation to access quickly all the constituent parts (components) of any product they deal with. It also forms a 'natural' and logical bond between the two entities (i.e product and component).

Figure 9.1(d) shows an ordinary set type called CUSTOMER-ORDERS where record type CUSTOMER is the owner and record types URGENT- ORDER and OPEN-ORDER are the members. This structure enables an organisation to separate the orders which are urgent, from the rest, while retaining record type CUSTOMER as the owner of both and therefore allowing customers to issue urgent orders (e.g with a deadline) and ordinary orders (e.g without a deadline).

Figures 9.1(c) and 9.1(d) present single-level hierarchies between two and three record types (Figures 9.1(a) and 9.1(b) are of course special cases). Let us use another example with a multi-level hierarchy as depicted in Figure 9.2 where, for each occurrence of record type COUNTRY, there are as many occurrences under record type COUNTY as there are counties in the country named. Similarly, for each occurrence of record type COUNTY, there are as many occurrences under record type CITY as there are cities within a given county. Finally, for each named city, there is a number of occurrences under record type STREET. The corresponding three sets are: COUNTY-SET, CITY-SET and STREET-SET.

Although the clauses SET, OWNER and MEMBER do not, by their respective definitions, create a network model, the rules that govern their utilisation enable the creation of a structure that resembles a network. The following are some of the characteristics of sets relevant to an understanding of the concept and its applicability:

(a)   A schema may contain an arbitrary number of sets.
(b)   A set must have an owner and one or more member record types.
(c)   Each set must have an order specified in the schema (this is discussed later).
(d)   Any record type may be declared as the owner record type of one or more sets.
(e)   Any record type may be declared as a member record type of one or more set types.

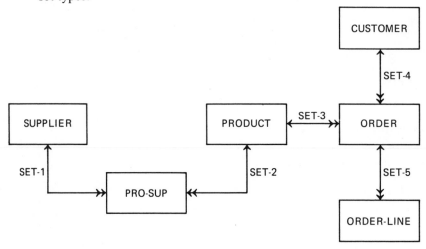

Figure 9.3 A network model.

These simple rules regarding the definition of sets enable us to create network models of some complexity. Figure 9.3 presents a network model with five different sets where record type PRODUCT is the owner of two sets, SET-2 and SET-3. Also, record type ORDER is a member record type in sets SET-3 and SET-4 but an owner record type in set SET-5.

The network in Figure 9.3 illustrates part of a database schema that is used to hold information on products supplied to customers who issue orders each of which may contain references to one or more different products, quantities, delivery notes, etc. Record type PRO-SUP is the 'link' record type of SUPPLIER and PRODUCT which are related by a many-to-many relationship, that is, a SUPPLIER may supply two or more different products (through set SET-1) and the same product may be supplied by two or more different suppliers (through set SET-2).

Link record types are frequently used to decompose a many-to-many relationship into two one-to-many relationships. The link record type components are usually the two primary keys of the corresponding two record types, but other components may also be defined when required.

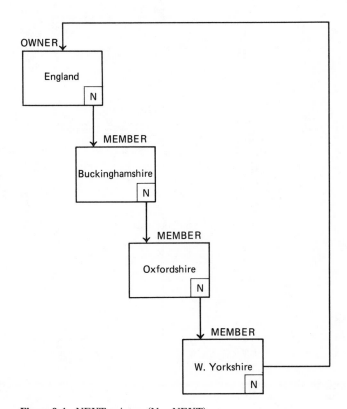

Figure 9.4   NEXT pointers (N = NEXT).

9.3 STRUCTURAL RELATIONSHIPS

Within the context of set, we envisage a number of possible linkage schemes whereby record occurrences can be interrelated and processed. To this end, we refer to Chapter 3 where we discussed three types of list structures: one-way, two-way, and circular. We are now in a position to discuss their utilisation by the syntax of the Network Database Language (NDL).

Record occurrences of member record types in a set can be linked together to form a linear structure similar to a one-way list. If the link mode of a set has been declared with the clause NEXT, then each member record type will be allocated an implicit pointer field that receives an appropriate value which can be used to access the next record occurrence within the set. Figure 9.4 shows a set occurrence with an owner (i.e England) and three member occurrences under record type COUNTY (i.e Buckinghamshire, Oxfordshire, and W. Yorkshire). The last occurrence (i.e W. Yorkshire) points to the owner occurrence (i.e England).

There are applications which process records in both NEXT and PRIOR modes, that is, bidirectionally. For example, if the occurrences of a set type CITY-

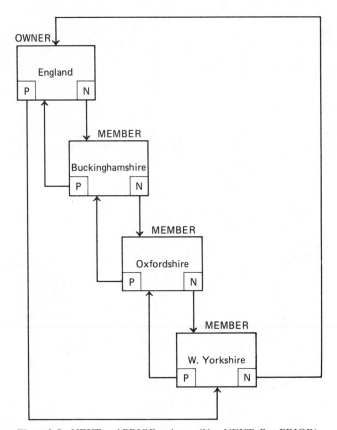

Figure 9.5   NEXT and PRIOR pointers (N = NEXT, P = PRIOR).

SET (see Figure 9.2) are ordered by the data item SIZE (i.e the population of each city), then the user can find out quickly the name of the city which is in the immediately preceding rank of Oxford. Each member record occurrence in a set will be linked to the immediately preceding occurrence provided the clause PRIOR has been included in the definition of the set. Figure 9.5 shows a structure that utilises both NEXT and PRIOR pointers. The PRIOR pointer of the owner occurrence (i.e England) points to the last occurrence in this set (i.e W. Yorkshire).

Where the owner occurrence of a set must be accessible directly from each of the member occurrences, then we utilise an owner pointer from each member occurrence. The clause OWNER creates a pointer to the owner occurrence from each member occurrence. Figure 9.6 shows a structure that utilises NEXT, PRIOR, and OWNER pointers; the owner occurrence does not have an owner pointer.

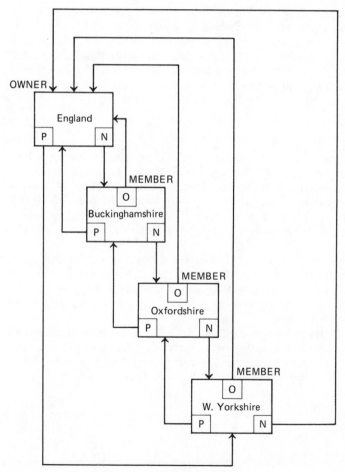

Figure 9.6   NEXT, PRIOR and OWNER pointers
            (N = NEXT, P = PRIOR, O = OWNER).

9.3.1 Order of Record Occurrences

It makes sense to declare in advance the order with which record occurrences are to be inserted within sets so that the DBMS carries out this task automatically when, for example, the CONNECT command of the data manipulation language is executed. A set order is best declared at the schema but the programmer should also be provided with appropriate commands that manipulate and sort record occurrences according to the criteria specified by a user within a session.

We are here discussing the *logical* order of records independent of their physical storage or linkage schemes. Thus, the same record occurrences of a member record type can participate in occurrences of two or more different sets and be ordered differently in each set.

It is important, at this stage, to distinguish between a *permanent* order declared within the schema and a *temporary* order established during a user-session. During a user-session there may be a number of temporary values held within what is called a User Work Area (UWA). A UWA is an area in memory or disk assigned to an executing program(s) and contains information on the current state of a subschema in use, current record type(s), data values, etc.

Generally speaking, a set order can be established on the basis of: (a) data values held under specific data items (e.g keys), (b) positioning of a record occurrence relative to the current record occurrence in the UWA, that is before or after it, and (c) a chronological or reverse chronological order. These considerations are captured effectively by the following order clause of NDL:

ORDER { FIRST | LAST | NEXT | PRIOR | SORTED |
        SORTED RECORD TYPE name...}

If the order is FIRST, then each incoming record occurrence in the set will be inserted at the top of the list. For example, if the incoming record is 'Cambridgeshire' (see Figure 9.4) then the owner record 'England' will point directly to 'Cambridgeshire', and 'Cambridgeshire' will then point to 'Buckinghamshire'. If the order is LAST, then 'W. Yorkshire' will point to 'Cambridgeshire' and 'Cambridgeshire' will then point to the owner record (i.e 'England').

If the order is NEXT and if the current record in the UWA is, say, 'Oxfordshire' (see Figure 9.4), then the incoming record will be inserted between 'Oxfordshire' and 'W. Yorkshire'. If the order is PRIOR and if the current record in the UWA is say, 'W. Yorkshire', then the incoming record will be inserted between 'Oxfordshire' and 'W. Yorkshire'.

When the option SORTED is specified, the DBMS will maintain the member records of a set in an order based on the sort key of each member record type. For example, if we wish to maintain occurrences under record type CITY of set CITY-SET (see Figure 9.2) in ascending order of population, we can write:

SET CITY-SET
   OWNER COUNTY
   ORDER SORTED
   MEMBER CITY
      KEY ASCENDING POPULATION

If the option SORTED RECORD TYPE name... is used, then the member record types will be used as key items in the sort keys defined in the key clauses of member record types. In other words, the order the names of record types appear in this option will be the order their corresponding occurrences are held. For example, if we wish to maintain the customer orders of set CUSTOMER-ORDERS (see Figure 9.1(d)) in the order urgent orders first and open orders second, we can write:

SET CUSTOMER-ORDERS
  OWNER CUSTOMER
  ORDER SORTED RECORD TYPE URGENT-ORDER OPEN-ORDER
  MEMBER URGENT-ORDER
    KEY ASCENDING DATE
  MEMBER OPEN-ORDER
    KEY ASCENDING DATE

Because a database can be used by a number of people at the same time, it is possible for two different operators to attempt to insert the same record occurrence in a set. By 'same' we mean that two or more record occurrences contain keys which are identical. This situation may or may not signify an error condition and so the database administrator must be given the option to either retain duplicate occurrences in the database for subsequent analysis, or to prohibit their storage altogether.

The ORDER clause can be extended to cater for duplicate occurrences according to the following format:

ORDER { FIRST ǀ LAST ǀ NEXT ǀ PRIOR ǀ SORTED { RECORD TYPE
     name... ǀ
     DUPLICATES { PROHIBITED ǀ FIRST ǀ LAST } } }

The option PROHIBITED states that no duplicates are to be stored. If the FIRST option of the DUPLICATES clause is specified, then member record occurrences that are duplicates will be ordered in reverse chronological order of insertion. If the LAST option of the DUPLICATES clause is specified, then member record occurrences that are duplicates will be ordered in chronological order of insertion (i.e every incoming duplicate will become the last member occurrence in the set).

Let us adopt set SET-1 of Figure 9.3 to illustrate the use of the ORDER clause with the DUPLICATES option. The following statements define set SET-1 and retain all duplicate occurrences under member record type PRO-SUP using the LAST option:

SET SET-1
  OWNER SUPPLIER
  ORDER SORTED DUPLICATES LAST
  MEMBER PRO-SUP
    KEY ASCENDING PRODUCT-CODE

Because two or more record occurrences are classed as duplicates when their key values are identical, an alternative place where the DUPLICATES clause can appear is within the clause that defines a data item as a key. The following format provides an alternative way to control duplicates:

KEY { ASCENDING ǀ DESCENDING } data items...
    [DUPLICATES { PROHIBITED ǀ FIRST ǀ LAST }]

The DUPLICATES clause here is similar to the one we described before. So, the previous statements that define set SET-1 of Figure 9.3 can now be rewritten as follows:

SET SET-1
    OWNER SUPPLIER
    ORDER SORTED
    MEMBER PRO-SUP
        KEY ASCENDING PRODUCT-CODE DUPLICATES LAST

9.3.2 Membership of Record Occurrences

In the previous two sections we described the structural relationships of record types and the possible ordering of record occurrences in sets. We can now discuss the membership modes of sets, that is, the insertion and retention characteristics of a record for each set in which it appears as a member record.

The basic idea behind storing values on database files is that each value is first stored under an appropriate data item (i.e the variable of a DBMS program) and after all the data items of a record type have received appropriate values, the complete record can be inserted or connected to a set type. Values for data items can be supplied by a user during an online session, or they can be read from database files. In practice, however, a complete block or a page of data is read or stored from or onto a database file.

Now, in many cases, the user creates a record and expects this to be inserted into an appropriate set automatically by the DBMS. Alternatively, he may wish to carry out a record insertion 'manually', that is, by issuing a specific INSERT or CONNECT command with a specific set type. Let us see how the NDL syntax deals with this matter and the options it offers the user or DBA.

The definition of a set type comprises the clauses SET, OWNER, ORDER and MEMBER. As we have seen, the MEMBER clause, in turn, incorporates the KEY clause to define a data item as a key and also to control duplication of value as under a key. If we extend the MEMBER clause to control the insertion and retention of record occurrences, we can achieve some of the membership characteristics we discussed above.

The following format of the member clause provides a simple syntax to: (a) specify a member record type of a set type, (b) define the insertion characteristics of a member record type, (c) define the retention characteristics of a member record type, (d) specify a uniqueness constraint for member records, (e) define the sort control key for a member record type, and (f) specify a validity condition on member records:

MEMBER record-name
    INSERTION { MANUAL |AUTOMATIC | STRUCTURAL
                Specification...}
    RETENTION { FIXED | MANDATORY | OPTIONAL }
    [UNIQUE data-item...]
    [KEY { ASCENDING | DESCENDING } data-item...]
        [DUPLICATES {PROHIBITED | FIRST | LAST }]
    [CHECK condition]...

If insertion is MANUAL, then record occurrences are inserted as members in a set only by an explicit CONNECT statement which we discuss later. If insertion is AUTOMATIC, then record occurrences are inserted automatically as members of a set when this is initially stored in the database. Under both insertion MANUAL and AUTOMATIC the owner record occurrence is identified by the application.

If insertion is STRUCTURAL, then record occurrences are inserted automatically as members of a set when this is initially stored in the database. Here, the owner record occurrence is identified by the DBMS through the 'structural specification'. The latter states that the owner record occurrence is selected by the DBMS to have values under specified data items *equal* to those of the record to be inserted.

Let us adopt set SET-2 (see Figure 9.3) to illustrate the use of the structural specification. Let a key item in record type PRODUCT be called PRODUCT-CODE, and a key item in record type PRO-SUP be called PRO-CODE: these two being used for similar purposes, that is, to distinguish between different products. Now, if records under PRODUCT contain the details of each and every product, then we may wish to check the incoming values under key PRO-CODE to ensure that these have already been included within the records of PRODUCT. The following statement defines this condition:

INSERTION STRUCTURAL PRO-SUP.PRO-CODE =
PRODUCT.PRODUCT-CODE

The notation: record-name.data-item specifies the complete name of a component; the full stop separates the record name from the data item name.

The RETENTION clause defines the retention characteristics of a member record type. When the retention mode is FIXED, then a record occurrence remains a member of the same set occurrence until it is erased from the database. When the retention mode is MANDATORY, then a record occurrence can become a member of another set occurrence within the same set type. When the retention mode is OPTIONAL, then a member occurrence need not remain within its current set occurrence or any other set occurrence of the same type.

The UNIQUE clause specifies a constraint on the data item named (a key) and states that its values must be unique, that is, duplicates are not allowed.

The CHECK clause enables the specification of an expression that will produce a result which can be true or false. This clause can be compared to an ordinary IF command in a high level programming language. Typical logical operators that can be utilised within an expression are: AND, OR and NOT. For example, if we wish to ensure that all occurrences under record type ORDER-LINE (see Figure 9.3) have a value under data item QUANTITY which is greater than zero and less than 9999, we can specify the following CHECK clause:

MEMBER ORDER-LINE
.
.
.
CHECK QUANTITY > 0 AND QUANTITY < 9999

9.4 NETWORK DATABASE LANGUAGE

In the previous sections we discussed the CODASYL architecture, paying particular attention to its logical and structural characteristics. The architectural features we presented are mostly integrity constraints that restrict the valid states of the database. For data items, we discussed the constraints UNIQUE values, CHECK condition and DEFAULT values. For record types we discussed the constraints SET membership, ORDER of record occurrences, INSERTION mode, and RETENTION mode.

In the following sections we are going to discuss the current NDL syntax under three major areas of interest to the CODASYL committee. These are, the schema and subschema definition, and data manipulation statements.

9.4.1 Schema Definition

The schema is the logical description of the database representing the record types of an organisation and all inter-record relationships. The latter are exemplified through the concept *set* which is of vital importance to the understanding of current network DBMSs.

The major entries of the schema definition are presented in the following brief syntax:

```
SCHEMA schema-name
  [ { RECORD record-name}
      { ITEM component-name }... |
    SET set-name
    OWNER owner-name
    ORDER order definition
    { MEMBER member-name}
        INSERTION clause
        RETENTION clause
        [KEY clause]
    }...
  }...
  ]
```

There are two basic components in the schema: (a) the RECORD entry that allows the definition of each record type, followed by the ITEM entry that allows the definition of each data item (attribute), and (b) the SET entry that allows the definition of a set including its OWNER, ORDER, MEMBER, and INSERTION and RETENTION clauses for each member.

In what follows we present the complete syntax of the schema definition sublanguage. The format of this presentation is an attempt to bring together all the architectural components of an NDL schema, our objective being to help the reader to gain an integrated view of the individual schema entries we discussed previously.

Format of schema definition

```
SCHEMA schema-name
  RECORD record name
    [{ UNIQUE { [ record-name. ] component-name [subscripts]
                 | component-name [subscripts] [OF record-name ]
              }...
      | ITEM component-name
        { CHARACTER [integer]
            | { FIXED integer [signed-integer] |
                NUMERIC integer [signed-integer] | INTEGER }
            | { FLOAT integer | REAL | DOUBLE PRECISION }
        }
        [OCCURS { integer }...]
        [DEFAULT { character-string-literal | numeric-literal }]
      | CHECK condition
    }...
    ]
  SET set-name
    OWNER{ record-name | SYSTEM }
    ORDER { FIRST | LAST | NEXT | PRIOR | DEFAULT
            | SORTED { RECORD TYPE { record-name }...
                       | DUPLICATES { PROHIBITED | FIRST | LAST |
                                       DEFAULT }
                     }
          }
    MEMBER record-name
      INSERTION  { AUTOMATIC | MANUAL}
                  | STRUCTURAL { member-component-identifier = }
                  owner-component-identifier | owner-component-
                  identifier = member-component-identifier }
                  [{ AND { member-component-identifier =
                           owner-component-identifier |
                           owner-component-identifier =
                           member-component-identifier }
                   }...]
                  }
      RETENTION  { FIXED | MANDATORY | OPTIONAL }
      [{ UNIQUE    { [{ record-name | OWNER | MEMBER }.]
                     component-name [subscripts]
                     | component-name [subscripts]
                     [OF { record-name | OWNER | MEMBER }]
                   }...
      }...
      ]
      [KEY { { ASCENDING | DESCENDING }
             { { [{ record-name | OWNER | MEMBER }.]
                 component-name [subscripts]
               | component-name [subscripts] [OF { record-name |
                 OWNER | MEMBER }]
             }
             | RECORD TYPE
           }...
         }...
      [DUPLICATES { PROHIBITED | FIRST | LAST | DEFAULT } ]
      ]
      [{ CHECK CONDITION }...]
```

NOTE: In the above format, the clauses CHARACTER, FIXED, NUMERIC,
       FLOAT, and OCCURS, specify a number entry as 'integer' which is
       expected to be an unsigned integer greater than zero.

9.4.2 Subschema Definition

The subschema is the logical description of that section of the database which is
relevant and available to an application. A subschema can of course be common
to two or more different applications. In what follows we present the syntax of the
NDL subschema definition.

Format of subschema definition

```
SUBSCHEMA { schema-name.subschema-name
                 I subschema-name OF schema-name }
[{ RECORD [record-name RENAMED] record-view-name
   [{ ITEM [component-name RENAMED] component-view-name }...
    I ALL]
   I SET [set-name RENAMED] set-view-name
  }...
]
```

The definition of a subschema comprises: (a) a SUBSCHEMA name as well as
the name of the schema from which it is derived, (b) one or more RECORD types
(otherwise referred to as record views), and (c) one or more SET types (otherwise
referred to as set views). The term 'view' is appropriate here since it corresponds
to that portion of the database the user sees or has available for processing using
data manipulation commands.

The NDL syntax allows the Database Administrator (DBA) to choose those
RECORD types from the schema which are relevant to a subschema (i.e an
application) and to RENAME these if necessary. The DBA may also select from
each record type in the schema only those data items (otherwise referred to as
component views) which are relevant to a subschema, and to RENAME these
accordingly; alternatively, the ALL keyword allows the inclusion of all data items
from a schema record type. Set types may also be renamed.

9.4.3 Data Manipulation

After appropriate subschemata have been defined and compiled by the DBMS,
application programs can be written to manipulate that portion of the database
specified in each subschema. What is therefore needed is a number of statements
(commands) that allow the programmer (or user) to manipulate record occurrences by applying the operational logic (the algorithm) of each application.
Example commands here are: 'connect' a record to a set, 'erase', 'modify', 'store'
a record, etc.

The relational Data Manipulation Language (DML) we discussed in Chapter 4
is of course intended to operate on user views (i.e component views, record views
and set views, in the present context) by means of high level commands that are
compatible with the logical model of the database, particularly the schema and

subschema DDL. Our interest here is in the network DML which has in the past formed the basis for the development of most business applications, although it is now widely accepted that the relational approach offers a better user interface to accessing databases. It is interesting to point out that several systems have been developed to decompile CODAŠYL DML into relational database interfaces [Demo, 1983; Demo & Kundu, 1984], and relational queries [Katz & Wong, 1982].

Because the DML commands offered by most vendors today are not sufficient to implement applications fully, it becomes necessary to use other programming languages, such as, COBOL and FORTRAN, and to include DML statements within the application programs which are developed using these high level programming languages. The latter are then referred to as *host languages*.

It should be explicitly noted that an application program written with host and DML statements must be compiled by a DBMS utility to produce the object (executable) code of the computer in use. The execution of the code will actually create what is called a SESSION state or run unit that starts with the first database operation and terminates after the last database operation. Figure 9.7 illustrates three active run units, two non-active run units, two applications (APL1 and APL2), and two subschemata.

A session consists of cursors, sets, and the list of all record types that have been prepared for processing (otherwise referred to as the *ready list*). A *session cursor* identifies the current record occurrence of the session, a *record cursor* identifies the current record occurrence of each record type in the subschema (independent of set membership), and a *set cursor* identifies the owner occurrence and the current member occurrence in each set type of the subschema.

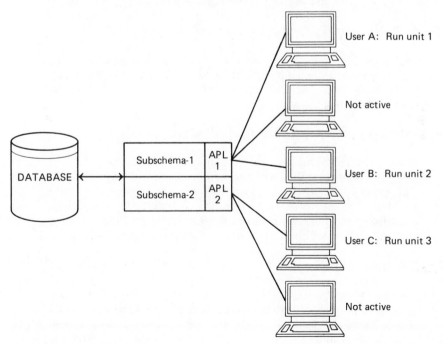

Figure 9.7   Illustration of run units.

In what follows we present the complete format of each DML statement, a brief description of its function and explanatory comments where necessary. The formal specification of the NDL standard [ANSI, 1986] is presented in the Backus Naur Form (BNF) which is not intended for the general reader but for the designer of compilers. Our main objective here, is to give the reader an overall view of each DML statement, its syntax and structural components so that he can assess the degree of operational compatibility of the NDL compilers that are available with the ANSI standard.

The notation we adopt to illustrate the format of each DML statement is as we discussed in the introduction of this chapter. The element 'database-key-identifier' implies the following:

{SESSION I record-view-name I { OWNER I MEMBER } set-view-name}

If SESSION is specified, then the database key of the session cursor will be used. If a record-view-name is specified, then the database key of the record cursor will be used. If OWNER or MEMBER is specified, then the corresponding database key of the owner or member occurrence in the set cursor of the set view specified will be used.

Data Manipulation Statements

COMMIT [FINISH]

> COMMIT: Terminate a transaction and make all changes to record occurrences permanent. If the FINISH option is specified, then all the record types currently held in the User Work Area (UWA) will be emptied after they have been stored in the database. That is, all files that were open during a transaction, will be closed.

CONNECT database-key-identifier TO set-view-name

> CONNECT: Connect a record occurrence to a set occurrence. This statment is used when a member record type has been defined with an INSERTION MANUAL statement or a RETENTION OPTIONAL statement.

DISCONNECT database-key-identifier FROM set-view-name

> DISCONNECT: Disconnect (remove) a record occurrence from a set, but do not erase the record occurrence itself from the database. This operation is eligible provided the retention clause of the record type has been specified as OPTIONAL (as discussed in the schema definition) and the record has also been prepared for processing with the UPDATE option (see under the FIND statement).

ERASE database-key-identifier WITH { FULL I PARTIAL } CASCADE

> ERASE: Erase (delete) records from set occurrences provided they have been prepared for processing with the UPDATE option. The sets affected by this operation are those whose owner record occurrence is identified by the database-key-identifier. With the FULL CASCADE option, all affected records are erased.

However, with the PARTIAL CASCADE option, only member occurrences that have been defined with the FIXED or OPTIONAL retention modes are erased. If any affected set member has been defined with the MANDATORY retention mode, then the erase operation is not eligible.

```
FIND { database-key-identifier
       I { FIRST I LAST I NEXT I PRIOR I
          { ABSOLUTE I RELATIVE } signed-integer }
       { record-view-name
          I [record-view-name] IN set-view-name
          I SUBSCHEMA RECORD
       }
       [WHERE condition]
     }
[FOR { RETRIEVE I UPDATE }]
[RETAIN ALL
   I { [AS MEMBER { set-view-name }...]
      [RETAIN RECORD
         I RETAIN SET { set-view-name }...
         I RETAIN RECORD SET { set-view-name }...
      ]
   }
]
```

FIND: Locate a record occurrence in the database, before it can be retrieved (the FOR RETRIEVE option), or updated (the FOR UPDATE option). The main task of the find statement is to update the cursors of the session so that the GET statement can then be issued to transfer database values to component views. If the database-key-identifier is supplied, then the record occurrence that matches the key is found. The options FIRST, LAST, NEXT and PRIOR utilise the structural characteristics of sets we discussed in Section 9.3 (the OWNER keyword is not part of this list because we can trace the owner through the specification of the 'database-key-identifier'). The value of the signed-integer corresponds to the absolute or relative position of the record in the set. The SUB-SCHEMA RECORD option specifies the subschema domain, that is, all the record occurrences of record-views. If a WHERE option is included, then 'condition' specifies the logic of the search (e.g FIND FIRST SUPPLIER WHERE CITY = 'BRADFORD'). Finally, the RETAIN Option is used to establish the cursor disposition for a record, a set or all record occurrences. In other words, the RETAIN option permits the retention of selected cursors.

```
GET record-view-name
    { SET parameter-name [subscripts] TO operand }...
```

GET: Transfer component values to the User Work Area (UWA)

and assign these to appropriate parameters. This command utilises the current cursors to carry out the transfer and is issued after a FIND command has been executed.

MODIFY record-view-name
  [{ SET { [record-view-name.] component-view-name [subscripts]
          [CURSOR]
        | component-view-name [subscripts] [OF record-view-name]
          [CURSOR]
        }
    TO operand
  }...
  ]

> MODIFY: Replace the current contents of selected component views, provided the affected record views have been prepared for processing with the UPDATE option. The replacement of the contents takes place according to the values contained in the operand. The modify operation changes data values of *existing* records and stores these in the database.

NULLIFY database-key-identifier

> NULLIFY: Set the cursor corresponding to database-key-identifier to null. As we have discussed previously, the database-key-identifier can specify the SESSION, a record-view-name, an OWNER or a MEMBER occurrence.

READY { record-view-name
         { EXCLUSIVE | PROTECTED | SHARED }
         { RETRIEVE | UPDATE }
       }...

> READY: Prepare one or more record views for processing, in other words, open the necessary database files and meta-files which contain the record views specified. At this stage, it makes sense to consider carefully the fact that the same record view(s) can be accessed concurrently by other users and that deadlocks can be created as a result of concurrent run units. The options EXCLUSIVE, PROTECTED and SHARED specify the access modes of record views under a concurrent user environment. The options RETRIEVE and UPDATE specify that the values of the record views are to be retrieved or updated respectively.

RECONNECT database-key-identifier IN set-view-name

> RECONNECT: Reconnect the occurrence of a record view (indicated by the database-key-identifier) in a set view. If the record view has a FIXED retention mode, then its occurrences cannot be reconnected to set views other than their own.

ROLLBACK [FINISH]

> ROLLBACK: Cancel all the changes made to occurrences of record views during a transaction. If the FINISH option is specified, then the UWA will also be emptied (i.e all the files that were opened with the READY statement will be closed). The execution of the ROLLBACK operation signifies unsuccessful completion of a transaction.

```
STORE record-view-name
   [{ SET { [record-view-name.] component-view-name [subscripts]
        [CURSOR]
        | component-view-name [subscripts] [OF record-view-name]
        [CURSOR]
        }
     TO OPERAND
   }...
   ]
   [{ RETAIN ALL}
     | RETAIN RECORD
     | RETAIN SET { set-view-name }...
     | RETAIN RECORD SET { set-view-name }...
   }
   ]
```

> STORE: Transfer values held in the UWA (under a record view) to the database, provided the record view has been prepared for processing with the UPDATE option. The SET option here permits the selective replacement of values under component views by values of the operand. The RETAIN option permits the selective retention of cursors. The store operation actually creates a *new* record occurrence and stores (inserts) this in the database, while obeying the rules that govern the processing of duplicates. Thus, if DUPLICATES PROHIBITED has been specified, then a duplicate occurrence will be flagged by the STORE command.

```
TEST { database-key-identifier-1 = database-key-identifier-2
     | NULL database-key-identifier
     | SET EMPTY set-view-name
     | SET set-view-name CONTAINS database-key-identifier
     }
```

> TEST: This operation is used to: (a) compare database keys and determine whether they identify the same record occurrence, (b) determine whether a database key is null, (c) determine whether a set view has any member occurrences, and (d) determine whether a record occurrence (identified by a database-key-identifier) is a member of some set occurrence.

9.5 SUMMARY

The network architecture is based on a multi-type data model where a record type may have more than one 'parent' record type associated with it. In this chapter, we discussed a simple network architecture exemplified by the CODASYL proposal for a Network Database Language (NDL).

The CODASYL proposal utilises the concept *set* to define inter-record relationships. Each set type is named and must have one record type declared as its *owner* and one or more record types declared as its *member* record types. Each set type must also have order, insertion and retention modes. A *singular set* has a special owner, the so called *system* that has no data items. A *recursive set* has the same record type as owner and member.

The structural features (i.e the way record occurrences are clustered) of the CODASYL proposal correspond to three main list structures: one-way, two-way and circular. The terms used to refer to records in sets are: FIRST (immediately after the owner), LAST (immediately before the owner), NEXT and PRIOR (these being relative to a record in the User Work Area (UWA)).

A DBMS is as good as the integrity constraints it provides and maintains. The CODASYL proposal discusses a number of constraints which restrict the valid state of the database. For data items, we presented the constraints UNIQUE values, CHECK condition and DEFAULT values. For record types, we presented the constraints SET membership, ORDER of record occurrences, INSERTION and RETENTION modes of record occurrences.

The American National Standards Institute (ANSI) is currently considering a proposal to standardise an NDL, particularly the schema and subschema definitions and the Data Manipulation Language (DML). In this chapter, we presented the current proposal, illustrating the complete format of most statements (clauses). Our main objective has been to give the reader the gist of the syntax of NDL, rather than its formal structure and detailed syntactical specification.

9.6 REFERENCES

ANSI, X3H2, 'Concepts and Terminology for the Conceptual Schema and the Information Base', (ISO TC97/SC5/WG3), 1985.

ANSI, X3H2 Technical Committee on Databases, 'Network Database Language', 1986.

CODASYL, Report of the CODASYL Data Description Language Committee, Pergamon Press, 1978.

Deheneffe, C. & Hennebert, H., 'NUL: A Navigational User's Language for a Network Structured Database', Proc. ACM SIGMOD, pp. 135-142, 1976.

Demo, B., 'Program Analysis for Conversion from a Navigation to a Specification Database Interface', Proc. IX International Conf. on VLDB, Florence, October, 1983.

Demo, B. & Kundu, S., 'A Basic System for Decompiling CODASYL DML into a Relational Interface', Proc. International Computer Symposium ICS, Taiwan, December 1984.

Gray, P. M. D., 'Efficient Access to CODASYL and FDM Databases', ACM SIGMOD, Vol. 14, No. 4, pp. 437-443, 1985.

Katz, R. H. & Wong, E., 'Decompiling CODASYL DML Into Relational Queries', ACM TODS, Vol. 7, pp. 1-23, 1982.

Sibley, E. H. (editor), 'Special Issue on Database Management Systems', ACM Computing Surveys, Vol. 8, No. 1, 1976.

Spaccapietra, S., et al., 'An Approach to Effective Heterogeneous Database Cooperation', In: Distributed Data Systems, Vol. 7, pp. 1-23, 1982.

Taylor, R. W. & Frank, R. L., 'CODASYL Database Management Systems', ACM Computing Surveys, Vol. 8, pp. 67-103, 1976.

Yannakoudakis, E. J. & Cheng, C. P., 'A Rigorous Approach to Data Type Specification', Computer Bulletin, Vol 3, Part 4, pp. 31-36, 1987.

10 DICTIONARY OF DATABASE TERMINOLOGY

ACCESS PATH

A physical level mechanism which establishes the route necessary for the identification of occurrences of records or tuples within the actual physical database. There may exist more than one access path for the identification of a given record or sets of records.

When a request for one or more records is issued by a program or user, the access method analyses meta-data and control information (e.g the length of records in a file, links, chains, pointers) and proceeds to establish appropriate record addresses. Depending on the type and method of access as well as relevant access paths, an address is reached through one or more of the following modes: sequential, indexed-sequential, hashed or direct.

AFTER IMAGE

A given record or sets of records can be modified/updated by an appropriate DBMS command at any point of time. At the end of the modification process a copy of the record or indeed its associated and complete physical block may be copied to a separate area. This becomes the after image copy of the data.

After image copies of data are necessary for a number of reasons. For example, if an error occurs while an original image is being overwritten or destroyed, then it will be impossible to recover its contents without of course the use of an earlier backup copy - provided it exists and it is also up to date.

APPLICATION GENERATOR

A software utility which may or may not be part of the DBMS, moulded to a specific applications environment. It offers the user a facility to enter the specification of an application and proceeds to: (a) interpret the specification to appropriate software modules, (b) link the modules together, (c) execute the desired functions.

Application generators appeared first in the market as tools for specialised environments, such as simulation, and are now part of many DBMSs guiding the user towards the specification of the problem and its subsequent solution with existing software.

AREA

A physical section of the database which can be considered synonymous to a 'file'. The area can therefore be 'opened', 'closed' or 'locked' as a complete and independent unit of data. It forms a convenient way to protect data as well as to recover or backup selected sections of the database.

A database area may contain multi-record type information, as well as extra control information necessary to establish appropriate access paths.

An alternative name for area is 'realm' often used with respect to a network model of data (e.g CODASYL).

ATTRIBUTE

A specific interpretation of the real world representing a meaningful object and its properties. An attribute has a name (e.g Department-name) and is based on a pre-specified domain (e.g CHARACTER(10) implying a 10-character string).

The concept of attribute must be studied in connection with the concept 'data item' as applied in the logical schema. An attribute is translated to a data item in a logical schema or subschema and is defined accordingly.

Where appropriate, and provided an attribute can be translated to exactly one data item in the logical schema, we will assume that the terms are synonymous. See also under 'data item'.

AUTHORISATION

A right an individual user, program, or process may have to access data for display, modification, insertion, deletion or processing. These levels of authorisation can be pre-defined or be allocated dynamically after the database has been set up. Usually, it is the responsibility of the database administrator to assign appropriate authorisation levels for accessing data.

The following is an example of an authorisation command that permits the user called 'John' to update the field 'Salary' in table 'Payroll':

GRANT UPDATE (Salary)
    ON Payroll
    TO John

AUTOMATIC MEMBERSHIP

To understand this it becomes necessary to introduce the concept of 'set', that is, a group of records (not necessarily of the same type) which are related logically. Take for example two record types, the PERSONAL (referring to name, address, age, etc) and the HISTORY (referring to dates, jobs held, salary, etc) details of individuals. An occurrence under PERSONAL and one, two or more occurrences under HISTORY ordered by date, may refer to a single person whose history details are updated during a transaction.

Now, automatic membership is a property of a set type enabling the placement of record occurrences (e.g history records) in sets to be carried out automatically rather than on demand as is the case with 'manual membership'.

An example statement forming part of the definition of a set is INSERTION AUTOMATIC (see also under 'set').

BACKOUT

Problems may arise as a result of modifying records, accidental invocation of processes or indeed system errors. It is therefore desirable, in many cases, to be able to revert back to the previous state of the database using 'before images' (previous copies of the data concerned) or to transfer control to the previous program module (e.g the calling segment of a data manipulation program). This process is called backout and must not be confused with 'rollback' which is specific to database transactions.

The following commands establish a condition within a transaction whereby the backout process is activated automatically if an error occurs:

```
PROCEDURE TRANSACT
            BEGIN TRANSACTION
            ON ERROR BACKOUT
            .
            . {program statements}
            .
            COMMIT
            END
```

BACKUP

The procedure whereby a copy of a section(s) of the physical database is made prior to or after the completion of a program which accesses it. A backup copy of the data can then be used to reconstruct the physical database if necessary.

The backup process can be activated periodically by the system automatically or by means of manual intervention by the user. We can thus talk of the 'backup copy' or the 'backup procedure'.

BASE TABLE

This term is used in connection with the relational database model and refers to a table which actually exists in the database in exactly the same format as that defined in the corresponding relation (i.e a record type defined with a data storage description language). So, the values and the order of the attributes in a given tuple of a base table, may be seen by the user exactly as they are stored.

Compare a base table with a view table. A view table is a 'virtual' table where its tuples are derived (synthesised) from one or more base tables. Moreover, the attribute order (horizontally) may be different, and subsets of attribute values may also exist in a view table.

It is important to emphasise here that differences between a tuple of a base table and what the user sees do exist. For example, a base tuple may be encoded or compressed, a base tuple may be spread between two or more physical slots (e.g sectors). See also under 'table' and 'view'.

BEFORE IMAGE

A copy of a section(s) of the database before it is actually processed or modified. This is a form of data safety in case of accidental loss or unintentional modification. Before image copies of data can subsequently be used to reconstruct the database.

A before image copy of data can be forced by the user/programmer through an explicit command, or it can be carried out automatically by the DBMS. The criteria (e.g volume and type of manipulations) whereby the latter takes place will be part of the storage schema of the database. It is the responsibility of the database administrator to ensure that before image copies are made as and where necessary.

BLOCK

A unit of input or output between main memory and the physical devices. A disk input/output unit can in fact comprise 1, 2, 4, 8, 16, etc blocks and is usually referred to as 'bucket'. In magnetic tapes however we only receive or transmit a single block at a time. The concept of block must be studied in connection with the concept 'track' which is more hardware-dependent and applies to disk packs or other direct access devices. See also under 'disk unit' and 'track'.

BOYCE-CODD NORMAL FORM (BCNF)

A relation may be in third Normal Form (3NF) but can still give rise to anomalies with certain manipulative operations upon the tuples. The anomalies occur when there are two or more candidate keys in a relation and when these have common or overlapping attributes. The Boyce-Codd normal form (the name is given after the authors who first investigated this problem) deals with multiple candidate keys by introducing a rule that states that a relation is in 'strong 3NF' or BCNF if and only if it is in 3NF and every determinant is a candidate key. A determinant is an attribute or group of attributes upon which some other attribute is fully functionally dependent.

BROWSING

Examining a list of data by going through a set of records/tuples one after the other in order to satisfy a given request. Browsing is usually associated with 'looking' at the data actually displayed on the screen or other output device.

BUCKET

A number of disk blocks which contain database records. The records in a bucket are usually allocated the same hash address. The size of the bucket increases by predefined multiples of a block (e.g 2, 4, 8, 16, etc). There are however disk systems which allow a variable block length to be created and maintained but these are cumbersome to program. See also under 'block'.

CANDIDATE KEY

One or more attributes which can be used to identify records uniquely. Thus, we talk of single or composite candidate keys. Candidate keys are studied at the data analysis stage and before the logical schema is implemented.

There may be more than one combination of attributes which have this property, but it is only one combination which is adopted as the primary key of the entity.

CANONICAL STRUCTURE

A structure which is consistent, free from duplicate material, contains only facts about an organisation or any type of entity, and forms a necessary and minimum structure for any demands that may be imposed upon it by software or organisational aspects.

The property of 'canonicity' is thus desirable and should be introduced in all database structures, especially the conceptual schema. We can therefore talk of a canonical schema which reflects all the views of the organisation accurately and efficiently and can evolve with changes in the applications using it.

A canonical structure can be synthesised by merging known views, analysing the relationships, the overlap and consistency of entities. The stability of the resultant structure can also be measured by examining whether it is affected substantially by the introduction of new views.

CARDINALITY

This is the number of tuples in a table. It can vary from application to application or from one run to another, in a dynamic fashion, reflecting the insertion and deletion of records in the database. For example, the cardinality of the following table is 4:

CAR-PLATES

Car-plate	Car-owner
ODB 492W	Stylios G
TAR 818B	Victoras P
VCR 804B	Edwards D A
WAR 322Z	Proteus F W

COMMIT

Most transactions involve the manipulation of one or more records which may also be updated, changed or modified as and where appropriate. For example, the salary of a group of employees may be altered following a decision to award a pay rise.

A transaction takes place at a specific point of time and has a defined beginning and end otherwise referred to as 'commit'. The commit command requests the system to commit itself to the transactions which have taken place and to create a permanent copy of the data. It actually signals the successful completion of a transaction.

Consider the following statements in pseudo-code whereby a transaction is defined and the updates are committed when no errors occur:

```
PROCEDURE TRANSACT
            BEGIN TRANSACTION
            ON ERROR ROLLBACK
            .
            . {program statements}
            .
            COMMIT
            END
```

See also under 'transaction' and 'rollback'.

COMPOSITE KEY

This is an identification key which comprises more than one attribute. The order of the attributes within the key may not be significant to the user, but may be important when the key is actually manipulated by a sublanguage function. An example of such a manipulation is hashing for address calculation where a well defined set of operations is performed upon the key in order to create the address of the corresponding record.

CONCEPTUAL SCHEMA

The complete and global definition of the real-world pertinent to an organisation, including all static as well as dynamic information types, structures, relationships and usage.

The conceptual schema aims to model the real-world by considering the information requirements of all users and applications without any reference whatsoever to the computer, operating system or DBMS. In a way, the conceptual schema attempts to document all user and organisation functional requirements and to communicate these to data processing staff for discussion.

In order to design the global conceptual data model, it becomes necessary to investigate each local conceptual data model and to proceed by analysing adjacent areas of the organisation. This process necessitates a lengthy data analysis excersise. Conceptual schema information can be recorded according to systems analysis and documentation techniques, but can also incorporate general statements such as:

1. Distinguish between full-time and part-time employees.
2. Distinguish between product types and components.
3. The payrates under incentive schemes are in pence per minute.
4. No order will be allowed without an associated customer name.
5. An order can be placed over the phone or in writing.
6. The age of an employee cannot exceed 99.

After the conceptual schema has been established and agreed upon with management and users, then the logical schema can be designed by considering the way data can be structured on the computer with the aid of a DBMS. We must emphasise here that the conceptual schema should not be affected by changes to the database software, logical or internal schemata.

CONCURRENT ACCESS

A database environment where users can access records at the same time and where the records can in fact be the same. Besides, with concurrent access multiple operations on data can take place.

Careful control of concurrency is necessary to avoid inconsistency in transactions where for example user X attempts to read a record which at the same time is being modified by user Y. Now, if user X receives the contents of the record and user Y modifies it and overwrites the previous contents, then user X will be processing an out of date version of the record.

CONSISTENCY

A characteristic of the database where all values are inserted, altered and retrieved in a consistent manner through intelligent data propagation techniques. Besides, no two different or conflicting facts should be allowed for the same object and conversely, no two different definitions should exist for the same object.

For example, when the value of an attribute 'hours worked' is altered to contain 35 under table TAB1 for employee X, then if another table, say TAB2, also contains the same attribute for the same employee, then its value should also be altered accordingly. Moreover, if the definition of attribute 'hours worked' is altered in any way (e.g from hours to minutes), then this should be propagated to all pertinent tables of the database.

A problem area where inconsistencies may arise is concurrent database transactions (see under 'transaction'). Here, it should not be possible for one user to receive data for further manipulation (e.g decision-making) while another is actually altering this data.

The term 'consistency' must be studied in connection with the term 'integrity' (see under 'integrity').

CONSTRAINT

A rule which imposes a restriction on the usage of the database and thereby ensures that its integrity and consistency are maintained. 'Usage', in the present context, implies the manipulative operations (e.g insert, update, delete) which take place upon one or more tables (or files) of the database.

We often talk of integrity and consistency constraints which are defined at the schema and subschema, but checked during the execution of appropriate data manipulation statements. Example rules (constraints) are presented under 'integrity'.

CURSOR

Most high level programming languages available today operate on a single record at a time, that is, a single tuple or record occurrence in a file. With a DBMS command we can scan either a complete table (file) or a section of this. By default, a DML command scans the complete table and so it becomes necessary to define subsets or proper subsets of record occurrences that can be manipulated as though they were individual tables. We can then carry out specific operations on each subset, again one record occurrence at a time, and thereby offer a means of interfacing a database language with a high level language (the host language).

A cursor is a set of record occurrences (tuples) which are extracted from one or more base or view tables and stored on a temporary table. The cursor table is created when the cursor is 'opened' and destroyed when the cursor is 'closed'.

Another way to visualise a cursor is to assume that the tuples in the source table(s) (i.e base or view table(s)) are 'marked' and declared as a named logical unit which can be processed further independent of any other tables.

So, a cursor is declared, opened and closed as required. While a cursor is open, an appropriate command (e.g FETCH) can be used to access a tuple at a time, starting from the beginning of the cursor table. Accessing of cursor tuples then takes place sequentially one after the other and at any point of time there will be a specific tuple which can be retrieved by the FETCH command (assume there is an 'invisible' current pointer to a tuple).

CYLINDER

A cylinder corresponds to a complete set of tracks on a disk unit, whether flexible or hard, which can be accessed without any read/write head movement. In other words, a cylinder comprises all the tracks in the same plane parallel to the rotation of the axis of the pack. Within a disk pack, each cylinder contains an equal number of tracks as well as sectors.

In the following table we present two example disk drives and their architectural characteristics:

Characteristics	Disk 1	Disk 2
Drive capacity	300 Mb	689 Mb
Data surfaces	12	20
Cylinders	1200	842

See also under 'disk unit'.

DATABASE

The physical structures and data associated with a given logical schema definition, that is, a complete and integrated set of record occurrences and relationships for a given organisation. It is important to emphasise that the database contains both 'stored values' and necessary control data to manipulate these.

A database is common to all programs and users and is accessed in a standardised manner. A DBMS is employed to: (a) design, (b) initialise, (c) manipulate, (d) update, (e) reorganise and (e) tune the database.

DATABASE ADMINISTRATOR (DBA)

The person responsible for the overall organisation of the database as well as the database management system which controls it. This person is a highly skilled software engineer and his role is technical rather than conventional managerial. The DBA is usually responsible for the major tasks of logical schema and subschema design, their compilation and maintenance.

The complexity of the above tasks has given rise to a number of posts under the main umbrella of database administration, such as, project DBA, functional DBA, consultant DBA, management DBA, and others. However, the different levels of abstraction regarding the database environment, namely, conceptual, logical, storage, physical, and possibly hardware, clearly define the nature of each post.

DATABASE MANAGEMENT SYSTEM (DBMS)

An integrated piece of software which enables the creation, manipulation, maintenance or reorganisation of a database at all levels (logical, external and internal) in a consistent, totally controlled, standardised and optimal manner.

The DBMS usually comprises a number of sublanguages such as, data definition, data manipulation, data storage definition, and query. These sublanguages may also be interfaced to other 'host' programming languages such as Pascal, FORTRAN or COBOL. A data dictionary system and appropriate software also form a vital part of the DBMS, offering, primarily, a means of documenting the entire database environment including schemata, subschemata, applications, programs, users, etc.

The DBMS must not be confused with the database which actually holds the 'values' pertinent to an organisation. Unfortunately, this distinction, or rather definitional aspect, is not always made clear by users or designers of software. In many cases, the term 'database system' refers to the DBMS rather than the stored values.

DATABASE UTILITY

A computer program which is part of the DBMS and which performs a well defined task. Examples of database utilities are the formatter (to set up and initialise/format database files), the loader (to transfer data on to the physical files), and the internal optimiser (to reorganise data at the physical level).

A database utility can be an integrated part of the DBMS, or it can be a stand-alone piece of software compatible with the DBMS of an organisation. Modular design of DBMSs enables vendors to offer, not only plug-compatible software, but also the facility for an organisation to expand its software in a step-wise fashion.

DATA DESCRIPTION LANGUAGE (DDL)

A programming sublanguage, part of the DBMS package, used to describe and define data and relationships at the logical level prior to any processing which may take place.

Depending on the architectural level of the database, we talk of the schema DDL, the subschema DDL, and the storage DDL otherwise known as the Data Storage Description Language (DSDL).

DATA DICTIONARY

This is a directory of all data types, attributes, entities, relationships, etc, and generally all logical, subschema, and internal schema entries of an organisation. Conceptual database information may also be recorded within the data dictionary.

The data dictionary aims to, primarily, store meta-information, act as an information resource directory, and communicate its contents to users, programmers and administrators alike. It also provides management with documentation and analysis of resources such as, schemata, programs and hardware.

Ideally, the data dictionary should be integrated with the DBMS and should also be maintained in conjunction with the database (i.e its definition, values, and usage).

DATA INDEPENDENCE

A feature of the DBMS allowing data to be manipulated on the devices independent of their logical definitions and relationships, and also the ability to manipulate data (views, subschemata) at the logical level independent of their storage definitions or physical structures.

This concept forms an essential aspect of all areas of software engineering and has been the guiding light for the design of DBMSs. Perhaps the architectural principles of database systems would have materialised earlier if computer professionals had studied data independence in the early days of programming language design and management information systems. See also under 'logical independence' and 'physical independence'.

DATA ITEM

The name given to an attribute within a logical schema which in turn is designed with a specific DBMS in mind. The data item is the smallest unit of data which can be manipulated and which has associated with it a specific type (e.g integer, real, string) as well as length in bits or bytes. In other words, the data type of a data item corresponds to a domain or range of acceptable values within the life-cycle of an application.

An example data item is 'Department-code' of type string, length 3 bytes. This can be a mnemonic code, such as, COM, FIN, MAN, referring to computing, finance and management, or it can be an index pointer to another data item, such as 'Dept-description' containing the values 'computing', 'finance' and 'management'.

Where appropriate, a data item can be considered synonymous to an attribute. See also under 'attribute'.

DATA MANIPULATION LANGUAGE (DML)

A programming sublanguage, part of the DBMS, which enables application programs to access and manipulate data that has already been defined at the logical level.

Ideally, the DML will be fully compatible with the query language of the DBMS offering a common structure and syntax to both query language users and application programmers. Equally desirable is that feature of the DBMS which enables DML statements to be invoked from other high level languages, such as, Pascal, FORTRAN and COBOL.

Examples of manipulative statements are: select records, delete records, insert records, cluster (link) records together, etc.

DATA MODEL

A structure defining the relationships among a set of entities or record types. These may be related in terms of a tree, a network or a set of relations as is the case with the relational model.

When the model contains conceptual or semantic information describing for example the conceptual schema, then it becomes the 'conceptual data model' of the organisation.

When the data model contains logical and structural information regarding the actual computerisation of the entities and their relationships using a DBMS, then it becomes the 'logical data model' of the organisation. Here, a data model contains a description of the database and reflects the informational structure of the organisation which uses the database.

DATA REDUNDANCY

A characteristic of a set of files or record occurrences where there is overlap of values at the physical level. As an example, consider files F1, F2 and F3 for application A1 and files F2A and F3 for application A2 where file F2A is an actual copy of F2.

At the relation level, data redundancy can be understood in terms of attributes which are not essential or where their presence creates duplicate entries in the corresponding columns.

Data redundancy can give rise to inconsistencies between different applications as well as duplicate effort where, for example, the same record occurrences have to be updated under two separate files. Database systems aim to minimise redundancy as much as possible.

DATA STORAGE DESCRIPTION LANGUAGE (DSDL)

A data sublanguage used to define storage details for a logical database schema. When a database is designed incrementally, or where application testing takes place, it may be desirable to define storage details of only a subset of the logical schema.

A DSDL schema may contain details for security control, storage pages, areas and sizes, storage area expansion increments, record packing densities, hashing items, indexes, set pointers for next, prior, first, last, etc.

Fundamental research in storage structures also attempts to define the various levels a DSDL should address. In order to understand this, consider the different levels of storage, physical and device record. The major question thus becomes how far down the storage level a DSDL can afford to go without re-inventing the wheel. In other words, is it worth implementing a software module in the DBMS that performs a task which is already available as part of the operating system software ?

DATA TYPE

The concept of data type is closely related to the concept 'domain' and ultimately defines the set of values a variable can take. A variable in turn may represent a data item or an attribute within an application program or database environment generally.

Certain commonly used and basic (primitive) data types are 'integer', 'real', 'string', 'boolean', and 'bit-pattern'.

A user-defined data type can comprise a combination of the above primitive data types aiming to represent a real-world item, aggregate of items or a complete entity.

Examples of data types, as they are defined in the Pascal and FORTRAN programming languages are presented below:

Pascal	FORTRAN
VAR salary, payrate: REAL	REAL salary, payrate
VAR counter, sum: INTEGER	INTEGER counter, sum
VAR dept-code: CHAR	CHARACTER dept-code*1

DEADLOCK

A concurrent processing environment resulting in a situation where two or more users wait for each other to release a section(s) of the database before proceeding further. This usually occurs when 'exclusive' or 'protected' locks are applied during the manipulation of record types within the same realm or record occurrences in the same file.

An example of a deadlock is when one user locks a record and proceeds to retrieve another which is already locked by a second user who, in turn, is attempting to access the record locked by the first user. When a complete database realm (file) is locked by a user, then others cannot of course retrieve any records held within it. An alternative name for a deadlock situation is 'deadly embrace'.

DECOMPOSITION OF RELATIONS

The process whereby a relation with two or more attributes is broken down into a number of other relations on the basis of certain criteria. The most frequently used criteria for decomposition fall under the main headings of first, second, third, fourth and fifth normal forms (see under each normal form).

Decomposition becomes necessary for a number of reasons, such as, the elimination of data redundancy, and the prevention of anomalies with update, insert and delete operations. For example, study the relation:

EMPLOYEES (Employee#, Department#, Manager, Contract details)

where '#' denotes a key attribute. When the manager of a department changes, then all tuples which refer to the manager have to be changed accordingly because 'Manager' is functionally dependent on 'Department', and 'Manager' and 'Contract details' are functionally dependent on 'Department'. However, if we decompose relation EMPLOYEES into the following relations, then this anomaly is eliminated:

EMPLOYEE (Employee#, Department#)
DEPARTMENT (Department#, Manager, Contract details)

DEGREE

The number of attributes in a relation. We say a relation is of degree n or a relation of n-th degree. For example, relation STYLE (Style-no, Duration, Pay-rate, Percent-allowances, Analyst-no) is of the 4-th degree.

DISK UNIT

This is a computer peripheral which is used as a storage medium. It can record data on one or more disks (coated by a magnetic oxide or other element) which are rotated as a disk pack, at a constant speed. Data is recorded on concentric tracks which may also be subdivided into sectors, each of a fixed capacity. As the disks rotate, a set of read/write heads move in unison between the surfaces and access the tracks. A complete set of tracks (in a vertical manner) which can be read or written onto without further movement of the read/write heads, is called a cylinder. The time it takes to move the read/write heads onto the cylinder that contains the required data, is otherwise referred to as the 'seek time'.

Disk drives are usually classified as floppy drives (when they can accept only floppy diskettes), fixed drives (when the disks are permanently fixed inside the drive), and exchangeable (when the disk pack can be interchanged by the user).

Recently, we have seen the introduction of optical disk drives where data is recorded using laser beams instead of magnetised spots on the coating of each surface. Instead of having a disk pack which rotates at a constant speed, we can have a laser beam unit which is directed to the required track.

Three example disk drives and their architectural characteristics are the following:

Characteristics	Disk 1	Disk 2	Disk 3
Drive capacity	20 Mb	300 Mb	689 Mb
Data surfaces	6	12	20
Cylinders	306	1,200	842
Bytes per track	10,416	21,000	40,960
Revs per min	3,600	3,600	3,600
Transfer rate	0.625 Mb/s	1.2 Mb/s	2.45 Mb/s
Av. seek time	85 ms	25 ms	18 ms

DISTRIBUTED DATABASE

A database stored on different locations and manipulated by a number of separately working computers or workstations. The distribution of data need not be obvious to the user.

The DBMS handling the distributed database offers:

(a) A communications facility for each location (including users and data) to communicate with each other.
(b) A facility which enables data to be shared between different locations.
(c) A utility which enforces integrity and consistency of data and processes.

DOMAIN

This is a complete set of values an attribute can receive throughout its processing cycle. A domain is usually defined in conjunction with the establishment of an attribute and can be integer, real, string, or any other data type defined within a schema. (Note that a domain can be specified within a conceptual, logical or storage schema.)

Thus, the definition of a domain comprises its name, type, length and values envisaged. The values are of course schema- and/or subschema-dependent but it should also be possible for different attributes to share the same domain. When attributes share a domain they can be manipulated by a join, union, or other functions. Otherwise, it does not make sense to operate on them with these commands. For example, if attribute 'Payrate' is integer and attribute 'Rate' is real it does not make sense to compare these for equality.

An example command defining a domain called 'Name', of type character, length 25 bytes is:

DOMAIN Name CHAR(25)

ELEMENTARY RELATION

The process of normalisation and the creation of groups of attributes, generally, aims to create stable relations, that is, relations which are not affected by operations such as, insert, delete, update, etc. The resultant groups of attributes correspond to real world objects which are in effect 'codified' by these. When a relation cannot be split any further (either because it will lose semantic information, or because it is a fifth normal form relation) it is called an elementary relation (ER). An ER can of course be used in conjunction with other relations to produce a relation in a lower normal form.

ENTITY

A set of attributes, specific to an application, representing a real-world object. An entity must be stable, functional and time-independent to a certain extent. The concept of entity can be studied in connection with the concept 'relation'.

The definition of an entity can comprise its name, attributes, type of each attibute, relationships of the entity with others, etc.

Unfortunately there is no clear-cut and objective technique for grouping attributes into entities although the relational model, to a certain extent, provides a discipline for the creation of relations which can in many cases refer to complete real-world entities.

We assume that a real-world entity comprises one or more entity-relations. Therefore, throughout this book we consider entity-relation (simply referred to as entity) as an object subtype of the real-world entity.

An example of an entity, in the present sense, is DEPARTMENT comprising the attributes: Department-code, Department-name, Department-location, Department-size and Department-head.

EQUIJOIN

This is a join operation where the *theta* operator is equality (see 'join'). By definition, the equijoin operation produces a relation which contains identical columns. If the resultant relation does not contain any identical columns, then it is said to be the result of a *natural join*.

EVOLUTIONARY STRUCTURE

This is a structure (model) which can evolve with time and organisational change, without a disproportionate change in the database. Each architectural level of the database environment (i.e conceptual, logical, external and internal) can utilise an appropriate evolutionary structure in order to cope with changes in the organisation.

When a structural change is unavoidable, then it must not have any unexpected side-effects and must also imply change to only those sections of the database which are actually affected. For example, when the logical schema changes as a result of including an extra data item, then the internal realm will be expected to deal with only that portion of the database which accepts the new field. Moreover, where the change must be propagated to other areas of the database, then this must be done automatically by the DBMS.

EXTENSION

This term is often used in connection with the concept 'set' of objects, values, etc. It refers to the representational property of a set, that is, the extension of the set. It specifies an actual occurrence of a set by stating its members explicitly. For example, the representation of the set:

$M = \{2, 4, 6, 8, 10, 12, 14, 16, 18, 20\}$

gives an extension of the set M. See also under 'intension'.

EXTERNAL SCHEMA

This describes the view an application has of the database. An alternative name for external schema is 'subschema'. See also under 'subschema'.

FIFTH NORMAL FORM (5NF)

A characteristic of a relation which is in 1NF, 2NF, 3NF and 4NF and which cannot be reconstructed from other relations each having fewer attributes than the original relation. By 'reconstruction' here we mean the manipulative operations necessary to create the table of a relation. Moreover, if a 5NF is decomposed into others, then the resultant relations may all have the same primary key.

Evidently, where a relation is in 4NF and of degree 2 (i.e with only two attributes), then this is also in 5NF since we cannot decompose it further without losing information.

FIRST NORMAL FORM (1NF)

A property of a relation comprising a number of attributes each based on a single domain, and which does not contain any 'repeating groups'. An extra requirement may be that a first normal form relation contains a primary key to identify each record occurrence uniquely.

FOREIGN KEY

A single or composite key which is present as an ordinary key in a relation but is (at the same time) the primary key of another relation.

Foreign keys are absolutely vital, particularly in the relational model, and can be used as the basis for establishing 'connections' or 'associations' between different relations. Care must be taken so that foreign keys are updated consistently throughout the database in order to maintain the integrity of data.

Evidently, a foreign key in a 'host' relation must be based on the same domain as the primary key of its 'home' relation, but a foreign key does not have to be a member of the primary key in the host relation.

Consider the following example of two relations where the symbol '#' indicates a key:

EMPLOYEE: E-code#, E-name, E-address, E-telephone, E-dept#
DEPARTMENT: D-code#, D-name, D-location, D-manager

Here, the primary key of EMPLOYEE is E-code#, and the primary key of DEPARTMENT is D-code#. From the foregoing, E-dept# in relation EMPLOYEE is a foreign key and can be used to access tuples under relation DEPARTMENT where it becomes equivalent to key D-code#.

FOURTH GENERATION LANGUAGE (4GL)

A very high level language offering, besides the traditional batch facilities, an interactive mode whereby logical structures can be: (a) defined, (b) initialised, (c) manipulated, and (d) reorganised. All these tasks can also be carried out without the use of a host language such as Pascal, FORTRAN or COBOL.

Besides, a 4GL offers a non-procedural approach to the development of applications, generally, and can be considered as a natural progressive step from ordinary high level languages.

FOURTH NORMAL FORM (4NF)

A characteristic of a relation which does not contain two or more independent facts about a real-world entity. The 4NF criterion thus attempts to separate individual facts from a single relation and to transfer these into independent relations. Besides, for a relation to be in 4NF, it must also be in first, second and third normal form.

Moreover, a 4NF relation is a relation which allows all sub-key attributes to be functionally dependent only on the primary key.

FUNCTIONAL DEPENDENCE

A relationship between two attributes, say ATR1 and ATR2, on the basis of their associated values where at any point of time there exists only one logical value under ATR2 with a given value under ATR1. We say, ATR2 is functionally dependent on ATR1 and denote this by ATR1----->ATR2, or ATR2 is not functionally dependent on ATR1 and denote this by ATR1--/-->ATR2. In other words, for every value under ATR1 there is one and only one value or factual information under ATR2. Thus, a value under ATR1 must always occur with the same value under ATR2.

ATR1 can be a composite attribute in which case we talk of 'full functional' dependence, or a single attribute in which case we talk of 'simple functional' dependence. When ATR1 is composite and only a subset of it gives functional dependence on ATR2, then we refer to this as 'partial dependence'.

HASH ADDRESS

A physical address calculated by a hashing function following appropriate manipulations on the key or identifier of a record.

Most high level languages offer a means of addressing each record directly, and on the basis of its relative position in a file. The hash address then becomes an integer number in the range 1...N where N is the prespecified maximum relative position (i.e maximum records in the file).

In many cases, different keys are transformed into the same hash address creating what is termed as 'collision'. Collisions must be resolved before the actual placement of the records takes place implying the allocation of new addresses to all colliding records (with the exception of the first record which remains in the hash address otherwise referred to as the 'home address').

HASHING

The process whereby a key or other identifier of a record is transformed into a physical address usually on a direct access device. We talk of the 'hashing function', that is, the process which performs the transformation.

Several hashing techniques have been tested and compared, examples of which are: prime division, squaring, truncation, folding and randomisation.

Two important qualitative criteria to judge the effectiveness of a hashing function are: (a) the minimisation of collisions (i.e different record keys that produce the same address), and (b) the uniformity of address-space utilisation (i.e the spread of the addresses generated). See also under 'hash address' and 'synonym'.

HOMONYM

One aspect of data analysis involves the identification of terms (e.g entity names, attribute names, data item names, etc) which are used to refer to two or more different objects (e.g entities) within the enterprise. In other words, a homonym is a term which is similar in form to another but not in meaning.

Homonyms can be defined by amplification (i.e extra and explicit definition) or by context (i.e through surrounding application-dependent information). For example, entity UNIT-DETAILS for application, say, APL1 may refer to the attributes: Manager, Location, Telephone, Number-of-staff. However, entity UNIT-DETAILS for application, say, APL2 may refer to the attributes: Product-made, Cost, Duration, Capacity.

HOST LANGUAGE

A programming language from which we issue calls to DBMS functions and procedures. The calls can be in the form of ordinary host language statements (e.g the CALL subroutine-name statement in FORTRAN) or they can be specially designed statements which are translated into host language statements through a DBMS utility. The latter is otherwise called 'pre-processor'.

Examples of host languages are Pascal, FORTRAN and COBOL. An example statement that can be included within a host language program calling the subschema 'sub1' of schema 'sch1' is:

INVOKE SUBSCHEMA sub1 OF SCHEMA sch1

The above statement can instruct the pre-processor to include appropriate data definition statements within, say, the DATA DIVISION of a source COBOL program.

See also under 'fourth generation language' and 'sublanguage'.

INDEX

A database area which holds information about specific attributes (usually keys) and corresponding addresses (or links) and where values under these can be located. Its primary aims are to speed the retrieval of record occurrences and to form links between record types, tables or files generally.

Where an index exists, the appropriate DBMS sublanguage function will always examine it first before retrieving the record occurrence(s). In the following example we show an index called CODES and associated file called BOOKS where the alphabetic author order is indicated by the order the link numbers appear in the index (in a top-down manner):

CODES

Key	Link
c200	1
c205	3
c210	2
c220	4
c230	5

BOOKS

Link	Author	Date	Edition	Title
1	Ayres F	1985	1	Librar. . .
2	Jones A	1985	1	The ar. . .
3	Emmanuel J	1986	1	The lo. . .
4	Knuth D	1984	2	Comput. . .
5	West J W	1983	3	Inform. . .

In this example, we can use values under the 'Link' attribute of the index to retrieve the corresponding records in the BOOKS file in alphabetical order. Besides, given a value under attribute 'Key' in the index we can retrieve the corresponding record in BOOKS directly.

INDEXING

The process whereby an index is established. This may be automatic or manual and can be applied under two stages:

(a)   The creation of new database areas holding columns/values of the indexed attributes.

(b)   The linking of the indexed values with their corresponding record
      occurrences in tables or files in general.

INFORMATION RESOURCE DICTIONARY SYSTEM (IRDS)

Computer software enabling the creation and maintenance of a data dictionary
(see under 'data dictionary') which forms the basis to document the information
system itself as well as provide a means to store meta-data (i.e data about data).
      We must point out here that the IRDS is nothing more than another software
utility which may be provided by the DBMS. Because the principles behind an
IRDS are equally important to non-database environments, it becomes feasible to
adopt it as a tool for any information system (regardless of whether a DBMS is
used or not).

INTEGRITY

A characteristic of the database where the accessing of data items by different
applications for display or alteration can be coordinated through the system so
that data input or output is checked consistently, and updates are propagated
globally rather than only within isolated database realms.
      Another important aspect of integrity involves the maintenance of a log of all
record accesses or updates so that recovery of lost or corrupted data becomes
possible.
      Integrity of relations and associated tables can be maintained on the basis of a
number of rules which are obeyed by all data manipulation operations. Example
rules are:

(a)   Every relation conforms with its definitional aspects and the primary key
      identifies all tuples uniquely.
(b)   Where an attribute (usually a key) is common to two or more relations,
      then its values appear consistently throughout the tables.
(c)   Where a table of a relation, say TAB1, contains a foreign key (i.e a key
      which is the primary key of another relation, say, TAB2), then all values
      under TAB1 must also exist under TAB2 or be null.
(d)   Where appropriate, attributes must be qualified by the statements 'NULL
      VALUES ALLOWED' or 'NULL VALUES NOT ALLOWED' so that
      the DBMS can detect operations (e.g insert, update) which break these
      rules.

      An example case (under category (c) above) where integrity is violated involves
the following two tables:

1.   A table called EMPLOYEES containing key 'Dept' and an associated
      value 'computer'.
2.   A table called DEPARTMENTS with a primary key called 'Dept-co' but
      without a tuple which contains the value 'computer' under 'Dept-co'.

So, the following request to display all attribute values (denoted by '*') from

DEPARTMENTS and where tuples contain the value 'computing' under attribute 'Dept-co', does not in fact produce any records:

SELECT *
    FROM DEPARTMENTS
    WHERE Dept-co = 'computing'

INTENSION

This term is often used in connection with sets of objects, values, etc. It corresponds to the definitional property of a set and defines the permissible occurrences of its entries, implicitly, by specifying a membership condition. For example, the set definition:

M = {a | where a is an even positive integer number}

represents the intension of set M. For a value to be a valid member of the set it must be an even, positive and integer number. See also under 'intension'.

INTERNAL SCHEMA

This describes how data is actually stored on the physical devices, and basically attempts to translate the logical schema into its internal equivalent. The transformations from logical to physical are not always one-to-one and major differences arise. For example, the physical order of data items can be different from their logical order, a logical record can be split into two or more physical records of different types, common data items between different logical records may not necessarily be duplicated.

In summary, the internal schema comprises definitions regarding stored record types, block lengths and distributions, security control, compression details, hashing of keys or other addressing schemes, such as, indexes, pointers, chains, etc.

Alternative names for internal schema are 'storage schema' and 'physical schema'. For our purposes, these terms are synonymous. See also under 'data storage description language'.

INTERSECTION TYPE

This is an independent relation or record type incorporating two primary keys from two separate relations. An intersection type may also incorporate extra attributes if necessary.

An intersection type can be used to manipulate the keys efficiently, without disturbing the 'parent' types. Once the desired keys have been isolated (marked), the corresponding tuples of the parent relations can be processed further.

For example, assume that an order is issued with a single supplier and that it can contain two or more items. If all necessary information is held within two relations, say, ORDER and ITEM, then the following relation becomes their intersection:

ORDER-ITEM (Order-no#, Item-no#, Date, Supplier)

The attribute Item-no# can be used to fetch further details on each item, such as description, quantity and price.

INVERTED FILE

A file organisation employing indexes on secondary keys. The use of indexes thus provides fast and efficient retrieval of records through boolean requests involving AND, OR, NOT and other logical relational operators.

INVOKE

To activate a process or task which has already been defined and compiled, directly or from within another process or task. For example, the subschema of an application can be invoked through an appropriate DML command incorporated within an application program. The following statement illustrates this:

INVOKE SUBSCHEMA sub1 OF SCHEMA sch1

The query language is also used to invoke appropriate subschemata, or processes directly.

JOIN

This is an operation whereby a new relation is created from others by concatenating (putting together) all the attributes from the relations used. For a join operation to take place there must exist a domain that is common to the relations used and which in effect links tuples together on the basis of some arithmetic comparison operator (e.g =, >, <, etc). The general case of a join operation that involves these arithmetic operators is frequently referred to as 'theta join'; we can of course be more specific and make use of the terms: 'greater-than-join', 'less-than-join', 'equijoin' (when the attributes are tested for equality), etc.

The join operation is the most powerful algebraic operation frequently used to synthesise relations/tables from others already available in the schema of the organisation. There are several types of join operations (e.g natural join, semijoin, etc) depending on what attributes/tuples are selected from the underlying relations (see under 'natural join', and 'semijoin').

JOIN DEPENDENCY

Join dependency is a property of a decomposed relation (i.e a relation that has been split via projections for reasons of normalisation) where the join of its projections produces the original relation. In other words, if the original relation can be reconstructed from its projections, then we say that there is 'lossless join'. If the original relation cannot be reconstructed from its projections, then we say that there is 'loss join'; this implies that the join of the projections either creates unwanted tuples or loses tuples that were present in the original relation.

The property of join dependency is in fact an argument against bad decompositions and therefore bad relational schema design. Because decomposition is unavoidable in many cases, it becomes necessary to restrict the number of combinations of tuples that can appear/disappear after joining the projections, by, for example, joining on keys rather than on non-keys.

KEY

An attribute which is used to identify a record or clusters of record occurrences within a table or file. Its value is symbolic rather than a physical address and remains constant and independent of physical storage or reorganisational functions.

Depending on the actual physical database implementation, particularly the way inter-relation links are maintained, a key attribute can be physically present in one place, but virtual in another. This may in fact be necessary if we wish to reduce key redundancy which is usually introduced when relations are decomposed (split into smaller units) during normalisation.

The value of a key can be a natural occurrence, such as 'computing', or it can be designed artificially, as for example, 'c101' referring to a logical object, say, department computing payroll code 101. In the latter case, a coding system can be utilised to define each key domain appropriately.

We have a number of different types of keys, such as primary, secondary, single and composite.

LOCK

A characteristic of a record type, data item, area, subschema, schema, application program, or process, indicating its level of accessibility. For example, data item 'Salary' for application 'Progress-reports' may be locked for 'updates' implying that the application cannot alter existing values. Another example is, realm 'R1' (containing employee salaries) is locked for 'access' by the subschema 'S1' which is used to print address labels.

Let us proceed to give examples of appropriate database commands which carry out the following: (a) invoke a database file for updating, (b) test to see whether this file is already locked or not (by another user), (c) proceed to update the file when not locked, and (d) unlock the file and make this available to other users:

```
INVOKE file1
IF LOCK (file1) THEN
     APPEND
     .
     . commands to append records to the file
     .
     UNLOCK
ELSE
     PRINT 'Database file is not available'
ENDIF
```

LOCK UNIT

A structural unit of the database environment locked at any point of time. Example units are the subschema, area, record type, etc.

The primary function of a lock unit is to protect the database from unauthorised access, or any conflicting concurrent demands made upon the data or associated structures.

LOG

A database area containing information about transactions; primarily the alterations which have taken place. The log file is normally used to reconstruct the database or certain sections of it when necessary. Also, the log file can be used as proof of operations which have taken place.

LOGICAL INDEPENDENCE

A characteristic of the database where data can be manipulated at the logical level, that is, the way users view it, without affecting the internal organisation of the database or indeed other applications and users.

The DBMS must provide a high degree of logical independence on data and structures alike so that the organisation can satisfy all applications in an incremental or evolutionary manner. See also under 'data independence' and 'physical independence'.

LOGICAL SCHEMA

The complete and integrated definition of organisational information, including logical structure, record types, data items and relationships. The logical schema must not incorporate physical definitions, such as record access mechanisms and indexes, and is established through a data description sublanguage which is part of the DBMS software.

The logical schema is designed on the basis of the information provided by the conceptual schema and only under exceptional circumstances should the DBA seek to incorporate information that is not already included in the conceptual schema. Its design then takes place with a specific DBMS in mind, and an appropriate utility (e.g DDL) is used to specify its contents and structure. Different subschemata can subsequently be derived from the same logical schema serving the applications of the organisation.

An alternative name for logical schema is 'logical database description'. For our purposes here, and unless otherwise stated, when we talk of the schema we imply the logical schema.

MANDATORY MEMBERSHIP

A property of a set type allowing a record occurrence to become a member of another set occurrence within the same set type. Compare this with the property 'fixed' membership where a record occurrence remains a member of the same set occurrence until it is erased from the database. The following example shows network database statements that define mandatory membership on record type 'Pro-description':

```
SET Set1
    OWNER Product
    ORDER SORTED
    MEMBER Pro-description
    RETENTION MANDATORY
    .
    .
    .
```

Now, if a particular record has to be placed in an alternative set occurrence, then we must (a) transfer it into the user work area, (b) delete it from the current set, (c) prepare the new set, and (d) transfer the record from the user work area onto the new set. See also under 'set'.

MANUAL MEMBERSHIP

A property of a set type enabling the placement (insertion) of record occurrences within a set to be carried out on request, that is, through a specific INSERT or CONNECT statement. Compare this with the property 'automatic' membership where record occurrences are inserted automatically as members of a set when this is initially stored in the database.

Under both 'manual' and 'automatic' modes the owner record occurrence must be identified by the application, in other words, the DBMS cannot identify the owner record occurrence automatically. The following are example network database commands that define manual membership on record type 'History':

```
SET Set1
    OWNER Employee
    ORDER SORTED
    MEMBER History
    INSERTION MANUAL
    .
    .
    .
```

See also under 'set'.

META-DATA

Data which describes and defines other data. For example, a schema can be thought of as a meta-data structure which contains the descriptions of data types, entities, record types, etc.

We also talk of meta-files, that is, files which describe other files and which must first be opened and read before the data files can actually be processed.

MULTI-USER ENVIRONMENT

An applications environment where the DBMS allows the concurrent and simultaneous access of the database by several users. This environment can comprise software, data, hardware and peripherals which are available to two or more users at the same time.

A multi-user environment imposes a greater demand on the designer of the database management system and programmer alike who have to consider the possibility of deadlocks and their resolution.

MULTIVALUED DEPENDENCE

A relationship among attributes in a relation where an attribute value has associated with it multiple values under another. In other words, an attribute, say, X, multidetermines another, say, Y. We denote this by $X---\gg Y$.

Suppose there is a relation R, and two subsets of attributes of R, namely, A and B. If $A---\gg B$ holds then there is a multivalued dependency in R if given values for the attributes of A there is a set of zero or more associated values for the attributes of B, and this set of B values is not related (logically) to the values of the attributes in R-A-B.

NATURAL JOIN

This is a join operation (see 'join') where the resultant relation does not contain any identical attributes. In this context, two or more attributes are said to be identical when the values under their respective columns are the same; identical attributes/columns can be eliminated via the project operation. Let a database contain the relations:

R1 (Key, Name, Status, Area)
R2 (Key, Key2, Quantity)

then the natural join on attributes R1.Key and R2.Key, that is, 'R1.Key *theta* R2.key' (see 'join') produces a relation, say, R3, where

R3 (Key, Name, Status, Area, Key2, Quantity)

The facility to produce natural joins from two or more tables is one of the most useful functions of a relational DBMS. It can form the basis to interrelate and cluster tuples in order to answer complex logical enquiries, and can also be used to suppress, at the logical level, the inherent duplication of attributes (e.g foreign keys) that the relational database approach introduces by definition.

NETWORK

A number of entities linked in a general fashion without any restrictions as to the number of links or connections each can have.

Networks are cumbersome to define and maintain but can be broken down into a number of hierarchical structures (trees) before they are structured onto computer files.

One way to specify the relationship between two entities is in terms of occurrences (values) under each in a uni- or bi-directional manner. In other words, given two entities 'A' and 'B' and pertinent values under each, we can have the following arrangements:

One value under 'A' many under 'B' (1:M)
One value under 'A' one under 'B' (1:1)
Many values under 'A' one under 'B' (M:1)
Many values under 'A' many under 'B' (M:M)

It is also possible to specify a zero occurrence (i.e the possibility of an unknown value under an entity) which must be treated as a special case.

Consider for example, the entities: STUDENT, COURSE, LECTURER, BOOKS-HELD and SUBJECT, and various relationships, such as, a COURSE may be given by two or more LECTURER(s), a LECTURER may give two or more COURSE(s), a SUBJECT may be taught by two or more LECTURER(s), etc. The following is an example of a network incorporating these entities linked in a general manner:

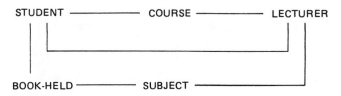

NON-KEY ATTRIBUTE

An attribute which cannot be used as a key to access records in a table. For example, consider the relation EMPLOYEE: Employee-code, Employee-name, Employee-address, Employee-telephone, Employee-department. 'Employee-code' is the primary key of the relation and all the rest are non-key attributes. Attribute 'Employee-department' may in fact be a key in its own right, or a primary key in another relation.

A non-key attribute is otherwise referred to as 'data attribute'. See also under 'key'.

NORMALISATION

A data analysis exercise which investigates the relationships of attributes in relations in terms of first, second, third, fourth and fifth normal forms. Thus, the main criteria used during normalisation are: attribute domains, functional dependence, transitive dependence and multivalued dependence.

Normalisation can be achieved by (a) splitting a relation into smaller relations, or (b) incorporating new attributes into a relation. Under (a) a key always forms the link between the resultant relations and can subsequently be used to synthesise the original relation. Correct synthesis, however, can only be achieved when the resultant relations conform with the above stated criteria.

A standard notation may be adopted during normalisation in order to clarify and establish the relationships between attributes. For example, A----->B can denote functional dependence of attribute B upon A. Also, A--/-->B can denote the absence of functional dependence of B upon A. When A is a composite attribute denoted by Aco, then we talk of full functional dependence and denote this by Aco=====>B, or Aco==/==>B.

OPERATING SYSTEM

A standard piece of software bonded with the physical architecture of a computer.

The operating system offers the infrastructure necessary for other programs to utilise computer resources in an efficient and productive manner. It also enables multi-user and concurrent environments to be set up and maintained effectively by enforcing standards and therefore ensures compatibility when programs or data are exchanged.

The operating system can be considered as the interface between user-written programs and the computer procedures built into the hardware.

In summary, the operating system performs two distinct and major tasks: (a) The control, allocation and efficient utilisation of all computer resources, and (b) The provision of a standard interface between hardware and computer users. The DBMS is here considered to be an extension of the latter task and offers an even higher level of man-machine communication.

Example trade mark operating systems are UNIX, PICK, MS-DOS or PC-DOS. These are supported by different software houses which also offer other related or plug-compatible system software.

PAGE

A subset of a database area otherwise referred to as 'realm'. Each page is numbered and accessed individually, and usually each realm consists of an integral number of pages each of the same storage capacity. With the majority of DBMS, the page forms the basic unit of input and output between the database and its associated buffers in the primary memory.

The concept page must be studied in connection with the concept 'bucket'. See also under 'bucket'.

PHYSICAL INDEPENDENCE

A characteristic of the database where data can be manipulated at the physical devices without affecting existing user views or applications which access it. Manipulations at the physical level can, for example, involve the re-structuring of data to optimise access, the introduction of new devices, and the re-arrangement or re-ordering of the data.

The DBMS must provide a high degree of physical independence so that the organisation can expand and upgrade its hardware and software without too much disturbance at the application level and generally the logical level.

PHYSICAL SCHEMA

The physical representation of the logical schema. See also under 'internal schema'.

PRIMARY INDEX

An index which holds information about the primary key of an entity and of course the associated addresses (links) of the records in the file proper. See also under 'index'.

PRIMARY KEY

A single or composite key which provides unique identification of all record occurrences within a file or table.

The primary key is chosen from a set of candidate keys and its composition remains unchanged throughout the life of an entity or relation.

For example, the primary key of relation DEPARTMENT (comprising the attributes: Department-code, Department-name, Department-location, and Department-size), is Department-code since this is the only attribute which can identify all tuples uniquely.

PRIVACY

A characteristic of data and software which refers to the degree of their accessibility by one or more users or programs.

A DBMS can offer different levels (modes) of privacy, such as read, write, insert, delete, update, or execute as is the case with software. A combination of these may also define the privacy mode of a record type, data item, realm, subschema, etc.

The following are three example DBMS commands which define privacy locks at the subschema, realm, and record-type level respectively:

SUBSCHEMA NAME IS sub-1 PRIVACY LOCK FOR ALTER IS 'password'
REALM IS realm-1 PRIVACY LOCK FOR DISPLAY IS 'password'
01 record-type-1 PRIVACY LOCK FOR DELETE IS 'password'

QUERY LANGUAGE

A sublanguage, part of the DBMS, which enables the interrogation of databases. In its original sense, the query sublanguage was available to the non-expert (non-programmer) for casual inquiries and simple and short transactions. However, recent developments established the query software as a common sublanguage for both user and programmer alike.

Thus, we find a number of DBMSs today which offer the same statements (syntactically and structurally) for use within host languages, or as directly executable commands which are usually interpreted by the system.

An example query sublanguage is SQL (Structured Query Language). A typical query formulation may be: find the address of the manufacturer of drug 'seroquoq'. Let a relation be called 'Manufacturer' and two attributes 'Manufacturer-address' and 'Drug-name'. The corresponding SQL statements to carry out the search and display of the address of the manufacturer(s) of drug 'seroquoq' are as follows:

SELECT Manufacturer-address
  FROM Manufacturer
  WHERE Drug-name = 'seroquoq'

QUERY BY EXAMPLE (QBE)

This is a domain-dependent approach to man-machine communication where the user is presented with 'software forms' which he fills in before a query is satisfied. A software form can be visualised as a two-dimensional table of a relation the values of which are filled in during a session with the user.

A QBE can therefore be considered as a 'friendly interface' for database interrogation.

The structure of a QBE interface to the database offers three basic levels of communication:

(a)   Simple operation/function commands, such as 'P' to print or display, 'D' to delete, 'I' to insert and 'U' to update.
(b)   Names of domains which are to be assigned values by the DBMS.
(c)   Actual values of domains for use by the DBMS to interrogate the database.

Consider an example of a 'form' containing four attributes (Car-plate, Car-owner, Car-address, and Car-tele) from relation CAR. If the query implies find the name and address of owner of car registration 'PJO 155T', then the user can fill in the entries 'Car-owner' and 'Car-address' with the letter 'P' and the entry 'Car-plate' with the string 'PJO 155T'. The following illustrates a form that has been filled in and is therefore ready for interpretation by the QBE system:

CAR	Car-plate	Car-owner	Car-address	Car-tele
	PJO 155T	P	P	

In this example, only the values under 'Car-owner' and 'Car-address' will actually be displayed on the screen (as instructed by the command 'P' for print) provided the search locates the required record occurrence.

REALM

A synonym of the term 'area' (see under 'area').

RECORD OCCURRENCE

A complete and single occurrence of values under a given record type. A set of record occurrences constitute the table or file of a database. An example record occurrence is

101, Russell, BAW, 1872-1970, British, Philosophy

referring to the attributes: Code, Name, Initials, Years-of-birth-death, Nationality, and Area-of-specialisation.

The term 'record occurrence' must not be confused with the term 'physical record' which is more closely related to the devices, nor with the term 'virtual record' which exists in virtual memory alone and may change dynamically (i.e from application to application or from session to session).

An alternative term for record occurrence is 'tuple', used frequently in connection with the relational model of a database.

RECORD TYPE

A number of data items or data aggregates known to the DBMS with a single collective name (the record type name). Data items can be related logically or physically and can represent a real-world entity although this is not always possible or even necessary. In other words, there are cases where two or more record types are necessary to represent accurately a real-world entity. However, for our purposes here, we will consider a record type as a synonym of sub-entity type.

A record type is defined at the logical schema using the Data Definition Language (DDL) and can then be utilised by a subschema to satisfy the needs of an application. The following are example statements in NDL (Network Database Language) that define record type 'Department' using the attributes: 'Department-code' (2 characters), 'Manager' (20 characters), 'Location' (10 characters), and 'Number-of-staff' (integer):

```
RECORD Department
      UNIQUE Department-code
      ITEM Department-code    CHARACTER 2
      ITEM Manager            CHARACTER 20
      ITEM Location           CHARACTER 10
      ITEM Number-of-staff    INTEGER
```

The statement UNIQUE defines the primary key.

RECOVERY

The process whereby a database or a section of it is reconstructed from an existing copy or after image file. The recovery operation is usually carried out when data has been corrupted or lost accidentally.

The recovery process may be activated automatically by the DBMS where possible, or it can be carried out manually by the user or applications staff. The latter is of course not desirable and can be avoided by careful planning and design of appropriate DBMS recovery procedures.

RELATION

A set of attributes each based on a single domain. One or more of the attributes becomes the primary key of the relation and establishes unique identification of all tuples under the associated table.

Repeating groups are not allowed within relations.Moreover, a relation does not incorporate definitions regarding pointers, access paths, positional, or other structural information.

A relation is said to be in first, second, third, fourth or fifth normal form and can be created and described as such following a data analysis exercise otherwise referred to as 'normalisation'. A relation is said to be of degree n where n is the number of attributes it contains.

An example of a relation called DOCTOR containing 4 attributes (i.e a relation of the 4th degree) where the symbol '#' indicates the primary key is presented below:

DOCTOR (Doctor-number#, Name, Speciality, Department)

See also under 'normalisation', 'functional dependence', 'transitive dependence' and 'multivalued dependence'.

RELATIONAL ALGEBRA

A well defined and disciplined system of operators which enable a number of functions to be performed on the relations. A relational algebra operator accepts one or more relations as its operands and constructs a new relation.

Example relational algebra operators are 'selection', 'projection', 'join', 'union', 'intersection', 'difference', 'product' and 'division'. An example relational statement may be: Join relations R1 and R2 where attribute A1 in R1 is equal to attribute A2 in R2.

Thus, relational algebra offers a procedural language for the manipulation of relations.

RELATIONAL CALCULUS

Whereas relational algebra provides a specific set of operators forcreating relations, relational calculus defines the characteristics of the relation to be created from others in a collection. It is then up to the system to determine what relational algebra operators need to be employed in order to create the defined relation.

An example relational calculus statement may be: Find all tuples in R1 where attribute A1 is equal to 'Bradford'.

Thus, relational calculus offers a non-procedural language for the manipulation of relations.

REORGANISATION

This usually refers to a revision of the physical part(s) of a database. A revision can be understood in terms of changes at the storage unit, record linkage, physical record order, block length, bucket size, overflow area, file size, area size, etc.

Reorganisation of the database may in fact be necessary from time to time (especially where run-time statistics can be collected) in order to optimise access time, as well as storage space.

REPEATING GROUP

One or more data items which are repeated within a single record type depending on the value of other data items. The number of repeats may vary from one record occurrence to another.

To understand this, consider the definition of the following record type as it can be created using the COBOL rather than a DBMS language:

```
01 ORDER-RECORD.
    05  ORDER-NUMBER            PIC 9(5).
    05  CUSTOMER-NUMBER         PIC 9(5).
    05  CUSTOMER-REFERENCE  PIC X(10).
    05  ORDER-ITEM-OCCURS       PIC 9(2).
    05  ORDER-ITEMS
        OCCURS 1 TO 40 TIMES DEPENDING ON ORDER-ITEM-
                                            OCCURS.
        10  STOCK-CODE          PIC X(6).
        10  STOCK-DESCRIPTION   PIC X(40).
        10  STOCK-MEASURE       PIC X(4).
        10  AMOUNT-ORDERED      PIC 9(4).
        10  AMOUNT-SHIPPED      PIC 9(4).
        10  STOCK-PRICE         PIC 9(2)V9(2).
```

In further analysis of a repeating group, we find that it can materialise at the physical level under two different modes:

(a) The intra-record mode where each record either expands dynamically and 'horizontally' as each value arrives, or is allocated a fixed number of expansion units in order to accommodate incoming values of data items.
(b) The inter-record mode where each incoming value is accommodated within a new record occurrence which is linked to the 'home' occurrence (i.e the values under the non-repeating data items of the record type).

Evidently, repeating groups can introduce redundancy. Besides, the implementation of dynamically expanding structures is no trivial task. Therefore, it becomes necessary to eliminate a repeating group by splitting the record type into two and by linking these through what is called an 'intersection' type. Alternatively, the two record types created from a split (decomposition) can be interrelated by means of chains, pointers, etc.

RESTART

A procedure which enables the functioning of the database to continue following a system crash, unresolved deadlock or any other interruption (intentional or unintentional).

There are basically two modes of restarting the system:

(a) Using a previous backup copy of the complete realm(s) affected.
(b) Rolling back from a transaction and therefore concentrating on only those record occurrences which have been affected. The 'rollback' operation is vital and is usually provided as a standard command of the Data Manipulation Language (DML) (See also under 'rollback').

In most DBMS environments the DBA will have the option to restart the application affected, or to restart the complete DBMS environment.

RESTRUCTURING

This refers to the reorganisation of the logical structure of the database and usually involves the revision of the logical schema and its recompilation. Where restructuring affects existing storage definitions or existing stored information, then the following tasks must be carried out in the order presented:

(a) Unload the physical database on temporary files
(b) Revise the schema
(c) Recompile the schema
(d) Reformat the database files
(e) Load (populate) the database using the temporary files

The DBMS must of course provide appropriate utilities to carry out the operations implied by the above tasks.

ROLLBACK

An operation which takes place after a transaction has failed and permits a database to revert back to its previous version. This is possible through 'before image' files.

The DBMS can in many cases detect inconsistency or lack of integrity and therefore rollback automatically. The user/programmer is however advised to trap all errors and to utilise appropriate data manipulation commands in order to force rollback where necessary.

The following data manipulation statements define a transaction and cancel all updates carried out on the database (during the transaction) when errors occur:

```
PROCEDURE TRANSACT
            BEGIN TRANSACTION
            ON ERROR ROLLBACK
            .
            . {program statements}
            .
            COMMIT
            END
```

When no errors occur during the transaction, then all changes carried out are made permanent (i.e the DBMS commits the updates). See also under 'transaction', 'commit' and 'backout'.

RUN UNIT

An application environment where a program or process is under execution and where all the necessary data and meta-data are assumed to be part of a single storage area. Moreover, a run unit manipulates only that section of the database which is offered by the subschema or view(s) in use.

Each run unit has its own, so called User Working Area (UWA) where all session-dependent details are kept. Thus, within a given run unit there will be a specific subschema, program(s) in execution, and all control information on current block/bucket, record type, identifying keys, linkage details, operation performed, etc. It is important to emphasise that processing details are as much part of the run unit as is control information.

SECOND NORMAL FORM (2NF)

A relationship among attributes where each non-key attribute provides a single fact or value about the whole primary key and not a subset of it. Besides, for a relation to be in 2NF, it must also be in first normal form. The 2NF criterion thus applies to situations where there is a composite key.

We can assume that, within a given 2NF relation there exist as many 'functional dependencies' as there are non-primary key attributes. We talk of 'full functional' dependence with composite keys, or 'simple functional' dependence with single keys.

SECONDARY INDEX

An index on secondary keys used as a means of manipulating index values efficiently before the required record occurrences are actually accessed from the database.

Secondary indexes provide a facility whereby access details of logically related records can be clustered together in order to speed their retrieval following appropriate boolean-type queries. For example, the query 'display all employees of the computing department' will proceed as follows:

(a)   Check whether an index on 'employees' or 'departments' is available.
(b)   Use the index to 'mark' the access details of relevant records.
(c)   Use marked index entries and retrieve the corresponding records from the database.

Generally, an index entry comprises the value of the key(s) and access details which may involve some form of hashing, or pointers to records in the data file. See also under 'index' and 'secondary key'.

SECONDARY KEY

A single or composite key which identifies more than one record occurrence within a table or file, compared to the primary key which identifies a single occurrence within a file.

Where available, secondary keys can form the basis for establishing whether a query can be satisfied or not before actual record occurrences are retrieved from the database. See also under 'index' and 'secondary index'.

SECTOR

A fixed storage area on a disk pack, and a subset of the track. Each track in a pack can be subdivided into an equal number of sectors creating what is otherwise referred to as the 'sector mode' pack. Alternatively, each track can be used as a continuous storage area and we can thus talk of the 'free format mode' pack.

It makes sense to allow only one of the above modes within each disk pack. The majority of disk units today offer the sector mode for formatting disk packs. See also under 'disk unit'.

SELF-CONTAINED LANGUAGE

A database language which offers all commands necessary to create, manipulate and maintain a database. It can however be thought of as a language which contains a number of sublanguages. See also under 'sublanguage' and 'host language'.

The three architectural levels of logical, storage and physical schema (or rather operational shells) as well as the different types of users (i.e DBA, programmer, application user and casual user), necessitate the design of appropriate sublanguages for each of these to adopt and utilise as and where appropriate. Therefore, a self-contained language offers an ideal environment for compatibility and consistency in programming database procedures.

SEMIJOIN

To understand this relational operation we give the following general case: Let two relations R1 and R2 be joined according to two compatible attributes R1.A and R2.B (see 'join'). The result of 'R1 semijoin R2' is that set of tuples extracted only from R1 where 'R1.A *theta* R2.B' is true.

The order the relations are specified in the semijoin statement is significant and therefore 'R1 semijoin R2' and 'R2 semijoin R1' are different (i.e the results produced in each case may be different). In other words, the equijoin is not a symmetric operation.

Let a database contain the following tables:

R1	Key1	Name	Location
	k1	Ayres	Oxford
	k2	Byron	London
	k3	Plato	Athens

R2	Key2	Key3	Class
	k1	m1	B
	k1	m2	B
	k2	m3	A
	k2	m4	A
	k2	m5	C

The semijoin: R1 semijoin R2 where R1.key1 = R2.key2 can be implemented with the following SELECT operation:

SELECT Key1, Name, Location
  FROM R1, R2
  WHERE R1.Key1 = R2.Key2

This semijoin produces a new table, say, R3 where

R3	Key1	Name	Location
	k1	Ayres	Oxford
	k2	Byron	London

SET

One or more different record types related hierarchically and where one of them is defined as the *owner* and each of the rest become the *member* record types of the set. The records in a set are strongly related, logically, but not necessarily physically. Thus, we can find members of a set placed in different realms of the database.

A set has a name, one or more members, an accessing mechanism, an order, a linkage type, a defined mode for inserting/updating records, and other DBMS-dependent properties.

To understand the definition of a set we present the following CODASYL example that defines a set type called 'Cust-ord-head' using the records: Customer (Customer-code, Name, Address, Balance, Credit-limit) and Order-header (Order-code, Date, Description):

SET Cust-ord-head
  OWNER Customer
  ORDER SORTED
  MEMBER Order-header
    INSERTION AUTOMATIC
    RETENTION OPTIONAL
    KEY ASCENDING Order-code

STORAGE SCHEMA

The physical representation of the logical schema. See also under 'internal schema'.

STRUCTURED QUERY LANGUAGE (SQL)

A query language, part of the DBMS software, with a well defined structure and syntax and very high level commands (well above ordinary programming language commands).

The IBM Corporation have designed an SQL that is currently being considered by the International Standards Organisation (ISO) as a standard DBMS language for both data definition and data manipulation functions within a relational DBMS environment. See also under 'query language'.

SUBLANGUAGE

A programming language forming a subset of the DBMS software used to communicate between different types of users and the system. Thus, it becomes possible to consider different types of sublanguages for different purposes, as for example, the DDL and DML.

The DBMS may offer: (a) several different sublanguages, or (b) a single language containing different user-languages. See also under 'self-contained language'.

SUBSCHEMA

A subset of the logical schema aiming to provide an interface between an application and the global database aspects. It can therefore be considered as an application-dependent structure which restricts a user's view of the database to only those relevant sections of the logical schema.

Being a subset of the logical schema, the subschema is also a logical structure with its associated sets, entities, data items and appropriate application-dependent relationships.

An arbitrary number of subschemata can be derived from a schema, and also, an arbitrary number of applications can share the same subschema. Besides, different subschemata may contain overlapping/duplicate definitional information but not necessarily duplicate occurrence data at the physical level.

Alternative names for subschema are 'external schema' and 'view'. For our purposes, the terms subschema, external schema and view are considered synonymous although differences in interpretation, particularly in connection with the concept 'run unit', do exist. See also under 'view'.

SYNONYM

One aspect of data analysis involves the identification of different terms (e.g entity names, attribute names, data item names, etc) which are used to refer to the same object (e.g entity, attribute) within the enterprise. In other words, one of the objectives of data analysis is to identify the cases where two or more different names (terms) are used with the same meaning, form and structure. The terms then become synonymous and must be defined as such within the database (explicitly or implicitly). For example, the terms 'Product-no' and 'Style-no' become synonymous when they both refer to the same object, say, the unique identifier of an item manufactured by the enterprise.

The term 'synonym' is also used frequently during the calculation of record addresses using their keys (i.e hashing). Sometimes two or more different record keys produce the same address. The first record to be allocated an address is described as the *home* record. Any subsequent record keys that produce an address that is already allocated are described as synonyms and have to be stored elsewhere.

TABLE

A two-dimensional structure consisting of one or more columns each with a predefined name, and zero or more rows each representing a tuple of a relation. In addition, the intersection of a given row and column contains one and only one value rather than a repeating group of values.

There are basically three different categories of tables:

(a)   Base table; as defined by the 'create table' statement. It exists permanently in more or less the same format.

(b)   View table; a named table which is derived as a result of the 'create view' statement, but which does not exist permanently as an individual table in the database. In other words, this is a virtual table.

(c)   Derived table; a table which is derived as a result of manipulative operations (e.g select, group). One or more tables can be used to establish a derived table.

Within a table, the ordering of rows or columns is not significant and duplicate rows (tuples) are not allowed. It is however essential for a table (especially a base table) to have one or more attributes defined as the primary key which is capable of identifying each tuple occurrence uniquely.

The number of tuples in a table is otherwise referred to as the 'cardinality' of the table, and the number of columns (attributes) is otherwise referred to as the 'degree' of the table. An example table called CAR-PLATES (i.e car registration numbers) with cardinality 4 and degree 2 is presented below:

CAR-PLATES

Car-plate	Car-owner
ODB 492W	Stylios G
TUG 811B	Victoras P
VCR 804B	Edwards D A
WAR 322Z	Proteus F W

THIRD NORMAL FORM (3NF)

A relationship among attributes where each non-key attribute is non-transitively dependent on the primary key. The 3NF criterion thus attempts to remove any functional dependency of a non-key attribute on another non-key attribute. Therefore, a 3NF relation allows each non-key attribute to be functionally dependent only on the primary key.

For a relation to be in 3NF, it must also be in first and second normal forms.

A third normal form is considered by many software engineers to be ideal for the creation of record types.

TRACK

A complete and circular strip on a recording surface of a disk pack. All the contents of a track can thus be accessed without any movement of the read/write heads of the drive.

The majority of disk drives today subdivide tracks into sectors, that is, fixed sections each with the same storage capacity throughout the disk pack. Otherwise, it becomes the responsibility of the programmer to allocate storage units within a track as and when required. The latter necessitates more complicated programming and the maintenance of extra control information. See also under 'disk unit'.

TRANSACTION

A sequence of operations upon record types and corresponding values producing a consistent and integrated version of the database. The operations are logically related and perform a specific task, such as, the updating of salary details of all employees by awarding, say, a 10% increase.

A transaction takes place at a specific point of time and has a defined beginning and end (referred to as 'commit'). The commit command requests the system to commit itself to the transactions which have taken place and to create a permanent copy of the data. It actually signals the successful completion of a transaction.

If an error occurs during a transaction, we can rollback (see under 'rollback' and 'commit'), that is, revert to the previous state of the database.

Nested transactions are not normally allowed but an application program may contain one or more independent transactions.

The following example statements define a transaction which updates record occurrences by giving a 10% increase to all employees in department 'Computer' using record type 'Employee-pay':

```
PROCEDURE TRANSACT
        BEGIN TRANSACTION
        ON ERROR ROLLBACK
        UPDATE Employee-pay
           SET Salary = Salary + 10 * Salary / 100
           WHERE Department = 'Computer'
        COMMIT
        END
```

TRANSITIVE DEPENDENCE

A relationship among attributes in a relation where an attribute is functionally dependent on another through a third. This is particularly obvious when a non-key attribute is a fact (i.e provides functional dependence) about another non-key attribute.

Transitive dependence can be denoted as A----->B----->C where A, B and C are all attributes implying that C is functionally dependent on B and B is functionally dependent on A.

As an example, consider the relation STYLE and its associated table where S-number is the primary key:

STYLE

S-number	Category	Location
s101	formal	Bradford
s102	casual	Leeds
s103	casual	Leeds
s104	formal	Bradford

Here, S-number----->Location and Location----->Category. Therefore, Category is transitively dependent on S-number through Location.

TREE

A structure involving a number of nodes, such as entities, attributes, record types or data items linked together to form a hierarchy. Hierarchies may form part of the conceptual, logical, storage and physical level of a database environment and have always been used to describe a particular type of linkage among these. A tree, in effect, forms a type of model that can be used reflect the organisation or database itself.

Depending on the number of links specified at each node, we have the following types of trees: *Binary* (two links per node), *Balanced* (an equal number of links per node), and *General* (a variable number of links per node).

An example general tree incorporating the entities DEPARTMENT, SUPERVISORS, COURSES and STUDENTS with two hierarchic levels is presented below:

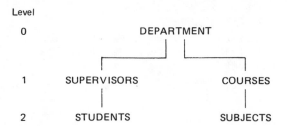

TUPLE

An occurrence or instance of values under all attributes of a relation. A tuple can be considered synonymous to record occurrence.

A tuple forms a complete row of a table in the relational model but may not necessarily have a one-to-one correspondence with its associated storage slot. For example, a tuple may be split between two or more sectors on a disk pack.

An example table called PAY-DETAILS with four tuples (or cardinality 4) is presented below:

PAY-DETAILS

Code	Surname	Initials	Department	Pay-code
100	Stone	BAW	Maths	3
105	Torsun	IT	Computing	4
110	Yannakoudakis	EJ	Computing	2
120	Wesley	TAB	Chemistry	1

See also under 'table', 'relation' and 'record occurrence'.

UNIVERSAL RELATION

A relation that is assumed to contain the attributes of the entire database, relieving the user of the requirement to master the logical structure of the database and its navigation. A universal relation can often be seen as the natural join of all the existing relations in the database.

This concept becomes necessary, particularly with natural language units, because the relational model expects the user to have knowledge of all the relations and the attributes in each before he can interrogate the database.

For a universal relation to make sense, while avoiding conflict with the architecture of the relational model of data, we must make various assumptions such as:

(a)   Universal relation scheme: the attributes of the entire database are available for the synthesis of relations.
(b)   Universal relation lossless join: if the universal relation is projected and the projections are then joined, the result is the original relation.
(c)   Weak instance assumption: an occurrence of the universal relation may contain tuples whose projections are not present in certain database relations.
(d)   Universal relation join dependency: the universal relation satisfies a single join dependency and a collection of functional dependencies.
(e)   Acyclic join dependency: a join dependency is acyclic if it is equivalent to a set of multivalued dependencies, implying that each query can be interpreted uniquely over the universal relation.

See also under 'join dependence', 'functional dependence' and 'multivalued dependence'.

VIEW

The concept of view is closely related to an application and refers to an actual subset of the database a user has for manipulation. The view is therefore application-dependent and can also be defined dynamically during a run unit.

To a certain extent, the concept 'view' is synonymous to 'subschema'. However, a subschema reflects the structural as well as functional requirements of a total and local user environment where the user/programmer does not need to create any new virtual relations. In other words, a subschema represents a complete application environment.

A data manipulation language can be used to define a view resulting in a relation and associated table(s) which may not necessarily exist permanently in the database but only in definition. In other words, the tables of a view may be derived upon the activation of the view itself creating what are known as *virtual tables*.

An arbitrary number of views can be derived from the same logical schema or indeed other views. Also, overlapping/duplicate information may exist among views but since the resulting tables are not actually stored, then duplicate data at the physical level does not exist.

Views can be shared by different applications and although, by default, the creator of a view is also its owner, he may grant permission to other users and at specific levels of authorisation, such as, 'select', 'insert', 'delete' and 'update'. See also under 'table' and 'base table'.

11 APPENDIX. EXAMPLE REPORTS FROM CANONICAL SYNTHESIS

Introduction

Our aim here is to present certain 'descriptive' reports produced by the canonical synthesis algorithm we have implemented in Pascal. Our system also produces 'graphical' reports on the derived schema showing clearly the logical clustering of the elements involved. Graphical reports have been omitted for reasons of space.

The example we have used shows a hospital database comprising 8 views, 19 keys and 58 attributes. The major original entities we analysed were: PATIENTS, GENERAL PRACTITIONERS, HOSPITALS, CONSULTANTS and DRUG SUPPLIERS. This is a realistic subset of what is required by an Area Health Authority in order to coordinate its resources.

Information on patients is described adequately by appropriate attributes. Because a patient can be an out-patient and/or an in-patient, there is a need to name each of these associations. To this end, the hospital database incorporates 'named associations' between elements; these appear in the reports under the heading of LINK NAME. The actual name is fed in as a string after the description of the type of association. So, to specify that the key NHS-NUMBER (National Health Service Number) of a patient (denoted by 'K') is associated with attribute CONSULTANT-NUMBER (denoted by 'A') in terms of a one-to-many link (1:M) which is named OUT-PATIENT, we write:

K NHS-NUMBER
A CONSULTANT-NUMBER 1 : M OUT-PATIENT

The corresponding diagrammatic form of the above becomes:

The primary key for each patient record in this database is the NHS number. However, it would be wise to allow access via their names since very few patients can actually remember their number. Each patient is assigned to a single consultant and hospital and can also be an in-patient and/or an out-patient, at any point of time.

Hospitals need to hold a variety of information on wards, in-patients, out-patients, operating theatres and their usage. Only the full address of each hospital needs to be stored and it is assumed that all hospitals within an Area Health Authority will have unique names. The wards are numbered throughout the area so only the ward number is required to identify uniquely any particular ward.

Prescriptions are written out to individual patients for a single drug at a time. In order to identify the quantity, dosage and hospital of a particular prescription we adopt a composite (concatenated) key comprising the NHS number, date and drug number.

In order to control the drug stock in each hospital we adopt a composite key comprising the drug number, the hospital and the expiry date of the drug. So, information on drugs supplemented by information on suppliers can aid the design of automatic re-order mechanisms within the database. The drug number is an imposed key used to identify a particular drug and its characteristics. An equivalent composite key can be made up of drug name, drug form (e.g tablet, ampoule, cream, powder) and concentration.

The Hospital Entities

In this section we discuss the hospital entities and their data elements including key attributes. An attempt has been made to adopt realistic information and data elements with meaningful names in order to demonstrate clearly the various stages of the synthesis algorithm. The main entities involved are:

1. Patients
   1.1 Case Histories
   1.2 X-Ray Dosages
2. General Practitioners (GPs)
3. Hospitals
   3.1 In-Patients
   3.2 Out-Patients
   3.3 Wards
   3.4 Operating Theatres
   3.5 Operating Theatre Bookings
   3.6 Prescriptions
   3.7 Drugs
4. Consultants
   4.1 Appointments
   4.2 Waiting Lists
5. Drug Suppliers
   5.1 Drugs

PATIENTS

The information held for each patient is as follows:-

1. National Health Service Number (KEY)
2. Patient Surname
3. Patient Forename(s)
4. Patient Title
5. Patient Address
6. Patient Telephone Number
7. Patient Sex

8. Patient Date-of-Birth
9. Patient's General Practitioner Number
10. Patient's ABO-Blood Group
11. Patient's Rhesus-Blood Group

There is also a need to hold information on case histories. To this end, the following attributes are used:-

1. NHS Number (KEY)
2. Diagnosis Date (KEY)
3. GP Number
4. Diagnosis Description (this may be a long piece of text)

Here, it becomes necessary to adopt a composite primary key, comprising the NHS Number and Diagnosis Date. The GP Number should not be made part of the key since it is assumed that only one GP will diagnose ailments on the same person on the same date. This is because a patient can be registered with only one GP at any time and it will be the GP who sends a patient to a consultant for further examination.

For each X-ray taken we need to store the year and the dosage so that overdoses can be avoided. Therefore the following attributes are necessary:-

1. NHS Number (KEY)
2. Year (KEY)
3. Dosage

GENERAL PRACTITIONERS

Under this entity we hold simple personal details for each GP so that we can link patients to GPs and make contact with them when necessary. The following attributes are used:-

1. GP Number (KEY)
2. GP Surname
3. GP Forename(s)
4. GP Address
5. GP Telephone Number

Although the primary key is the imposed GP Number, a secondary index for the name is advisable.

HOSPITALS

For each hospital we need to hold a variety of information such as, Wards, In-patients, Out-patients, Operating Theatres and Usage of each.
The Hospitals:-

1. Hospital (KEY)
2. Hospital Address

For each hospital we need to hold the address and a hospital name which is assumed to be unique within the Area Health Authority.
The Wards:-

1. Ward Number (KEY)
2. Hospital
3. Ward Name
4. Beds Available

The assumption made here is that wards are numbered throughout the Health Authority so that only the ward number is required to identify uniquely any particular ward.
The In-Patients:-

1. NHS Number (KEY)
2. Consultant Number
3. Ward Number

These attributes aim to associate consultants with wards and patients. The NHS Number is the only key necessary for unique identification of records.
The Out-Patients:-

1. NHS Number (KEY)
2. Consultant Number
3. Hospital

This is similar to the in-patients except that each out-patient is 'admitted' to a particular hospital rather than to a ward. For the purposes of this example it is assumed that a patient may be an in- and/or out-patient for only one hospital at a time and have only one consultant in each. This is practical for in-patients since it is impossible for a person to reside in more than one ward, although each may have more than one consultant. If, however, an out-patient is allowed for examination in two or more hospitals and with two or more consultants, then the out-patient relation would have to be all key.
The Operating Theatres:-

1. Theatre Number (KEY)
2. Hospital
3. Theatre Name
4. Special Equipment

This implies that each operating theatre is assigned a unique Health Authority number for identification. The attribute 'Special Equipment' is required for those theatres that have more than the usual facilities.
Operating Theatre Usage:-

1. Theatre Number (KEY)
2. Date (KEY)
3. Time (KEY)
4. NHS Number

5. Operation Type
6. Special Requirements

The primary key consists of the Theatre Number plus the Date and Time of the operation. This should provide unique identification of records because it is assumed that each operating theatre can accommodate a single operation at any time. Under this composite key we can then hold the type of operation and any special requirements.

Prescriptions:-

1. NHS Number (KEY)
2. Date (KEY)
3. Drug Number (KEY)
4. Hospital obtained from
5. Quantity
6. Dosage

Prescriptions are written out to individual patients for one drug only. In order to identify the quantity, dosage and the hospital of a particular prescription a composite key of NHS Number, Date and Drug Number is required. Specifying the hospital allows for a close check to be kept on the drug stocks of individual hospitals.

Drug Re-ordering:-

1. Drug-Number (KEY)
2. Hospital (KEY)
3. Re-order Level

This enables each hospital to have different re-order levels for each of the drugs held. It would also seem sensible to have an attribute for the current stock under this key, but each drug has a limited life span. Therefore, it is necessary to hold the stock of each drug and its expiry date.

Drug Stocks:-

1. Drug-Number (KEY)
2. Hospital (KEY)
3. Expiry Date (KEY)
4. Stock

Here, a composite key of Drug-Number, Hospital and Expiry Date is used to find the quantity of each drug held at a hospital with a particular expiry date. There would be two main access routes; the first would be by drug number and hospital to find the hospital and total amount of that drug over all expiry dates, and the second would be by the full key to update the stock entries as drugs are given out by the hospital. A further function would be required to scan through the drugs, writing off all those which are near or over their expiry dates.

CONSULTANTS

The information held for each consultant is:-

1. Consultant Number (KEY)
2. Consultant Surname
3. Consultant Forename(s)
4. Consultant Address
5. Consultant Telephone Number

As is the case with GPs, a consultant would be identified by a unique number, although a secondary key on Consultant Surname is also advisable.

The consultants appointments:-

1. Consultant Number (KEY)
2. Appointment Date (KEY)
3. Appointment Time (KEY)
4. NHS Number

There are several possible arrangements for this information. A composite key of NHS Number and Consultant Number will identify the appointments by date and time, but there is a possibility of arranging several appointments for the same consultant (say a visit every month for several months). However, the patient's number and an appointment date and time will uniquely identify the consultant to be seen. Also, a composite key of Consultant Number, Date and Time will identify all patients, dates and times for each consultant. Since each consultant is likely to see several patients but each patient will never have appointments for more than two or three consultants, then a composite key of Consultant Number, Date and Time is required. This also allows quick checking on what times a consultant is free.

Consultant's waiting lists:-

1. Consultant Number (KEY)
2. NHS Number (KEY)
3. Wait Date
4. Wait Reason

There are two cases here: (a) consultants are fully booked for a period of time (say one or two years!) beyond which definite appointments may not be made, or (b) a patient has had some treatment and will need to be examined again at some future time. In both of these cases consultants set up a waiting list that consists of the date each person was put on the waiting list plus the reason for doing so. If we assume that no patient can be put on any consultant's waiting list twice, then a key of Consultant Number and NHS Number is sufficient to uniquely identify the date and reason for examination of a patient. Since patients will usually be removed from the waiting list in the order their details were recorded, then a second access path is required to rank the patients by date.

DRUG SUPPLIERS

The Health Authority will need to hold details on every drug kept in their hospitals along with details of quantities, re-order levels and suppliers.

The Drugs:-

1. Drug Number (KEY)

    2. Drug Name
    3. Drug Form
    4. Concentration
    5. Storage Conditions
    6. Lifespan
    7. Administration
    8. Type

Drug Number is an imposed key used to identify a particular drug and its characteristics. An equivalent composite key can be made up of Drug Name, Drug Form (tablet, ampoule, cream, powder, etc.), and Concentration.
The supplier's drugs:-

    1. Drug Number (KEY)
    2. Supplier Number (KEY)
    3. Price
    4. Lead Time

Here, a composite key of Drug Number and Supplier Number is used in order to obtain the price of that drug from that supplier as well as the time it would take to deliver the drug.
The suppliers:-

    1. Supplier Number (KEY)
    2. Supplier Name
    3. Supplier Address
    4. Supplier Telephone Number

These details are usually adequate for communication between hospitals and suppliers.

The Notation Adopted

The notation we adopted during the implementation of the algorithm, and which appears in the reports, is as follows:

H	Heading
V	View
K	Key
A	Attribute
*	Comment line
1 : 1	One-to-one
1 : M	One-to-many
M : 1	Many-to-one
M : M	Many-to-many
1 : 0	One-to-unspecified
M : 0	Many-to-unspecified
0 : 1	Unspecified-to-one
0 : M	Unspecified-to-many

+   A key concatenated with the following element
(1)   Possible redundant '1' link
(M)   Possible redundant 'M' link

Reports Produced by Canonical Synthesis Software

The following reports are reproduced here exactly as printed by the system. These are self-explanatory and the attributes appear in their full name. Each element, view, cluster, etc, is given a sequence number which is then used for cross-referencing where appropriate. The reader should therefore be able to understand the process of canonical synthesis, the various stages it goes through and the statistics it produces.

The first report entitled VIEWS READ is actually the same as the source (input) file prepared by the analyst (only the sequence number is added by the system).

```
VIEWS READ
==========

     1   H MEDICAL DATA SYSTEM                  PREFIX IS:  MED
     2   *
     3   *
     4   *
     5   V SUPPLIER-INFORMATION
     6   *
     7   K SUPPLIER-NUMBER
     8   A SUPPLIER-NAME                1  :  0
     9   A SUPPLIER-ADDRESS             1  :  0
    10   A SUPPLIER-PHONE               1  :  0
    11   A DRUG-NUMBER                  M  :  0
    12   *
    13   *
    14   *
    15   V DRUG-INFORMATION
    16   *
    17   K DRUG-NUMBER                  +
    18     SUPPLIER-NUMBER
    19   A COST                         1  :  0
    20   A LEAD-TIME                    1  :  0
    21   *
    22   K DRUG-NUMBER
    23   A TYPE                         1  :  0
    24   A DRUG-NAME                    1  :  0
    25   A DRUG-FORM                    1  :  0
    26   A CONCENTRATION                1  :  0
    27   A STORAGE-CONDITIONS           1  :  0
    28   A LIFESPAN                     1  :  0
    29   A ADMINISTRATION               1  :  0
    30   *
    31   K DRUG-NUMBER                  +
    32     HOSPITAL                     +
    33     EXPIRY-DATE
    34   A STOCK                        1  :  0
    35   *
    36   K DRUG-NUMBER                  +
    37     HOSPITAL
    38   A RE-ORDER-LEVEL               1  :  0
    39   *
    40   *
    41   *
    42   V PRESCRIPTIONS
```

```
43    *
44    K  NHS—NUMBER                        +
45       PRESCRIPTION—DATE                 +
46       DRUG—NUMBER
47    A  HOSPITAL—OBTAINED—FROM             1  :  0
48    A  QUANTITY                           1  :  0
49    A  DOSAGE                             1  :  0
50    *
51    *
52    *
53    V  PATIENTS
54    *
55    K  NHS—NUMBER
56    A  PATIENT—SURNAME                     1  :  0
57    A  PATIENT—FORENAMES                   1  :  0
58    A  PATIENT—TITLE                       1  :  0
59    A  PATIENT—ADDRESS                     1  :  0
60    A  PATIENT—PHONE                       1  :  0
61    A  PATIENT—SEX                         1  :  0
62    A  DATE—OF—BIRTH                       1  :  0
63    A  GP—NUMBER                           1  :  M
64    A  ABO—BLOOD—GROUP                     1  :  0
65    A  RHESUS—BLOOD—GROUP                  1  :  0
66    *
67    K  GP—NUMBER
68    A  GP—SURNAME                          1  :  0
69    A  GP—FORENAMES                        1  :  0
70    A  GP—ADDRESS                          1  :  0
71    A  GP—PHONE                            1  :  0
72    *
73    K  NHS—NUMBER                        +
74       CASE—HISTORY—DATE
75    A  DIAGNOSIS—GP—NUMBER                 1  :  0
76    A  DIAGNOSIS                           1  :  0
77    *
78    *  IN PATIENTS
79    K  NHS—NUMBER
80    A  CONSULTANT—NUMBER                   1  :  M  IN—PATIENT
81    A  WARD—NUMBER                         1  :  M  IN—PATIENT
82    *
83    *  OUT PATIENTS
84    K  NHS—NUMBER
85    A  CONSULTANT—NUMBER                   1  :  M  OUT—PATIENT
86    A  HOSPITAL                            1  :  M  OUT—PATIENT
87    *
88    K  NHS—NUMBER                        +
89       YEAR
90    A  X—RAY—DOSAGE                        1  :  0
91    *
92    *
93    *
94    V  HOSPITALS
95    *
96    K  HOSPITAL
97    A  HOSPITAL—ADDRESS                    1  :  0
98    A  WARD—NUMBER                         M  :  1
99    *
100   K  WARD—NUMBER
101   A  HOSPITAL                            1  :  0
102   A  WARD—NAME                           1  :  0
103   A  BEDS—AVAILABLE                      1  :  0
104   *
105   *
106   *
107   V  CONSULTANTS
108   *
109   K  CONSULTANT—NUMBER
110   A  CONSULTANT—SURNAME                  1  :  0
```

```
111  A  CONSULTANT—FORENAMES              1  :  0
112  A  CONSULTANT—TITLE                  1  :  0
113  A  CONSULTANT—ADDRESS                1  :  0
114  A  CONSULTANT—PHONE                  1  :  0
115  *
116  *
117  *
118  V  APPOINTMENT—&—WAITING—LISTS
119  *
120  K  CONSULTANT—NUMBER                 +
121     APPOINTMENT—DATE                  +
122     APPOINTMENT—TIME
123  A  NHS—NUMBER                        1  :  M
124  *
125  K  NHS—NUMBER                        +
126     CONSULTANT—NUMBER
127  A  WAIT—DATE                         1  :  0
128  A  WAIT—REASON                       1  :  0
129  *
130  *
131  *
132  V  OPERATING—THEATRE
133  *
134  K  THEATRE—NUMBER
135  A  HOSPITAL                          1  :  0
136  A  THEATRE—NAME                      1  :  0
137  A  SPECIAL—EQUIPMENT                 1  :  0
138  *
139  K  THEATRE—NUMBER                    +
140     OPERATION—DATE                    +
141     OPERATION—TIME
142  A  NHS—NUMBER                        1  :  M
143  A  OPERATION—TYPE                    1  :  0
144  A  SPECIAL—REQUIREMENTS              1  :  0
145  *
```

MERGING OF THE VIEWS
===============

THE VIEWS READ IN ARE:—

```
          1       SUPPLIER—INFORMATION
          2       DRUG—INFORMATION
          3       PRESCRIPTIONS
          4       PATIENTS
          5       HOSPITALS
          6       CONSULTANTS
          7       APPOINTMENT—&—WAITING—LISTS
          8       OPERATING—THEATRE
```

```
STATISTICS PRODUCED:—
NUMBER OF VIEWS READ IN —      8
NUMBER OF COMMENT LINES —      43
TOTAL NUMBER OF KEYS    —      19
NO. OF CONCATENATED KEYS—       9
TOTAL NO. OF ATTRIBUTES —      58
NO. OF CONCAT. ATTRIBUTES—      0
TOTAL NO. OF COMPONENTS
OF CONCATENATED ELEMENTS—      13
```

THE STATE OF THE SCHEMA AFTER MERGING OF VIEWS
=====================================

ELEM. NO.	ELEMENT NAME(S)	LINK TO NO.	TYPES TO : FROM	LINK NAME
1	SUPPLIER—NUMBER			
		2	1 : 0	
		3	1 : 0	
		4	1 : 0	
		5	M : 0	
2	SUPPLIER—NAME			
		1	0 : 1	
3	SUPPLIER—ADDRESS			
		1	0 : 1	
4	SUPPLIER—PHONE			
		1	0 : 1	
5	DRUG—NUMBER			
		1	0 : M	
		9	1 : 0	
		10	1 : 0	
		11	1 : 0	
		12	1 : 0	
		13	1 : 0	
		14	1 : 0	
		15	1 : 0	
6	DRUG—NUMBER SUPPLIER—NUMBER	+		
		7	1 : 0	
		8	1 : 0	
7	COST			
		6	0 : 1	
8	LEAD—TIME			
		6	0 : 1	
9	TYPE			
		5	0 : 1	
10	DRUG—NAME			
		5	0 : 1	
11	DRUG—FORM			
		5	0 : 1	
12	CONCENTRATION			
		5	0 : 1	
13	STORAGE—CONDITIONS			
		5	0 : 1	
14	LIFESPAN			
		5	0 : 1	
15	ADMINISTRATION			
		5	0 : 1	
16	DRUG—NUMBER HOSPITAL EXPIRY—DATE	+ +		
		17	1 : 0	
17	STOCK			
		16	0 : 1	
18	DRUG—NUMBER HOSPITAL	+		
		19	1 : 0	
19	RE—ORDER—LEVEL			
		18	0 : 1	
20	NHS—NUMBER PRESCRIPTION—DATE DRUG—NUMBER	+ +		
		21	1 : 0	
		22	1 : 0	
		23	1 : 0	
21	HOSPITAL—OBTAINED—FROM			
		20	0 : 1	

22	QUANTITY				
		20	0 : 1		
23	DOSAGE				
		20	0 : 1		
24	NHS—NUMBER				
		25	1 : 0		
		26	1 : 0		
		27	1 : 0		
		28	1 : 0		
		29	1 : 0		
		30	1 : 0		
		31	1 : 0		
		32	1 : M		
		33	1 : 0		
		34	1 : 0		
		42	1 : M	IN—PATIENT	
		43	1 : M	IN—PATIENT	
		42	1 : M	OUT—PATIENT	
		44	1 : M	OUT—PATIENT	
		55	M : 1		
		62	M : 1		
25	PATIENT—SURNAME				
		24	0 : 1		
26	PATIENT—FORENAMES				
		24	0 : 1		
27	PATIENT—TITLE				
		24	0 : 1		
28	PATIENT—ADDRESS				
		24	0 : 1		
29	PATIENT—PHONE				
		24	0 : 1		
30	PATIENT—SEX				
		24	0 : 1		
31	DATE—OF—BIRTH				
		24	0 : 1		
32	GP—NUMBER				
		24	M : 1		
		35	1 : 0		
		36	1 : 0		
		37	1 : 0		
		38	1 : 0		
33	ABO—BLOOD—GROUP				
		24	0 : 1		
34	RHESUS—BLOOD—GROUP				
		24	0 : 1		
35	GP—SURNAME				
		32	0 : 1		
36	GP—FORENAMES				
		32	0 : 1		
37	GP—ADDRESS				
		32	0 : 1		
38	GP—PHONE				
		32	0 : 1		
39	NHS—NUMBER CASE—HISTORY—DATE	+			
		40	1 : 0		
		41	1 : 0		
40	DIAGNOSIS—GP—NUMBER				
		39	0 : 1		
41	DIAGNOSIS				
		39	0 : 1		
42	CONSULTANT—NUMBER				
		24	M : 1	IN—PATIENT	
		24	M : 1	OUT—PATIENT	
		50	1 : 0		
		51	1 : 0		
		52	1 : 0		
		53	1 : 0		
		54	1 : 0		

```
43    WARD—NUMBER
                            24       M  :  1        IN—PATIENT
                            44       1  :  M
                            48       1  :  0
                            49       1  :  0
44    HOSPITAL
                            24       M  :  1        OUT—PATIENT
                            47       1  :  0
                            43       M  :  1
                            59       0  :  1
45    NHS—NUMBER            +
      YEAR
                            46       1  :  0
46    X—RAY—DOSAGE
                            45       0  :  1
47    HOSPITAL—ADDRESS
                            44       0  :  1
48    WARD—NAME
                            43       0  :  1
49    BEDS—AVAILABLE
                            43       0  :  1
50    CONSULTANT—SURNAME
                            42       0  :  1
51    CONSULTANT—FORENAMES
                            42       0  :  1
52    CONSULTANT—TITLE
                            42       0  :  1
53    CONSULTANT—ADDRESS
                            42       0  :  1
54    CONSULTANT—PHONE
                            42       0  :  1
55    CONSULTANT—NUMBER     +
      APPOINTMENT—DATE      +
      APPOINTMENT—TIME
                            24       1  :  M
56    NHS—NUMBER            +
      CONSULTANT—NUMBER
                            57       1  :  0
                            58       1  :  0
57    WAIT—DATE
                            56       0  :  1
58    WAIT—REASON
                            56       0  :  1
59    THEATRE—NUMBER
                            44       1  :  0
                            60       1  :  0
                            61       1  :  0
60    THEATRE—NAME
                            59       0  :  1
61    SPECIAL—EQUIPMENT
                            59       0  :  1
62    THEATRE—NUMBER        +
      OPERATION—DATE        +
      OPERATION—TIME
                            24       1  :  M
                            63       1  :  0
                            64       1  :  0
63    OPERATION—TYPE
                            62       0  :  1
64    SPECIAL—REQUIREMENTS
                            62       0  :  1

THE TOTAL NUMBER OF UNIQUE LINKS IS —    65

     THE TOTAL NUMBER OF ELEMENTS IS —    64
```

FIND ALL UNKNOWN KEYS
================

THE NEW KEYS FOUND ARE:-

```
  1 :  SUPPLIER-NUMBER

  5 :  DRUG-NUMBER

  6 :  DRUG-NUMBER                        +
        SUPPLIER-NUMBER

 16 :  DRUG-NUMBER                        +
        HOSPITAL                          +
        EXPIRY-DATE

 18 :  DRUG-NUMBER                        +
        HOSPITAL

 20 :  NHS-NUMBER                         +
        PRESCRIPTION-DATE                 +
        DRUG-NUMBER

 24 :  NHS-NUMBER

 32 :  GP-NUMBER

 39 :  NHS-NUMBER                         +
        CASE-HISTORY-DATE

 42 :  CONSULTANT-NUMBER

 43 :  WARD-NUMBER

 44 :  HOSPITAL

 45 :  NHS-NUMBER                         +
        YEAR

 55 :  CONSULTANT-NUMBER                  +
        APPOINTMENT-DATE                  +
        APPOINTMENT-TIME

 56 :  NHS-NUMBER                         +
        CONSULTANT-NUMBER

 59 :  THEATRE-NUMBER

 62 :  THEATRE-NUMBER                     +
        OPERATION-DATE                    +
        OPERATION-TIME
```

THE TOTAL NUMBER OF KEYS FOUND IS   -   17

THE NUMBER OF KEYS IN THE SCHEMA IS -   17

CHECK COMPOSITE ELEMENTS FOR LINKS TO THEIR COMPONENTS
==

THE CONCATENATED ELEMENTS FOUND ARE:-

```
  6 :  DRUG-NUMBER                        +
        SUPPLIER-NUMBER

       LINKS TO COMPONENTS ARE:-
  COMPONENT FOUND -      5
  COMPONENT FOUND -      1
```

```
16 :  DRUG—NUMBER                          +
      HOSPITAL                             +
      EXPIRY—DATE

         LINKS TO COMPONENTS ARE:—
   COMPONENT FOUND —     5
   COMPONENT FOUND —    44

18 :  DRUG—NUMBER                          +
      HOSPITAL

         LINKS TO COMPONENTS ARE:—
   COMPONENT FOUND —     5
   COMPONENT FOUND —    44

20 :  NHS—NUMBER                           +
      PRESCRIPTION—DATE                    +
      DRUG—NUMBER

         LINKS TO COMPONENTS ARE:—
   COMPONENT FOUND —    24
   COMPONENT FOUND —     5

39 :  NHS—NUMBER                           +
      CASE—HISTORY—DATE

         LINKS TO COMPONENTS ARE:—
   COMPONENT FOUND —    24

45 :  NHS—NUMBER                           +
      YEAR

         LINKS TO COMPONENTS ARE:—
   COMPONENT FOUND —    24

55 :  CONSULTANT—NUMBER                    +
      APPOINTMENT—DATE                     +
      APPOINTMENT—TIME

         LINKS TO COMPONENTS ARE:—
   COMPONENT FOUND —    42

56 :  NHS—NUMBER                           +
      CONSULTANT—NUMBER

         LINKS TO COMPONENTS ARE:—
   COMPONENT FOUND —    24
   COMPONENT FOUND —    42

62 :  THEATRE—NUMBER                       +
      OPERATION—DATE                       +
      OPERATION—TIME

         LINKS TO COMPONENTS ARE:—
   COMPONENT FOUND —    59

        NUMBER OF CONCATENATED ELEMENTS IS —    9

        NUMBER OF COMPONENTS LINKED TO   IS —   14

NO. OF NON—KEY COMPONENTS/CONCATENATIONS —    0

TOTAL NUMBER OF KEYS IN THE SCHEMA IS      —   17
```

SEARCH FOR ALL ISOLATED ATTRIBUTES
=========================:

THERE WERE   0 ISOLATED ATTRIBUTES

DELETE ALL ILLEGAL LINKS TO ATTRIBUTES
=============================

THE TOTAL NUMBER OF ILLEGAL LINKS IS -   0

SEARCH FOR ALL ONE-WAY LINKS BETWEEN TWO KEYS
================================

THE MISSING ASSOCIATIONS ARE ASSUMED TO BE 'M' LINKS -

BETWEEN   1 : SUPPLIER-NUMBER
* AND *   5 : DRUG-NUMBER

BETWEEN   59 : THEATRE-NUMBER
* AND *   44 : HOSPITAL

THE TOTAL NUMBER OF ONE WAY LINKS BETWEEN KEYS IS -   2

CONCATENATE THOSE KEYS ONLY WITH M : M ASSOCIATIONS
=====================================

THE KEYS WHICH HAVE SUCH ASSOCIATIONS ARE:-

BETWEEN -   1 : SUPPLIER-NUMBER
* AND * -   5 : DRUG-NUMBER

THE RELATIONSHIP IS M : M

THE CONCATENATION ALREADY EXISTS AS -   6

THE TOTAL NUMBER OF CONCATENATIONS EXAMINED IS -   1

SEARCH FOR DIRECT IDENTICAL KEYS
=======================

NUMBER OF PATHS FOLLOWED =   796
THERE WERE   0 IDENTITIES.

SEARCH FOR ALL REDUNDANT '1' ASSOCIATIONS
=============================

POSSIBLE REDUNDANCY DETECTED BETWEEN:-
 24 : NHS-NUMBER
AND
 44 : HOSPITAL
THE DIRECT RELATIONSHIP OF - 1,OUT-PATIENT - IS IMPLIED BY :-
PATH NO.   1 :   FROM 24 TO   43(1,IN-PATIENT) TO 44(1)

```
POSSIBLE REDUNDANCY DETECTED BETWEEN:-
  55 : CONSULTANT-NUMBER                    +
       APPOINTMENT-DATE                     +
       APPOINTMENT-TIME
AND
  42 : CONSULTANT-NUMBER
THE DIRECT RELATIONSHIP OF - 1 - IS IMPLIED BY :-
PATH NO.   1 :   FROM   55 TO   24(1) TO   42(1,IN-PATIENT)
PATH NO.   2 :   FROM   55 TO   24(1) TO   42(1,OUT-PATIENT)


POSSIBLE REDUNDANCY DETECTED BETWEEN:-
  56 : NHS-NUMBER                           +
       CONSULTANT-NUMBER
AND
  42 : CONSULTANT-NUMBER
THE DIRECT RELATIONSHIP OF - 1 - IS IMPLIED BY :-
PATH NO.   1 :   FROM   56 TO   24(1) TO   42(1,IN-PATIENT)
PATH NO.   2 :   FROM   56 TO   24(1) TO   42(1,OUT-PATIENT)


NUMBER OF PATHS FOLLOWED          - 264

NUMBER OF LINKS INVESTIGATED      - 19

NUMBER OF LOOPS FOUND             -  0

NUMBER OF REDUNDANCIES FOUND      -  3

NUMBER OF REDUNDANCIES REMOVED -     0
```

SEARCH FOR ALL REDUNDANT 'M' ASSOCIATIONS
==============================

```
POSSIBLE REDUNDANCY DETECTED BETWEEN:-
  42 : CONSULTANT-NUMBER
AND
  24 : NHS-NUMBER
THE DIRECT RELATIONSHIP OF - M,IN-PATIENT - IS IMPLIED BY :-
PATH NO.   1 :   FROM   42 TO   55(M) TO   24(1)
PATH NO.   2 :   FROM   42 TO   56(M) TO   24(1)


POSSIBLE REDUNDANCY DETECTED BETWEEN:-
  42 : CONSULTANT-NUMBER
AND
  24 : NHS-NUMBER
THE DIRECT RELATIONSHIP OF - M,OUT-PATIENT - IS IMPLIED BY :-
PATH NO.   1 :   FROM   42 TO   55(M) TO   24(1)
PATH NO.   2 :   FROM   42 TO   56(M) TO   24(1)


POSSIBLE REDUNDANCY DETECTED BETWEEN:-
  44 : HOSPITAL
AND
  43 : WARD-NUMBER
THE DIRECT RELATIONSHIP OF - M - IS IMPLIED BY :-
PATH NO.   1 :   FROM   44 TO   24(M,OUT-PATIENT) TO   43(1,IN-PATIENT)
```

```
NUMBER  OF  PATHS  FOLLOWED          -  185

NUMBER  OF  LINKS  INVESTIGATED      -    7

NUMBER  OF  LOOPS  FOUND             -    0

NUMBER  OF  REDUNDANCIES  FOUND      -    3

NUMBER  OF  'REDUNDANCIES'  REMOVED  -    0
```

SEARCH FOR ALL INTERSECTING ATTRIBUTES
============================

```
NO.  INTERSECTING  ATTRIBUTES  FOUND  -      0
```

FINAL STATE OF THE SCHEMA
====================

ELEM. NO.	ELEMENT NAME(S)	LINK TO NO.	TYPES TO	FROM	LINK NAME
1	SUPPLIER–NUMBER				
		2	1 :	0	
		3	1 :	0	
		4	1 :	0	
		6	M :	1	
2	SUPPLIER–NAME				
		1	0 :	1	
3	SUPPLIER–ADDRESS				
		1	0 :	1	
4	SUPPLIER–PHONE				
		1	0 :	1	
5	DRUG–NUMBER				
		9	1 :	0	
		10	1 :	0	
		11	1 :	0	
		12	1 :	0	
		13	1 :	0	
		14	1 :	0	
		15	1 :	0	
		6	M :	1	
		16	M :	1	
		18	M :	1	
		20	M :	1	
6	DRUG–NUMBER SUPPLIER–NUMBER	+			
		7	1 :	0	
		8	1 :	0	
		5	1 :	M	
		1	1 :	M	
7	COST				
		6	0 :	1	
8	LEAD–TIME				
		6	0 :	1	
9	TYPE				
		5	0 :	1	
10	DRUG–NAME				
		5	0 :	1	
11	DRUG–FORM				
		5	0 :	1	
12	CONCENTRATION				
		5	0 :	1	
13	STORAGE–CONDITIONS				
		5	0 :	1	

14	LIFESPAN				
		5	0 : 1		
15	ADMINISTRATION				
		5	0 : 1		
16	DRUG–NUMBER	+			
	HOSPITAL	+			
	EXPIRY–DATE				
		17	1 : 0		
		5	1 : M		
		44	1 : M		
17	STOCK				
		16	0 : 1		
18	DRUG–NUMBER	+			
	HOSPITAL				
		19	1 : 0		
		5	1 : M		
		44	1 : M		
19	RE–ORDER–LEVEL				
		18	0 : 1		
20	NHS–NUMBER	+			
	PRESCRIPTION–DATE	+			
	DRUG–NUMBER				
		21	1 : 0		
		22	1 : 0		
		23	1 : 0		
		24	1 : M		
		5	1 : M		
21	HOSPITAL–OBTAINED–FROM				
		20	0 : 1		
22	QUANTITY				
		20	0 : 1		
23	DOSAGE				
		20	0 : 1		
24	NHS–NUMBER				
		25	1 : 0		
		26	1 : 0		
		27	1 : 0		
		28	1 : 0		
		29	1 : 0		
		30	1 : 0		
		31	1 : 0		
		32	1 : M		
		33	1 : 0		
		34	1 : 0		
		42	1 : (M)	IN–PATIENT	
		43	1 : M	IN–PATIENT	
		42	1 : (M)	OUT–PATIENT	
		44	(1): M	OUT–PATIENT	
		55	M : 1		
		62	M : 1		
		20	M : 1		
		39	M : 1		
		45	M : 1		
		56	M : 1		
25	PATIENT–SURNAME				
		24	0 : 1		
26	PATIENT–FORENAMES				
		24	0 : 1		
27	PATIENT–TITLE				
		24	0 : 1		
28	PATIENT–ADDRESS				
		24	0 : 1		
29	PATIENT–PHONE				
		24	0 : 1		
30	PATIENT–SEX				
		24	0 : 1		
31	DATE–OF–BIRTH				
		24	0 : 1		

32	GP–NUMBER						
		24	M	:	1		
		35	1	:	0		
		36	1	:	0		
		37	1	:	0		
		38	1	:	0		
33	ABO–BLOOD–GROUP						
		24	0	:	1		
34	RHESUS–BLOOD–GROUP						
		24	0	:	1		
35	GP–SURNAME						
		32	0	:	1		
36	GP–FORENAMES						
		32	0	:	1		
37	GP–ADDRESS						
		32	0	:	1		
38	GP–PHONE						
		32	0	:	1		
39	NHS–NUMBER	+					
	CASE–HISTORY–DATE						
		40	1	:	0		
		41	1	:	0		
		24	1	:	M		
40	DIAGNOSIS–GP–NUMBER						
		39	0	:	1		
41	DIAGNOSIS						
		39	0	:	1		
42	CONSULTANT–NUMBER						
		24	(M)	:	1	IN–PATIENT	
		24	(M)	:	1	OUT–PATIENT	
		50	1	:	0		
		51	1	:	0		
		52	1	:	0		
		53	1	:	0		
		54	1	:	0		
		55	M	:	(1)		
		56	M	:	(1)		
43	WARD–NUMBER						
		24	M	:	1	IN–PATIENT	
		44	1	:	(M)		
		48	1	:	0		
		49	1	:	0		
44	HOSPITAL						
		24	M	:	(1)	OUT–PATIENT	
		47	1	:	0		
		43	(M)	:	1		
		59	M	:	1		
		16	M	:	1		
		18	M	:	1		
45	NHS–NUMBER	+					
	YEAR						
		46	1	:	0		
		24	1	:	M		
46	X–RAY–DOSAGE						
		45	0	:	1		
47	HOSPITAL–ADDRESS						
		44	0	:	1		
48	WARD–NAME						
		43	0	:	1		
49	BEDS–AVAILABLE						
		43	0	:	1		
50	CONSULTANT–SURNAME						
		42	0	:	1		
51	CONSULTANT–FORENAMES						
		42	0	:	1		
52	CONSULTANT–TITLE						
		42	0	:	1		
53	CONSULTANT–ADDRESS						
		42	0	:	1		

54	CONSULTANT–PHONE			
		42	0 :	1
55	CONSULTANT–NUMBER	+		
	APPOINTMENT–DATE	+		
	APPOINTMENT–TIME			
		24	1 :	M
		42	(1):	M
56	NHS–NUMBER	+		
	CONSULTANT–NUMBER			
		57	1 :	O
		58	1 :	O
		24	1 :	M
		42	(1):	M
57	WAIT–DATE			
		56	0 :	1
58	WAIT–REASON			
		56	0 :	1
59	THEATRE–NUMBER			
		44	1 :	M
		60	1 :	O
		61	1 :	O
		62	M :	1
60	THEATRE–NAME			
		59	0 :	1
61	SPECIAL–EQUIPMENT			
		59	0 :	1
62	THEATRE–NUMBER	+		
	OPERATION–DATE	+		
	OPERATION–TIME			
		24	1 :	M
		63	1 :	O
		64	1 :	O
		59	1 :	M
63	OPERATION–TYPE			
		62	0 :	1
64	SPECIAL–REQUIREMENTS			
		62	0 :	1

THE TOTAL NUMBER OF UNIQUE LINKS IS –   87

NUMBER OF POSSIBLE REDUNDANT LINKS IS –   6

THE TOTAL NUMBER OF ELEMENTS IS –   64

THE CANONICAL SCHEMA GENERATED
======================

DATA GROUP –   1
****

CLUSTER –   1   LEVEL –   1
 KEY   FIELD(S)
 _____

 SUPPLIER–NUMBER

      OWNED   ATTRIBUTES
 _____

 SUPPLIER–NAME
 SUPPLIER–ADDRESS
 SUPPLIER–PHONE

```
        LINKS  TO  AND  FROM  OTHER  GROUPS
        ─────────────────────────────────────
        DATA        LINK        LINK
        GROUP       TYPE TO     TYPE FROM    LINK NAME
        ─────       ───────     ─────────    ─────────
          3         MANY          ONE
        ── SECONDARY  KEY  LINKS ──
```

DATA GROUP ─   2
****

CLUSTER ─   2 LEVEL ─   1
    KEY FIELD(S)
    ─────────────────────────────────────

    DRUG─NUMBER

        OWNED   ATTRIBUTES
        ─────────────────────────────

        TYPE
        DRUG─NAME
        DRUG─FORM
        CONCENTRATION
        STORAGE─CONDITIONS
        LIFESPAN
        ADMINISTRATION

        LINKS TO AND FROM OTHER GROUPS
        ─────────────────────────────────────

```
        DATA        LINK        LINK
        GROUP       TYPE TO     TYPE FROM    LINK NAME
        ─────       ───────     ─────────    ─────────
          3         MANY          ONE
          4         MANY          ONE
          5         MANY          ONE
          6         MANY          ONE
        ── SECONDARY  KEY  LINKS ──
```


DATA GROUP ─   3
****

CLUSTER ─   1 LEVEL ─   2
    KEY FIELD(S)
    ─────────────────────────────────────

    DRUG─NUMBER
    SUPPLIER─NUMBER

        OWNED   ATTRIBUTES
        ─────────────────────────────

        COST
        LEAD─TIME

        LINKS TO AND FROM OTHER GROUPS
        ─────────────────────────────────────

```
        DATA        LINK        LINK
        GROUP       TYPE TO     TYPE FROM    LINK NAME
        ─────       ───────     ─────────    ─────────
          1         ONE           MANY
          2         ONE           MANY
        ── SECONDARY  KEY  LINKS ──
```

```
DATA GROUP -    4
*****************
```

```
CLUSTER -   2  LEVEL -   2
   KEY  FIELD(S)
```
_____

```
DRUG-NUMBER
HOSPITAL
EXPIRY-DATE
```

OWNED   ATTRIBUTES
_____

STOCK

LINKS TO AND FROM OTHER GROUPS
_____

DATA GROUP	LINK TYPE TO	LINK TYPE FROM	LINK NAME
2	ONE	MANY	
12	ONE	MANY	

— SECONDARY   KEY   LINKS —

```
DATA GROUP -    5
*****************
```

```
CLUSTER -   2  LEVEL -   2
   KEY  FIELD(S)
```
_____

```
DRUG-NUMBER
HOSPITAL
```

OWNED   ATTRIBUTES
_____

RE-ORDER-LEVEL

LINKS TO AND FROM OTHER GROUPS
_____

DATA GROUP	LINK TYPE TO	LINK TYPE FROM	LINK NAME
2	ONE	MANY	
12	ONE	MANY	

— SECONDARY   KEY   LINKS —

```
DATA GROUP -    6
*****************
```

```
CLUSTER -   2  LEVEL -   2
   KEY  FIELD(S)
```
_____

```
NHS-NUMBER
PRESCRIPTION-DATE
DRUG-NUMBER
```

OWNED   ATTRIBUTES
_____

```
HOSPITAL-OBTAINED-FROM
QUANTITY
DOSAGE
```

LINKS TO AND FROM OTHER GROUPS

DATA GROUP	LINK TYPE TO	LINK TYPE FROM	LINK NAME
2	ONE	MANY	
7	ONE	MANY	
— SECONDARY	KEY	LINKS —	

DATA GROUP —   7
****

CLUSTER —   3   LEVEL —   2
   KEY   FIELD(S)

NHS—NUMBER

OWNED   ATTRIBUTES

PATIENT—SURNAME
PATIENT—FORENAMES
PATIENT—TITLE
PATIENT—ADDRESS
PATIENT—PHONE
PATIENT—SEX
DATE—OF—BIRTH
ABO—BLOOD—GROUP
RHESUS—BLOOD—GROUP

LINKS TO AND FROM OTHER GROUPS

DATA GROUP	LINK TYPE TO	LINK TYPE FROM	LINK NAME
6	MANY	ONE	
8	ONE	MANY	
9	MANY	ONE	
10	ONE	(MANY)	OUT—PATIENT
10	ONE	(MANY)	IN—PATIENT
11	ONE	MANY	IN—PATIENT
12	(ONE)	MANY	OUT—PATIENT
13	MANY	ONE	
14	MANY	ONE	
15	MANY	ONE	
17	MANY	ONE	
— SECONDARY	KEY	LINKS —	

DATA GROUP —   8
****

CLUSTER —   3   LEVEL —   1
   KEY   FIELD(S)

GP—NUMBER

OWNED   ATTRIBUTES

GP—SURNAME
GP—FORENAMES
GP—ADDRESS
GP—PHONE

LINKS TO AND FROM OTHER GROUPS

DATA GROUP	LINK TYPE TO	LINK TYPE FROM	LINK NAME
7	MANY	ONE	

— SECONDARY KEY LINKS —

DATA GROUP –   9
****

CLUSTER –   3   LEVEL –   3
   KEY FIELD(S)

NHS–NUMBER
CASE–HISTORY–DATE

OWNED   ATTRIBUTES

DIAGNOSIS–GP–NUMBER
DIAGNOSIS

LINKS TO AND FROM OTHER GROUPS

DATA GROUP	LINK TYPE TO	LINK TYPE FROM	LINK NAME
7	ONE	MANY	

— SECONDARY KEY LINKS —

DATA GROUP –   10
****

CLUSTER –   4   LEVEL –   1
   KEY FIELD(S)

CONSULTANT–NUMBER

OWNED   ATTRIBUTES

CONSULTANT–SURNAME
CONSULTANT–FORENAMES
CONSULTANT–TITLE
CONSULTANT–ADDRESS
CONSULTANT–PHONE

LINKS TO AND FROM OTHER GROUPS

DATA GROUP	LINK TYPE TO	LINK TYPE FROM	LINK NAME
7	(MANY)	ONE	OUT–PATIENT
7	(MANY)	ONE	IN–PATIENT
14	MANY	(ONE)	
15	MANY	(ONE)	

— SECONDARY KEY LINKS —

```
DATA GROUP —  11
******************

CLUSTER —  5  LEVEL —  2
    KEY  FIELD(S)
    _____

    WARD—NUMBER


        OWNED  ATTRIBUTES
        _____

        WARD—NAME
        BEDS—AVAILABLE

        LINKS TO AND FROM OTHER GROUPS
        _____
```

DATA GROUP	LINK TYPE TO	LINK TYPE FROM	LINK NAME
7	MANY	ONE	IN—PATIENT
12	ONE	(MANY)	
— SECONDARY KEY LINKS —			

```
DATA GROUP —  12
******************

CLUSTER —  5  LEVEL —  1
    KEY  FIELD(S)
    _____

    HOSPITAL


        OWNED  ATTRIBUTES
        _____

        HOSPITAL—ADDRESS

        LINKS TO AND FROM OTHER GROUPS
        _____
```

DATA GROUP	LINK TYPE TO	LINK TYPE FROM	LINK NAME
4	MANY	ONE	
5	MANY	ONE	
7	MANY	(ONE)	OUT—PATIENT
11	(MANY)	ONE	
16	MANY	ONE	
— SECONDARY KEY LINKS —			

```
DATA GROUP —  13
******************

CLUSTER —  3  LEVEL —  3
    KEY  FIELD(S)
    _____

    NHS—NUMBER
    YEAR


        OWNED  ATTRIBUTES
        _____

        X—RAY—DOSAGE
```

```
         LINKS  TO  AND  FROM  OTHER  GROUPS
         ─────────────────────────────────
         DATA      LINK       LINK
         GROUP     TYPE TO    TYPE FROM     LINK NAME
         ────      ──────     ──────        ────────
           7        ONE        MANY
         ── SECONDARY   KEY  LINKS ──
```

DATA GROUP – 14
****

CLUSTER – 4 LEVEL – 2
   KEY FIELD(S)
   ────────────────────────────

   CONSULTANT–NUMBER
   APPOINTMENT–DATE
   APPOINTMENT–TIME

```
         OWNED   ATTRIBUTES
         ─────────────────────────────

         LINKS  TO  AND  FROM  OTHER  GROUPS
         ─────────────────────────────────
         DATA      LINK       LINK
         GROUP     TYPE TO    TYPE FROM     LINK NAME
         ────      ──────     ──────        ────────
           7        ONE        MANY
          10       (ONE)       MANY
         ── SECONDARY   KEY  LINKS ──
```

DATA GROUP – 15
****

CLUSTER – 4 LEVEL – 2
   KEY FIELD(S)
   ────────────────────────────

   NHS–NUMBER
   CONSULTANT–NUMBER

```
         OWNED   ATTRIBUTES
         ─────────────────────────────

         WAIT–DATE
         WAIT–REASON

         LINKS  TO  AND  FROM  OTHER  GROUPS
         ─────────────────────────────────
         DATA      LINK       LINK
         GROUP     TYPE TO    TYPE FROM     LINK NAME
         ────      ──────     ──────        ────────
           7        ONE        MANY
          10       (ONE)       MANY
         ── SECONDARY   KEY  LINKS ──
```

DATA GROUP – 16
****

CLUSTER – 5 LEVEL – 2
   KEY FIELD(S)
   ────────────────────────────

   THEATRE–NUMBER

```
            OWNED   ATTRIBUTES
            _____  __

            THEATRE–NAME
            SPECIAL–EQUIPMENT

            LINKS  TO  AND  FROM  OTHER  GROUPS
            _____

            DATA       LINK         LINK
            GROUP     TYPE TO     TYPE FROM    LINK NAME
            ____      _____    _____    _____

             12        ONE          MANY
             17        MANY         ONE
            — SECONDARY   KEY   LINKS —
```

```
DATA GROUP –   17
*****************
```

```
CLUSTER –   3  LEVEL –   3
   KEY   FIELD(S)
   _____

   THEATRE–NUMBER
   OPERATION–DATE
   OPERATION–TIME
```

```
            OWNED   ATTRIBUTES
            _____

            OPERATION–TYPE
            SPECIAL–REQUIREMENTS

            LINKS  TO  AND  FROM  OTHER  GROUPS
            _____

            DATA       LINK         LINK
            GROUP     TYPE TO     TYPE FROM    LINK NAME
            ____      _____    _____    _____

              7        ONE          MANY
             16        ONE          MANY
            — SECONDARY   KEY   LINKS —
```

ELEMENT TO FINAL DATA GROUPS INDEX
========================

ELEMENT NAME	DATA GROUPS
ABO–BLOOD–GROUP	7
ADMINISTRATION	2
APPOINTMENT–DATE	14
APPOINTMENT–TIME	14
BEDS–AVAILABLE	11
CASE–HISTORY–DATE	9
CONCENTRATION	2
CONSULTANT–ADDRESS	10
CONSULTANT–FORENAMES	10
CONSULTANT–NUMBER	10, 14, 15
CONSULTANT–PHONE	10
CONSULTANT–SURNAME	10
CONSULTANT–TITLE	10
COST	3
DATE–OF–BIRTH	7
DIAGNOSIS–GP–NUMBER	9
DIAGNOSIS	9
DOSAGE	6
DRUG–FORM	2
DRUG–NAME	2

```
DRUG—NUMBER                     2,    3,    4,    5,    6
EXPIRY—DATE                     4
GP—ADDRESS                      8
GP—FORENAMES                    8
GP—NUMBER                       8
GP—PHONE                        8
GP—SURNAME                      8
HOSPITAL—ADDRESS                12
HOSPITAL—OBTAINED—FROM          6
HOSPITAL                        4,    5,   12
LEAD—TIME                       3
LIFESPAN                        2
NHS—NUMBER                      6,    7,    9,   13,   15
OPERATION—DATE                  17
OPERATION—TIME                  17
OPERATION—TYPE                  17
PATIENT—ADDRESS                 7
PATIENT—FORENAMES               7
PATIENT—PHONE                   7
PATIENT—SEX                     7
PATIENT—SURNAME                 7
PATIENT—TITLE                   7
PRESCRIPTION—DATE               6
QUANTITY                        6
RE—ORDER—LEVEL                  5
RHESUS—BLOOD—GROUP              7
SPECIAL—EQUIPMENT               16
SPECIAL—REQUIREMENTS            17
STOCK                           4
STORAGE—CONDITIONS              2
SUPPLIER—ADDRESS                1
SUPPLIER—NAME                   1
SUPPLIER—NUMBER                 1,    3
SUPPLIER—PHONE                  1
THEATRE—NAME                    16
THEATRE—NUMBER                  16,   17
TYPE                            2
WAIT—DATE                       15
WAIT—REASON                     15
WARD—NAME                       11
WARD—NUMBER                     11
X—RAY—DOSAGE                    13
YEAR                            13
```

12 ACRONYMS

1NF	First Normal Form
2NF	Second Normal Form
3NF	Third Normal Form
4NF	Fourth Normal Form
5NF	Fifth Normal Form
ANSI	American National Standards Institute
BASIC	Beginners All-purpose Symbolic Instruction Code
BCNF	Boyce-Codd Normal Form
BNF	Backus Naur Form
COBOL	COmmon Business Orientated Language
CODASYL	Conference On DAta SYstems Languages
CPU	Central Processing Unit
DBA	Data Base Administrator
DBCS	Data Base Control System
DBMS	Data Base Management System
DBTG	Data Base Task Group
DDBMS	Distributed Data Base Management System
DDL	Data Definition Language
DDP	Data Dictionary Processor
DMCL	Device Media Control Language
DML	Data Manipulation Language
DSDL	Data Storage Description Language
ER	Elementary Relation
FIFO	First In First Out
FORTRAN	FORmula TRANslation
HDAM	Hierarchic Direct Access Method
HIDAM	Hierarchic Indexed Direct Access Method
HISAM	Hierarchic Indexed Sequential Access Method
HSAM	Hierarchic Sequential Access Method
I/O	Input or Output
IPSE	Integrated Program Support Environment
IRDS	Information Resource Dictionary system
ISO	International Standards Organisation
LAN	Local Area Network
LIFO	Last In First Out
LISP	LISt Processing language
NDBMS	Network Database Management System
NDL	Network Database Language

NLU	Natural Language Unit
OS	Operating System
OSI	Open Systems Interconnection
PROLOG	PROgramming in LOGic
QBE	Query By Example language
QUEL	QUEry Language
RDBMS	Relational Database Management System
RDL	Relational Database Language
SPARC	Systems Planning And Requirements Committee
SQL	Structured Query Language
SSE	System Software Engineer
UWA	User Work Area
VDU	Visual Display Unit
WAN	Wide Area Network

SUBJECT INDEX